Early Start: Preschool Politics in the United States

In the United States, preschool education is characterized by the dominance of a variegated private sector and patchy, uncoordinated oversight of the public sector. As this is unusual compared to systems in other Western industrialized nations, how did such an arrangement develop? Tracing the history of the American debate over preschool education, Andrew Karch argues that the current state of decentralization and fragmentation is the consequence of a chain of reactions and counterreactions to policy decisions dating from the late 1960s and early 1970s, when preschool advocates did not achieve their vision for a comprehensive national program but did manage to foster initiatives at both the state and the national level. Over time, beneficiaries of these initiatives and officials with jurisdiction over preschool education have become ardent defenders of the status quo. Today, advocates of greater government involvement must take on a diverse and entrenched set of constituencies resistant to policy change.

This study proves the value of a developmental approach that treats social policymaking as a long-term causal chain. In his close analysis of the politics of preschool education, Karch demonstrates how to apply the concepts of policy feedback, critical junctures, and venue shopping to the study of social policy.

ANDREW KARCH is Arleen C. Carlson Associate Professor in the Department of Political Science at the University of Minnesota.

Early Start

Preschool Politics in the
United States

Andrew Karch

THE UNIVERSITY OF MICHIGAN PRESS

Ann Arbor

Published in the United States of America by
The University of Michigan Press
Manufactured in the United States of America
♾ Printed on acid-free paper

2016   2015   2014   2013   4   3   2   1

A CIP catalog record for this book is available from the British Library.

Library of Congress Cataloging-in-Publication Data

Karch, Andrew.
    Early start : preschool politics in the United States / Andrew Karch.
        pages   cm
    Includes bibliographical references and index.
        ISBN 978-0-472-11872-4 (cloth : alk. paper) — ISBN 978-0-472-02907-5 (e-book)
        1. Education and state—United States.   2. Early childhood education—United States.
    I. Title.
    LC89.K365   2013
    372.210973—dc23

                                                            2012047397

For Dahlia and Jonah

Contents

Acknowledgments

During my first semester in graduate school, I took a course on education policy and a course on the politics of the welfare state. These courses piqued my interest in early childhood education and the potential insight it offered into the politics of social policy in the United States. Surprised by how little the courses overlapped, I set that interest aside. That turned out to be a temporary decision. As state lawmakers, national officials, and (eventually) political scientists devoted considerable attention to preschool education in the early 2000s, I decided to embark on a project investigating the political origins of early childhood policy in the United States.

Many individuals provided helpful comments and suggestions at various stages of the project. This book evolved out of several conference papers, chapter drafts, and presentations, and I would like to thank Jal Mehta, Elizabeth Rigby, Shanna Rose, Ken Wong, Marty West, Sandy Schneider, Jim Guthrie, Jill Clark, Stephanie Rubin, Dick Winters, Nancy Martorano Miller, Scott Abernathy, and seminar participants at the University of Texas at Austin and Southern Methodist University for their valuable feedback. I would also like to thank Barbara Beatty, Jane Gingrich, and Maris Vinovskis, all of whom graciously read the entire manuscript and provided constructive suggestions that enhanced its historical and theoretical richness. I am also grateful to the many reference librarians who helped me navigate the archival materials on which I relied: Jennie A. Levine at the University of Maryland, Jim Lavisher at the National Library of Medicine, Alan Walker at the National Archives, Katie Senft at the New York University Archives, Kathy Christie at the Education Commission of the States, Steve Nielsen at the Minnesota Historical Society, and Carolyn Hanneman at the Carl Albert Congressional Research and Studies Center. This project would not have come to fruition without the generous guidance, support, and encouragement I received from everyone mentioned here, though, of course, none of them should be held responsible for any shortcomings that remain in the final product.

Several institutions provided support that made this project possible. I wish to thank the University of Texas at Austin, the University of Minnesota, and the Carl Albert Congressional Research and Studies Center for providing research funds. I am also grateful for my ongoing association with the University of Michigan Press. Melody Herr provided a perfect combination of enthusiasm and extraordinary patience at every stage of the publishing process, and Susan Cronin provided useful assistance as I worked on the final manuscript. I would also like to acknowledge permission to use material that appeared in two previously published articles: "Policy Feedback and Preschool Funding in the American States," *Policy Studies Journal* 38, no. 2 (May 2010): 217–34; and "Venue Shopping, Policy Feedback, and American Preschool Education," *Journal of Policy History* 21, no. 1 (2009): 38–60.

My family remains the most important source of support in my life. When I began this project, my wife, Kaori, and I were newly married and learning to appreciate our new surroundings in Austin. As I finally write these acknowledgments, a few years and one major change of climate later, we have our own personal stake in early childhood policy. With the arrival of our daughter, Dahlia, and our son, Jonah, our lives have changed in ways that we never could have imagined. We sleep less (sometimes much less) but smile and laugh more than ever, as we watch our wonderful preschoolers figure out the ways of the world. It is a trade-off we would make again and again without hesitation. This book is dedicated to Dahlia and Jonah. Their arrival did not facilitate its completion, but it did serve as a reminder of why I think the issues it addresses are so significant.

Introduction: The Preschool Puzzle

On April 1, 1968, the U.S. commissioner of education, Harold Howe II, was supposed to address the annual meeting of the Department of Elementary School Principals of the National Education Association in Houston, Texas. When his presence was required at an appropriations hearing in Washington, Howe was unable to make the trip. Instead, his speech was read to the principals. It contained a bold prediction: "I would predict that by the year 2000 most children in the United States will be attending regular public school starting at the age of four."[1]

Two elements of the commissioner's prediction are noteworthy. First, he foresaw a society in which preschool attendance for four-year-old children would be nearly universal. This element of his prediction was bold, because only 15.7 percent of three- and four-year-olds in the United States were enrolled in school in 1968.[2] Second, Howe envisaged a preschool system that would be an extension of the government-operated system of elementary and secondary education. Preschool would be publicly provided. This element of the prediction was also bold in 1968, when private nursery school enrollment outnumbered public enrollment by more than a two-to-one margin. Of the 816,000 children enrolled in nursery school that year, 554,000 (68 percent) attended a private school.[3] Undaunted by these statistics, Howe nonetheless envisioned a universal, publicly provided system of preschool education.

In the late 1960s, many individuals shared Howe's enthusiastic support of preschool education but were more pessimistic about its prospects. Representative Albert Quie (R-MN), a leading congressional expert on education policy, worried about the future. In a memorandum to members of the House Republican Task Force on Education, which he chaired, Quie observed, "Preschool education has not come of age in America, and unless several major problems are recognized and effectively counteracted, it may well die an infant."[4] The congressman argued that such issues as teacher training, parental roles, and educational effectiveness might lead to disillusionment.

More than four decades later, the specifics of both officials' predictions remain unfulfilled. As Howe predicted, preschool attendance increased substantially between 1968 and 2000, from 15.7 percent of all three- and four-year-olds in 1968 to 52.1 percent in 2000.[5] Enrollment expanded nearly fivefold among three-year-olds, and the enrollment rate of four-year-olds rose from 23 percent in 1968 to 65 percent in 2000 (Bainbridge et al. 2005, 730). By the turn of the twenty-first century, preschool enrollment had become an increasingly common part of early childhood in the United States. The universal, government-administered preschool system that the commissioner envisaged, however, did not exist. Contemporary American preschool policy consists of a fragmented amalgamation of programs and services that are funded and delivered in different ways in the public and private sectors. This complicated system remains bedeviled by many of the issues that Quie raised. Debates over teacher training, parental roles, and the effectiveness of preschool programs are as divisive today as they were during the late 1960s. Yet these ongoing controversies have not caused preschool education to "die an infant." Both enrollment in and public spending on preschool programs increased dramatically in the early 2000s.[6]

Policymakers, advocates, providers, and citizens continue to advance competing visions of the appropriate governmental role in early childhood policy. Some parties favor increased public investment, while others advocate general deference to parental autonomy and the private sector. This debate has never been resolved, and the contemporary preschool system has been described as an "uneven patchwork of public and private programs" (Barnett and Hustedt 2003, 60). Its fragmentation has repeatedly frustrated supporters of a more comprehensive and unified approach. A recent report concludes, "While nearly every level of government and sector of society has a stake in improving early care and learning, the responsibilities are so fragmented that no single actor holds enough of the levers for change to get it done."[7] This book attempts to isolate the political sources of the current system and its fragmentation.

Implicit in Howe's speech and Quie's memorandum is the notion that the late 1960s and early 1970s represented a key moment for preschool in the United States. Even though the two officials did not accurately predict the future, they correctly recognized that the decisions their contemporaries made would have enduring consequences. Indeed, the structure and politics of contemporary American preschool education can be traced to the early 1970s. At that time, multiple efforts to create a national framework for the universal provision of preschool services fell short, but several smaller programs at the national and state levels were created or expanded. The beneficiaries of those programs became ardent defenders of the status quo. Their mobilization prevented officials from adopting a more coherent approach to preschool service delivery and contributed to the fragmentation that is a defining feature of the present system.

Contemporary American Preschool Education

This book emphasizes a specific subset of programs that often fall under the broader heading of early childhood care and education. Preschools include "programs offered under public and private education auspices or providing compensatory education under special legislation" (Kamerman and Gatenio 2003, 1–2).[8] The key attribute of these programs is their educational emphasis. Regardless of whether it is called a prekindergarten, a nursery school, or something else, the main focus of a preschool is preparing children for their enrollment in kindergarten and elementary school.[9] Preschools in the United States typically serve children who are three or four years old. They may be either half-day or full-day, public or private; and they may operate year-round or cover the conventional academic year. The line between preschool and other forms of child care is often blurred, and this book emphasizes governmental policies toward educational programs at the expense of center-based child care or family child care approaches that are often described as custodial.[10]

Most contemporary assessments of American preschool education emphasize its complexity. In the absence of a comprehensive national policy, one scholar describes early childhood programs as a "mishmash of financing mechanisms and funding streams" (Fuller 2007, 285). Another calls preschool "education's version of the Wild West" (Kirp 2007, 25). Many observers agree that the contemporary preschool system is not really a coherent system at all, and some scholars have inferred that its development has been "unsystematic [and] chaotic" (Kagan and Neuman 2003, 60).

Preschool education in the United States differs from that of other countries along two main dimensions. First, the private sector plays a prominent role in preschool service provision. The Current Population Survey (CPS) has tracked nursery school enrollment in the United States since 1964. Using these data, figure 1 illustrates how private nursery school enrollment exceeded enrollment in government programs for most of the late twentieth century. Spending patterns also illustrate the importance of the private sector. Whereas parents' fees cover between 10 and 30 percent of the costs of early care and education in most European countries, with governments paying the remaining costs, parents are responsible for roughly 60 percent of the costs in the United States (A. D. White 2005, 1).[11] In some other countries, preschool is the preserve of the public sector, with the private sector playing a circumscribed role. In the Czech Republic, for example, early education and care is "almost entirely a public service" (Organization for Economic Cooperation and Development 2001, 157). In the United States, by contrast, both the public sector and the private sector are heavily involved in preschool education.

The distinction between the public and private sectors is important because the two sectors serve different constituencies in the United States. The programs administered by the national, state, and local governments are generally targeted initiatives that make services available to "disadvantaged" children. Public preschool programs mainly serve children from low-income families, children with learning disabilities, and children in areas with limited private-sector preschool availability. These compensatory programs, the most famous of which is Head Start, are an attempt to level the educational playing field and to promote equality of opportunity. Their chief objective is to prepare children for school, and this emphasis on "school readiness" has been a defining feature of preschool politics since the late 1980s.

Economically secure families are more likely to rely on the private sector for preschool services. As a result, some observers characterize early childhood policy in the United States as a "two-tiered" system stratified by class. Targeted government programs serve poor families and their children, while the private market serves more-affluent families. The government encourages well-off families to rely on the private sector by providing an income tax credit for child and dependent care. Initially established as a tax deduction in 1954, this tax expenditure historically has "mainly benefited middle- and upper-income families and spurred the growth of both voluntary and commercial services in the private sector" (Michel 1999, 5). Supporters of this approach argue that it promotes parental autonomy, allowing parents to choose a particular type of program or provider. Another justification for this tax expenditure is that it subsidizes third-party providers who furnish services that benefit society as a whole. In this case, the tax code underwrites private preschool (and child care) providers.

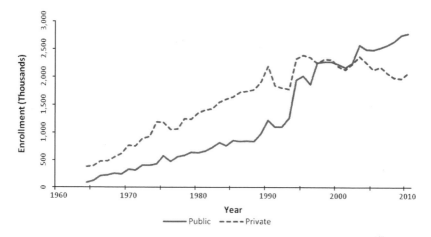

Fig. 1. Nursery school enrollment, 1964–2010. (Data from Current Population Survey.)

The second dimension along which preschool education in the United States differs from that of other countries is its public-sector decentralization. Government programs are administered at the national, state, and local levels. Dozens of national programs provide or support education and care for children under the age of five. They are administered by the Department of Education, the Department of Health and Human Services, and other agencies. In addition, many programs exist at the state level. During the 2009–10 academic year, forty states funded one or more prekindergarten initiatives (Barnett et al. 2010). One scholar characterizes this crowded landscape of governmental activity as a "hodgepodge of federal, state, and local funding streams and regulations" (Finn 2009, 27). This book focuses on national and state initiatives. Decentralization is a defining attribute of preschool education in the United States, whereas countries like France operate more-centralized systems.

The decentralization of preschool education allows subnational officials to design and administer programs that are consistent with the needs or preferences of their jurisdictions. As a result, preschool programs in the United States vary widely in their eligibility requirements, quality standards, resources, and other characteristics. The states have been an especially important locus of policymaking in the early 2000s, with enrollment in and spending on public-sector programs rising considerably. During the 2005 legislative sessions, for example, officials in twenty-six states boosted preschool funding by a total of approximately six hundred million dollars. In some states, including Colorado, Florida, Louisiana, Nebraska, and Pennsylvania, spending on preschool increased by at least 30 percent.[12] Although the economic recession that began in 2007 slowed the pace of change, the past two decades represent a period of significant state-level innovation in early childhood policy.

Many observers believe that this fragmented system produces undesirable outcomes. Reform advocates frequently describe the present patchwork approach as both administratively burdensome and counterproductive. According to the National Education Association, it is "out-of-date, inconsistent, and represents a tragically missed opportunity to improve children's chances for success later in school."[13] A coalition of educational associations argued that a lack of program coordination "often results in duplicate services, a convoluted number of programs and policies that are largely divorced not only from each other but also from the K–12 system, and contradictory policies that ultimately are not in the best interest of taxpayers or children and their families."[14] Advocacy groups are not the only ones who worry about the negative impact of program fragmentation. The Organization for Economic Cooperation and Development has described American preschool education as a "patchwork of services, regulations, and funding sources [that] leads to confusion, uneven quality, and inequality of access" (Organization for Economic Cooperation and Development 2001, 184).[15] The structure of American preschool education, in short, affects who gains access to programs and the quality of the services they receive.

In sum, preschool education in the contemporary United States is distinguished by its fragmentation. This complexity is a by-product of both its reliance on private-sector service providers and the decentralization of the government programs that do exist. The overlapping prerogatives of the private and public sectors and of national, state, and local governments result in an unusually complex system that many observers find problematic. During the late 1960s, neither Howe nor Quie foresaw the emergence of such complexity. How and why did preschool education in the United States take on its distinctive contemporary shape? That is the primary question that motivates this book.[16] In other words, it offers a "political analysis" rather than a "policy analysis" of preschool education (Sroufe 1995). It does not assess the desirability of government involvement in this policy sector. Nor does it evaluate the effectiveness of the contemporary preschool system (though it does investigate the political impact of such program evaluations when relevant). Instead, this book seeks to illuminate how political factors contributed to the distinctive features of the contemporary preschool system and what their impact reveals about the current prospects for significant reform.[17]

Such an endeavor seems especially important since so many actors agree that the status quo is undesirable. In light of this consensus, the stability of the fragmented system is somewhat puzzling.[18] To explain its emergence and persistence, we must examine key policy decisions, the reactions they spawned, and the ways in which these decisions and reactions created stakeholders whose mobilization constrained subsequent possibilities for change. Only by treating policymaking as an iterative process that plays out over considerable periods of time is it possible to isolate the political origins of the contemporary American preschool system.

Policy Development and Preschool Education

The American preschool system was not put into place at a single moment in time by self-conscious politicians who believed that a combination of public-sector and private-sector programs was the most effective way to deliver services to young children. In order to explain the current system and its implications for future reform possibilities, it is necessary to treat policymaking as a long-term causal chain. In keeping with recent research on policy development (Pierson 2005; Hacker 2005), this book focuses on how early childhood policy unfolded over time. It argues that its contemporary fragmentation can be traced to the temporally distant events of the early 1970s. Three concepts help explain this long-term causal chain: critical junctures, venue shopping, and policy feedback.

Critical junctures are founding moments that fix into place basic political orientations and institutions. They are "periods of significant change that produce distinct legacies" (Mayes 2004, 5). Critical junctures establish the organizational logic of a social policy, and subsequent changes tend to be variations or extensions of that logic. They are important in and of themselves and because they have significant and long-lasting consequences. In the late 1960s and early 1970s, several forces placed preschool education on the national political agenda. The mothers of young children entered the workforce in large numbers, cognitive psychology research suggested that the early years were a critical period for child development, and the political environment was conducive to major expansions of government activity.

In 1971, Congress considered the Comprehensive Child Development Act. The bill would have provided wide-ranging educational, nutritional, and health services to preschool-aged children. Both supporters and opponents viewed it as a step toward the universal public provision of preschool services, precisely the kind of program envisioned by Howe in his April 1968 address. It marked a dramatic departure from the temporary targeted initiatives that characterized previous national government programs. The legislation passed both houses of Congress with bipartisan support, but President Richard Nixon vetoed the bill and denounced it in harsh terms, due in part to pressure from conservatives.

Existing scholarship correctly acknowledges the significance of Nixon's veto but underestimates its short- and long-term consequences. The early 1970s have been called "the high-water mark" in efforts to establish public responsibility for the education and care of young children (Beatty 1995, 199), and the veto itself has been recognized as a "watershed" moment (Olmsted 1992, 5; E. Rose 2010, 9). The veto was not the final word on the issue, because the demographic, intellectual, and political forces that had placed preschool education on the national agenda remained in effect. The veto therefore spurred a series of reactions and counterreactions that affected the subsequent evolution of American preschool education. The absence of a comprehensive national policy facilitated the growth of private-sector programs to meet growing demand for preschool services. Meanwhile, advocates of government intervention, frustrated by their prospects at the national level, turned to other institutional settings to pursue their goals. This dynamic is known as venue shopping.

Important public policy decisions are made in various institutional settings in the United States. This decentralization gives policy advocates an incentive to focus on the arena in which they are most likely to be successful. After losing a congressional battle, for example, reformers can turn to the executive branch or to the state or federal courts. They can shift their focus to another institutional setting because "there are no immutable rules that spell out which institutions in society must be charged with making decisions" (Baumgartner and Jones 1993, 31). Venue shopping has long been recognized as an important element of the policymaking process.

Preschool advocates engaged in venue shopping after the veto of the Comprehensive Child Development Act. The coalition of interest groups supporting the bill had been unable to achieve their most ambitious goals at the national level, so some members shifted their attention to the states. The states represented fertile terrain for their efforts, because many state officials felt the vetoed legislation privileged localities and community organizations at their expense. They introduced numerous measures to allow greater governmental intervention in the education and care of young children, and these measures bore substantial fruit. Several states established offices of child development or preschool projects or commenced preschool activity in the early to mid-1970s. In addition to this state-level innovation, preschool advocates refocused their congressional efforts and won several smaller victories at the national level. Head Start was placed on surer footing, and the Child and Dependent Care Tax Credit was dramatically expanded.

The successful venue shopping that occurred during the 1970s had profound long-term consequences. By succeeding in multiple venues, preschool advocates established the foundation for the fragmentation of the contemporary system. Their successes generated policy feedback. A key element of the developmental perspective, policy feedback is the notion that "policies with specific qualities can produce social effects that reinforce their own stability" (Pierson 2005, 37). The adoption of a public policy can facilitate the organization and empowerment of its beneficiaries, as these constituencies mobilize to protect it against attack and press for its extension. Policymakers who wish to alter the status quo often must overcome the opposition of groups that benefit from existing arrangements. Their political power can constrain the options that future generations of officials possess, and it can make the retrenchment of existing policies difficult (Pierson 1993, 1996). Three groups played such a role in preschool politics: state and local government officials, Head Start supporters, and private-sector preschool providers.

State and local officials generally value money and authority. When programs are established at the subnational level, officials with jurisdiction over them may defend their authority against encroachment by their counterparts at the national level. They may be loath to cede policymaking authority to actors in another institutional venue. Several state and local preschool programs were created during the early- to mid-1970s. They gave subnational officials a stake in this policy arena that they did not previously possess. When members of Congress later returned to the issue of preschool services, state and local officials appeared at congressional hearings to defend their prerogatives, urging Congress to provide more funding for existing state programs. They argued that the national government's role should consist of agenda setting and financial support, that it should strengthen and not supplant state efforts. This form of policy feedback shifted the terms of the political debate and constrained reformers' options. It proved difficult for congressional reformers to overcome the opposition of the policymakers empowered by existing arrangements.

In terms of its political impact, Head Start is the most important preschool program at the national level. It is a targeted program through which the national government distributes grants to local community organizations to provide health, nutrition, and other social services to disadvantaged children and their families while preparing the children for primary education.[19] Head Start centers share a name, a mission, and a philosophy; receive training and technical assistance; and meet uniform performance standards. Established as part of the War on Poverty in 1965, Head Start maintained a tenuous existence during its early years. Supporters succeeded in placing the national program on surer footing in the 1970s, and today it retains strong public support (Vinovskis 2005; Zigler and Muenchow 1992).

The existence of Head Start mobilized another set of stakeholders. Head Start prioritizes parental and community involvement. It views parental involvement as a way both to empower parents and to educate and counsel them. In terms of planning and program governance, the families who participate in Head Start are an "integral part of the decision-making process" (Grotberg 1981, 12). Head Start also provides parents with career development opportunities. Historically, most of its employment and training efforts have focused on careers in early childhood (Zigler and Muenchow 1992, chap. 5). As a result, Head Start parents are staunch defenders of the program both because they value its educational and other services and because they are protecting their decision-making authority and their jobs.

The formation of the National Head Start Association (NHSA) in the early 1970s illustrates how public policies can lead to the organization of their beneficiaries. The organization viewed defending Head Start as its primary mission. Ironically, its formation contributed to a fissure within the early childhood policy community. The NHSA, like other Head Start supporters, has frequently called for additional public investment in preschool but tends to view new programs as a financial and existential threat. This competitive dynamic has affected preschool politics at both the national and the state level.

Finally, the importance of private-sector preschool providers is an outgrowth of the Child and Dependent Care Tax Credit. The tax credit dates to 1954, when the federal tax code was revised to allow a tax deduction for employment-related expenses for dependent care. Eligibility was initially limited to gainfully employed women, widowers, and legally separated or divorced men. The Revenue Act of 1971 made any individual maintaining a household eligible, raised the deduction limit, modified the legal definition of a dependent, and raised the income level at which the deduction began to be phased out. These changes sought to provide tax relief to middle- and low-income taxpayers. Additional reforms in 1975 and 1976 nearly doubled the income limit for phasing out the deduction and replaced the deduction with a nonrefundable tax credit. It was believed that these reforms would benefit taxpayers in the lower brackets by expanding the tax credit's reach to those who did not itemize deductions.[20]

The number of returns on which the Child and Dependent Care Tax Credit was claimed more than doubled between 1976 and 1988, and the aggregate amount of credit claimed rose even more sharply.[21] In 2008, an average credit of $535 was claimed on 6.587 million returns.[22] Credit claimants are not the only source of policy feedback. The tax credit is politically significant because it facilitated the growth of early childhood services in the private sector. These private-sector programs met the needs of many middle- and upper-income families, making those groups less likely to demand further governmental action (Morgan 2006; E. Rose 2010). Even more important, the service providers themselves emerged as key stakeholders and active participants in preschool politics.[23] Providers "grew into a constituency to be reckoned with when questions about public funding for young children moved onto federal and state agendas" (E. Rose 2010, 224). They often lobbied Congress and state legislatures to protect their interests. Most public programs therefore incorporate private-sector providers for both logistical and political reasons. As a result, recent reforms tend to preserve, rather than mitigate, the fragmentation of the contemporary preschool system.

In sum, the main argument of this book is that the contemporary structure of preschool education in the United States can be traced to developments in the early 1970s. A critical juncture occurred in 1971, when Nixon vetoed legislation that would have provided a permanent framework for the universal provision of preschool services. The absence of a comprehensive national policy, in combination with revisions in the federal tax code, contributed to the growth of the private sector. Meanwhile, supporters of increased public investment, largely stymied at the national level, engaged in venue shopping in disparate institutional settings. Their successes at the state level and their ability to put national programs like Head Start on more-secure political footing had important long-term political consequences, because the constituencies who benefited from these arrangements subsequently mobilized to defend the status quo. Lobbying by state officials, Head Start supporters, and third-party providers in the private sector made it more difficult for the national government to adopt a more unified approach to the provision of preschool services. Subsequent political discussions therefore occurred on a different political terrain than had the discussions of the late 1960s and early 1970s. In short, the venue shopping that occurred after a critical juncture generated policy feedback that both contributed to the contemporary fragmentation of American preschool education and constrained reformers' options as they sought major policy change.

Plan of This Book

In recent years, many scholars have noted the unusual blend of public and private social benefits that characterizes social policymaking in the United States (Gottschalk 2000; Hacker 2002; Howard 2007). Indeed, the private sector plays an essential role in preschool education. Moreover, the targeted and residual nature of existing public programs also resonates with conventional portrayals of the American welfare state (Michel 1999, 9). Scholars have advanced several explanations of American social policy, and chapter 1 of this book assesses their applicability to preschool education. It examines the strengths and weaknesses of accounts based on political culture, interest group politics, and the institutional structure of the American political system. Each of these perspectives helps explain elements of preschool politics, yet none of them provides a complete and convincing account. They are largely static explanations that cannot capture the dynamism that characterizes this policy arena. Explaining the origins and contemporary complexity of American preschool education requires a developmental perspective that treats the making of public policy as a long-term causal chain. Chapter 1 describes the merits of the developmental approach and three of its central concepts. It argues that critical junctures, venue shopping, and policy feedback help account for the emergence and persistence of the contemporary preschool system.

In keeping with the developmental perspective, the remaining chapters of this book proceed chronologically. Chapter 2 describes American early childhood policy prior to the late 1960s. These historical episodes represent the antecedent conditions against which the impact of a critical juncture must be assessed (Collier and Collier 1991). The emergency nursery schools of the New Deal, the wartime child care centers of the 1940s, and Head Start shared two key attributes. They were targeted and temporary (Beatty 1995; Lazerson 1972; Slobdin 1975). They neither promoted universal access to preschool services nor established the framework for a permanent national policy.[24]

The Comprehensive Child Development Act of 1971 broke sharply with the past, because it attempted to create a permanent national framework for the universal provision of preschool services. Chapter 2 concludes by examining the demographic, intellectual, and political forces that placed this landmark proposal on the national agenda, and chapter 3 describes the remarkable political dynamics that surrounded it. After extensive debate and negotiations, the bill received bipartisan congressional support only to be vetoed and denounced in very harsh language. The veto is a critical juncture because it provoked responses in alternate institutional venues that affected the subsequent evolution of American preschool evolution.

When examining critical junctures, scholars must distinguish between their aftermath and their heritage (Collier and Collier 1991, 8). The aftermath of critical junctures refers to their immediate and short-term consequences. Chapters 4 and 5 analyze the aftermath of Nixon's veto. The early and mid-1970s included important developments both at the state level, the subject of chapter 4, and in Congress, the subject of chapter 5. State officials, due to prodding by preschool advocates and their own belief that the vetoed legislation privileged other actors at their expense, expanded their involvement in early childhood policy. Meanwhile, various initiatives faltered in Congress. Preschool advocates scored important victories by creating or defending more-limited governmental interventions, but these victories, in combination with the state activity described in chapter 4, contributed to the dissolution of the coalition that had come together to support comprehensive change. They both fragmented public-sector activity and gave disparate actors conflicting stakes in existing arrangements.

The heritage of a critical juncture refers to its long-term consequences and the extent to which it affects temporally distant events. Chapters 6, 7, and 8 examine the heritage of Nixon's veto. Chapter 6 examines the limited policy changes that occurred at both the national and state level during the 1980s. Preschool advocates made little progress, in part because they were unable to coalesce into a unified force for reform. They agreed on the merits of additional public investment but disagreed on the form that it should take. Those who benefited from existing arrangements often viewed both comprehensive and incremental reforms as threats to their interests.

Over the last two decades, early childhood policy has received substantial attention from national and state policymakers. Chapter 7 describes the demographic, intellectual, and political factors that returned the topic to the political agenda. It then turns to recent congressional discussions of preschool education and demonstrates how previous policy decisions constrained policymakers' and reformers' options. Congress held several hearings that suggest a general interest in preschool education but evince little interest in an expanded national government role. The hearings focused on program coordination and the perceived deficiencies of the fragmented status quo. They both invoked administrative concerns and highlighted the political challenges involved in altering existing arrangements. Despite bipartisan agreement on the need for reform, the past two decades have been a period of limited congressional innovation.

Chapter 8 assesses the long-term consequences of Nixon's veto at the state level. In recent years, state officials have endorsed new preschool initiatives and expanded access to and increased spending on existing programs. This extensive state-level activity caused multiple scholars to identify the emergence of a preschool movement (Finn 2009; Fuller 2007, 5; Kirp 2007, 100). Chapter 8 combines secondary and case study evidence with a quantitative analysis of preschool funding decisions to illustrate how the existing slate of service providers affected early childhood policymaking. The major state-level shifts of the late 1990s and early 2000s built on or combined existing public and private programs, an approach that was a logistical and political necessity.

The concluding chapter of this book draws two types of lessons. First, it reassesses the developmental approach to the study of American social policy. Foundational concepts of this approach, including critical junctures, venue shopping, and policy feedback, help explain the fragmentation that characterizes the contemporary preschool system. The developments profiled in this book suggest that scholars should examine a wider range of programs and time periods in their efforts to develop generalizations about policymaking in the United States. They also suggest that scholars should devote more attention to the interactive relationship between episodes at the national and state level, to the role of subnational units as autonomous actors in a federal system, and to policy variation among the American states.

The second set of lessons with which this book concludes is more speculative. The past fifteen years have been a period of heightened interest in the education and care of young children. State and national officials have considered several different approaches to service delivery. Many states have acted, Congress has held multiple hearings on the issue, and some gubernatorial and presidential candidates have pledged to create voluntary prekindergarten programs for all four-year-olds. The evolution of

American preschool education, however, suggests that contemporary advocates of greater governmental involvement face significant hurdles. The prospects for a comprehensive and unified approach are not as bright as they were when Howe and Quie made their respective predictions in the late 1960s. A more diverse and entrenched set of constituencies now has a stake in preschool education, and accommodating them in pursuit of policy change will not be an easy task.

1 | Early Childhood Policy and the American Welfare State

Scholars have long been captivated by the distinctive features of the American welfare state. One recent focus has been the pronounced role of the private sector in the pursuit of social policy objectives. The American welfare state is a divided one in which many of the duties carried out by governments elsewhere are left in the hands of the private sector.[1] Various tax subsidies and regulations encourage private actors, such as employers, to provide benefits like health insurance and pensions (Hacker 2002, 7). As a result, the American economy is characterized by a "comparatively high level of private-sector spending upon health, education, and savings for old age" (R. Rose 1989, 113). The private sector plays a large role in early childhood policy. Of the 4,835,000 American children who attended nursery school in 2010, 2,059,000 (42.6 percent) were enrolled in private schools.[2] Private enrollment outnumbered public enrollment for most of the late twentieth century. As late as 1999, the majority of children in nursery school attended private institutions.

Most public early childhood programs in the United States are targeted initiatives that serve children who are from low-income families or who are considered disadvantaged. Dozens of public programs at the national and state levels are compensatory rather than universal. The decentralization of these government programs highlights the role of state governments as an important locus of decision making. State governments are "integral to almost all means-tested and some social insurance programs" (Howard 1999, 424), yet their impact is often overlooked. A complete understanding of American social policy necessitates attention to both private-sector activity and state politics. Conventional explanations of welfare state development offer limited insight into these two defining features of contemporary early childhood policy. This chapter reviews their strengths and weaknesses before turning to the analytical advantages of a developmental perspective that treats policymaking as a long-term causal chain. Critical junctures, venue shopping, and policy feedback help explain the current structure and politics of preschool education in the United States.

Conventional Explanations: Political Culture, Interest Groups, and Institutions

Education policy is difficult to categorize. Some scholars describe investments in education as developmental initiatives designed to spur economic activity, noting that they rank among the best predictors of economic growth and productivity (Peterson 1995, 65). Others focus on the distributive implications of education spending, arguing that "skills and education are at the core of the welfare state" (Iversen and Stephens 2008, 602). Both arguments contain a grain of truth. Education spending is related to economic performance, but it is also a free public service that can have redistributive consequences.

The overlapping objectives of educational programs help explain why this policy sector has long fit uneasily into comparative scholarship on social policy. One pioneering study concluded that "education is special" and excluded it from its study of the welfare state (Wilensky 1975, 3). The status of education policy represents a particular challenge for scholars interested in the United States. The American welfare state has been called "underdeveloped" and "incomplete" (Orloff 1988, 37), yet the country created the most comprehensive system of public schooling in the world (Tyack and Cuban 1995). This section reviews three prominent explanations of welfare state development. While each of them offers insight into early childhood policy in the United States, none provides a complete and convincing account.

Political Culture

Cultural accounts attribute policy outcomes to societal values and beliefs about the operation and justification of government. Values like individualism and an emphasis on private property and the free market cause Americans to place a greater emphasis on personal responsibility than on collective responsibility. Americans believe that hard work and personal effort are the keys to success. They view government as wasteful and inefficient and as something that should be used in emergency situations only.

The distinctive structure of American social policy might therefore be attributed to Americans' core beliefs about the justification and operation of government. According to one cultural account, "[T]he state plays a more limited role in America than elsewhere because Americans, more than other people, want it to play a limited role" (King 1973, 418).

Values like individualism and limited government intervention seem especially resonant in the context of early childhood policy. They imply that child-rearing practices should remain the private province of parents, and they suggest that government involvement is appropriate only when families are in crisis. Indeed, opponents of public investment often caution against government encroachment on parental prerogatives and argue that parents' educational choices should generally be free from either direct or indirect state interference (Cobb 1992; Gilles 1996). In the early 1970s, for example, one critic of child development legislation asserted that "autonomy of decision making must be an essential part of any child care arrangement . . . because it is right and just that Americans control their own lives" (Rothman 1973, 42). The primary strength of cultural accounts is their ability to account for these ubiquitous rhetorical claims.

The cultural explanation of American early childhood education is problematic for several reasons.[3] Values like individualism and equality can be interpreted in different ways that are not necessarily consistent with one another (Verba and Orren 1985). The state is the major supplier of education in the United States, and one cultural account attributes this outcome to the triumph of equality over other cherished American values like limited government. Education was portrayed as the great equalizer, and the state only competed with private institutions in a very small way (King 1973, 420). Contemporary analyses of public opinion suggest that large majorities of Americans view education as a government responsibility and favor greater spending on it (Howard 2007, 113). A comprehensive system of public education represents a challenge for the cultural perspective.

In addition, the connection between broad ideals and concrete policy solutions is often tenuous. The outcome with which this book is concerned is a complex amalgamation of national, state, and local government programs supplemented by private-sector service providers. Furthermore, governmental initiatives like Head Start and state prekindergarten programs directly provide education and care for young children. Other programs, including the Child and Dependent Care Tax Credit, provide indirect support to the private sector. The mechanism linking values like autonomy to this wide-ranging public-sector activity remains opaque.[4]

Political culture connotes deep and enduring beliefs about the proper role and scope of government. It is difficult to link those beliefs to concrete outcomes.

Another weakness of cultural accounts is their inability to explain policy change or its timing. The deep and enduring beliefs that make up a political culture are not susceptible to change. Cultural accounts are therefore "too holistic and essentialist to give us the explanatory leverage we need to account for variations in the fate of different social policies, or for changes over time in the fate of similar proposals" (Skocpol 1992, 17). They struggle to explain both the existence of an extensive public system of elementary and secondary education and the complicated mixture of public and private programs that exist in preschool education. Values and beliefs provide limited analytical leverage over new directions in policymaking or the emergence of new issues on the political agenda.

Finally, political culture cannot explain the near passage of the Comprehensive Child Development Act of 1971, a foundational moment in American early childhood policy. Both supporters and opponents viewed the bill as a step toward the creation of a permanent national framework for the universal provision of preschool services, and it received bipartisan support in both houses of Congress before being vetoed by President Richard Nixon. The congressional endorsement suggests that deep-seated beliefs about the proper role of government are insufficient to account for outcomes in this policy arena. One historian explains, "That Congress could be convinced to accept legislation even hinting at altering many of the strongest and most fervently held values about the role of government and the family was remarkable" (McCathren 1981, 120). In sum, while supporters and opponents of public investment frame their arguments in terms of equality and autonomy, respectively, the value content of their arguments cannot explain the fate of various proposals to expand the governmental role in early childhood policy.

Interest Groups

Interest group activity may help explain the contemporary fragmentation of early childhood policy in the United States. Specifically, the respective political strength of advocates and opponents of governmental intervention may account for the absence of a permanent national framework for the universal provision of preschool services.[5] The nominal beneficiaries of early childhood programs are "children [who] don't vote; thus, their political cause has always been weak" (Grubb 1987, 1). In 1975, Senator

Walter Mondale (D-MN) explained, "There is something about the politics of children we have yet to solve; maybe it's very simple. A friend of mine, a very conservative one, once said, 'You know, you should do more for old people and forget these kids, they can't vote,' and maybe that's the answer."[6]

Several observers describe the absence of a strong, cohesive children's lobby as important. Jule Sugarman, who directed the Office of Child Development during the Nixon administration, explained, "I think the advocates for children have never been organized in a way to sustain public pressure, and that is why children do get short-shrifted in this country."[7] Longtime advocate Marian Wright Edelman concurred, "Kids have been outside the political process and they've not had the kind of systematic advocacy that's required of any group in this country that's going to have any chance of anything."[8] The interest groups that lobby on behalf of young children and their families tend to be small organizations that compete with one another, such as the liberal Children's Defense Fund and the conservative Family Research Council.

A lack of unity among advocates of government intervention has exacerbated their political weakness. They have been described as a "divided constituency" (Michel 1999). For example, they have long disagreed about the appropriate content of early childhood programs. The split in the early twentieth century between educational and custodial programs has evolved into a conflict between the communities concerned with elementary school and early childhood education, over purposes, methods, and control (Grubb 1987). Constituencies who share the goal of expanding access to preschool services often work at cross-purposes, taking different sides on proposals that attempt to serve this objective.

The coalition opposing government intervention, in contrast, has been more cohesive. The mid-1970s marked the beginning of a conservative resurgence in American politics.[9] Ambitious initiatives in early childhood policy offended economic and social conservatives, who derided them as an undesirable expansion of the public sector and governmental interference in the family. Opponents viewed themselves as defending the prerogatives of stay-at-home mothers and the general principle of parental choice in all matters of child rearing (Morgan 2006). Their grassroots mobilization efforts sparked an avalanche of letters to Congress in the 1970s, and they continue to be active on matters of gender and family issues.

Interest group activity is an important part of preschool politics in the United States, but it is important not to overstate its significance as a causal factor. Even in the absence of a unified coalition, advocates of increased public investment have achieved several important victories over the past four decades. National programs like Head Start and the Child and Dependent Care Tax Credit have grown significantly since the 1970s, and enrollment in and funding of state prekindergarten programs expanded dramatically in the 2000s. Much of this recent activity occurred at the state level.[10] Interest group accounts struggle to explain why leading innovators in this policy arena include such conservative states as Georgia and Oklahoma.

Furthermore, congressional passage of the Comprehensive Child Development Act suggests that, despite their lack of unity, supporters of increased public investment were sufficiently effective to move an ambitious piece of legislation through Congress. A coalition headed by Marian Wright Edelman was instrumental in drafting the proposal and formulating the legislative strategy that resulted in its passage. Although Nixon vetoed the bill, the content of the legislation and its passage represented a major break with the past. The veto predated the political mobilization of social conservatives. In fact, it contributed to their activation. It is therefore problematic to attribute the veto to interest group politics.

Interest groups affect the formation of public policy, but public policies also affect the positions that groups take and the strategies they employ. Supporters of increased public investment adjusted their interests, objectives, and political strategies as mothers of young children entered the workforce, preschool attendance soared, and public policies addressed these trends. Reformers accommodated their institutional and policy context, leading to shifting fault lines within the community concerned with early childhood education. The creation and expansion of various initiatives gave them distinct turf to defend. Supporters sometimes critiqued expansive proposals out of the concern that they would divert resources from their preferred program. Even limited government intervention in early childhood policy facilitated the organization and empowerment of constituencies with a stake in the status quo and fostered the fragmentation of the preschool coalition. As subsequent chapters of this book will demonstrate, this lack of unity among advocates is better characterized as an outgrowth of public policies than as their cause.

Institutions

Institutional accounts attribute policy outcomes to the constitutional structure that mediates societal demands. They focus on the extent to which this structure centralizes decision-making authority. The American political system is noteworthy for its decentralization, which provides opponents of policy initiatives with multiple opportunities to block them. Opponents can defeat proposals at any of these veto points, whereas supporters must clear every hurdle if their proposal is to become law. In political systems with a large number of veto points, like the United States, the potential for policy change decreases (Tsebelis 1995). This institutional arrangement affords defenders of the status quo "a multiplicity of access points at which [they] can modify or exercise a veto over policy change" (Thomas 1975, 232). Due to their decentralizing impact, the core features of the American political system have been described as "inimical to welfare state expansion" (Huber, Ragin, and Stephens 1993, 721).[11]

Federalism, the balance of policymaking authority between the national government and the states, seems especially crucial in the context of education policy. Education periodically becomes a national issue, but "policy talk and policy action have taken place mostly at the state and local levels" (Tyack and Cuban 1995, 43). The vast majority of the cost of public education is paid out of state and local budgets, and local school boards and state departments of education exercise considerable discretion. One might trace the contemporary fragmentation of American early childhood policy to the decentralization of decision-making authority in the United States, placing special emphasis on federalism.[12]

The institutional perspective accounts convincingly for a foundational moment in early childhood policy. The near passage of the Comprehensive Child Development Act illustrates the significance of the country's constitutional structure. A presidential veto prevented the creation of a permanent national framework for the universal provision of preschool services, suggesting that the decentralization of decision-making authority can stymie major policy change. Additional efforts to create a comprehensive national system were also defeated, and institutional accounts attribute these repeated defeats to the existence of a large number of veto points.

Institutional accounts are incomplete, however. Institutions reveal little about the preferences, identities, and resources of key political actors (Pierson 1995). Institutional accounts also struggle to explain policy change and its timing. The constitutional structure of the United States has been stable, but while some policy initiatives successfully navigated this institutional labyrinth, others did not. Institutional accounts struggle to explain this variation, because they shed limited light on the actual decision-making processes that determine policy outcomes.

Furthermore, the national government has been increasingly active in education policymaking. National officials are "increasingly willing to suggest that [they] should have a significant role in decisions about important [education] matters" (Stout, Tallerico, and Scribner 1995, 14). According to one account, a "gradual process of nationalization occurred and transformed the politics of education from dominantly a local enterprise" (Cibulka 2001, 19).[13] The No Child Left Behind Act, signed into law by President George W. Bush during his first term, represents "the most significant intrusion of federal power in the history of American education" (Viteritti 2004, 80). Given this overall trend of increased national government involvement in education policymaking, the limited national movement in early childhood policy is all the more puzzling.

Policy Development and Preschool Politics

To isolate the origins of public policies, it is often necessary to "pay attention to processes that play out over considerable periods of time" (Pierson 2005, 34). A developmental approach must be "particularly sensitive to the temporal sequencing of causal factors and to the combination of distinct causal processes that become conjoined at distinct periods" (Katznelson 2003, 391). At a fundamental level, the main shortcoming of the three frameworks profiled in the preceding section is their inability to account for change over time. Cultural values are deep and enduring, multiple scholars describe long-standing dissension within the early childhood policy community (Michel 1999; Grubb 1987), and institutions are defined by their durability. Yet early childhood policy is a lively arena characterized by complicated social and political dynamics.

Forward-looking lawmakers did not establish the contemporary amalgamation of private-sector and public-sector preschool programs at a single moment. This complex and fragmented system evolved over time as various stakeholders reacted to shifting institutional terrain and to what had already transpired. The existing policy repertoire constrained the possibility of major shifts, serving as a "vital force shaping the alternatives perceived and the policies adopted" (Heclo 1974, 156). The durability of public policies can affect the likelihood of major change by altering the incentives and resources of political actors (Hacker 2002; Pierson 1993; R. Rose 1990). The contemporary fragmentation of early childhood policy is a by-product of the interactive relationship between politics and public policy, and accounts that do not take history into account overlook this crucial relationship.

This book argues that three concepts—critical junctures, venue shopping, and policy feedback—help explain the evolution of early childhood policy in the United States. These concepts provide a common analytical framework through which the historical complexities of social policy can be examined. By constructing and testing general claims about processes of long-term policy development, it becomes possible to develop a genuinely analytical history that is attentive to substantively and theoretically challenging questions of temporality and periodicity (Katznelson 2003, 391).[14] The developmental approach represents an especially important shift for the study of education policy, where existing research typically focuses on policy analysis. Policy analysis provides valuable insights about how programs function but, unfortunately, "leads one toward static snapshots of phenomena that are more accurately represented as being in motion" (Sroufe 1995, 79).

Critical Junctures

Critical junctures are "crucial period[s] of transition" (Collier and Collier 1991, 29). They are important not only in and of themselves but also because they produce durable legacies. Embedded in this concept is the notion that several institutional or policy options are feasible at a given moment but that any actions taken or decisions made at that time will profoundly affect subsequent developments. These crucial founding moments send institutions or public policies down particular developmental paths and constrain future possibilities. Critical junctures are "leading determinants of how programs and policymaking develop, with outcomes during a crucial transition establishing distinct pathways or trajectories of growth" (Mayes 2004, 18). They leave a lasting mark on the political landscape, one that constrains future reform possibilities.

Critical junctures provide an opening for institutional or policy change, but they do not determine the form that it will take. Only the more limited claim that a significant change occurred is embedded in the concept. Critical junctures "do not guarantee any particular institutional outcome" (Jones-Correa 2000–2001, 567). The institutions or public policies that exist after a critical juncture differ from what preceded them. Thus the antecedent conditions that precede a critical juncture represent the baseline against which its consequences must be assessed (Collier and Collier 1991, 30).

The notion that decisions made or actions taken at a particular moment have long-term consequences makes intuitive sense. The concept of critical junctures contributes to scholars' understanding of policy or institutional development by placing political developments "in historical context and in terms of processes unfolding over time and in relation to each other, within a broader context in which developments in one realm impinge on and shape developments in others" (Thelen 1999, 390). It emphasizes the importance of timing, sequencing, and the interaction of ongoing processes in political life. The impact of interest group activity or political alignments, for example, may depend on the institutional context and on what has already transpired. Understanding these interactions between ongoing political processes is a prerequisite for any effort to explain long-term outcomes.

The significance of antecedent conditions and change may seem problematic for an account of early childhood policy that describes a presidential veto as a critical juncture. A veto, by definition, leaves the status quo intact. The concept of venue shopping, however, helps explain why the veto did not halt the movement to increase the governmental role in preschool services. Instead, it redirected that movement by spurring advocates to seek more favorable institutional terrain for their policy goals. This venue shopping sparked reactions and counterreactions that shaped developments in this policy arena over the long term.

Venue Shopping

American political institutions diffuse power to a remarkable degree, and this decentralization is a double-edged sword. The dispersal of political authority provides multiple veto points for reform opponents, as institutional accounts emphasize, but each of these settings is also a point of access for reformers. Frustrated in one institutional venue, reformers can try to achieve their goals in another setting. In fact, the "many venues of American politics also allow new policy to find niches within which to flourish" (Baumgartner and Jones 1991, 1071). After losing a congressional battle, for example, advocates can turn to the executive branch, the federal courts, or state and local authorities. Decentralization can therefore lead to venue shopping, as advocates focus on the institutional setting in which they believe they are most likely to experience success.

Venue shopping implies that reformers can be strategic in pursuit of their goals. One study explains how "lobbyists themselves frequently speak of designing their advocacy strategies as if they were preparing for war, carefully selecting battlefields that play to their strengths at the expense of their enemies" (Holyoke 2003, 325). Such strategizing is possible because policy issues may be assigned to and decided in various institutional settings. Changes in venue can occur even when issues have traditionally been assigned to specific institutions. For example, the traditional preeminence of subnational governments in education policymaking has recently been challenged by such national legislation as the No Child Left Behind Act (Viteritti 2004; McDonnell 2005).

Reformers who engage in venue shopping do not need to know in advance how their proposals will be received. They may search for favorable venues in several arenas simultaneously, or they may search through a trial-and-error process. They may continue their searches where they find initial success, and they may abandon efforts where their ideas are rejected (Baumgartner and Jones 1991, 1048). Changes in the Aid to Families with Dependent Children (AFDC) program in the 1960s and early 1970s illustrate how reformers can experience success by venue shopping after their initial efforts have been defeated. Those "seeking to make AFDC more nationally uniform, more generous, and more widely available turned to the courts because their efforts had repeatedly met with failure in Congress" (Melnick 1994, 67). Their successes in the judicial system had profound consequences for welfare policy. Those who lose a policy debate have an incentive to change or attempt to change the venue in which the relevant decisions are made.

Venue shopping implies that studies of policy development in the United States must look beyond congressional and presidential activity to understand the dynamics of policymaking. The recent attention paid toward the role of the private sector in social provision is therefore a promising trend (Hacker 2002; Gottschalk 2000; Howard 1997). Other institutional venues, such as subnational governments, have received less attention. Studies of American federalism typically portray it as an impediment to the adoption of social policy (Robertson 1989; Hacker and Pierson 2002), but states and localities also represent an alternate institutional venue in which important policy decisions are made.

Recent research suggests that federalism can create opportunities for major policy change. It allows politicians at one level to build on the ideas and actions of their counterparts at other levels, generating positive feedback by accelerating certain trends and creating a bandwagon effect. Manna (2006) describes a process of "borrowing strength" whereby policy entrepreneurs working at one level of government can affect the policymaking agenda by leveraging the license and capacity that exist at another level. His compelling study of federalism and the national education policy agenda suggests that it is a mistake to view federalism solely as an obstacle to policy change. This insight is especially important for scholars of education policy, an arena in which "playing-field boundaries are in perpetual motion, and political arenas are constantly shifting boundaries where governing powers between national, state and local units of government are shared" (Scribner, Reyes, and Fusarelli 1995, 203). Early childhood policy exemplifies this dynamic, with a history that has taken place on several terrains in the public and private sectors (Michel 1999, 6).

The opportunities provided by American federalism help explain why it is appropriate to describe Nixon's veto as a critical juncture. The veto provoked responses in alternate institutional venues that provided the framework within which early childhood policy subsequently evolved. Thwarted at the national level, at least in terms of their most ambitious goals, preschool advocates modified their congressional campaign and sought more-favorable institutional venues for their concerns. Their successes, many of which occurred at the state level, had profound long-term consequences for the evolution of preschool education and the politics surrounding it.

Policy Feedback

Critical junctures are periods of change or transition that manifest lasting political legacies. Without this long-term impact, they would not be critical (Pierson 2000, 263). Existing research on critical junctures has been criticized, however, for inadequately specifying "the mechanisms that translate critical junctures into lasting political legacies" (Thelen 1999, 388). Studies invoking this concept must explain what sustains the institutional arrangements that emerge. Mechanisms of production link the critical juncture to its legacy, and mechanisms of reproduction perpetuate the ongoing institutional or political processes (Collier and Collier 1991, 31). This book uses the concept of policy feedback to denote these mechanisms of production and reproduction.

Public policy has traditionally been treated as the outcome of broader social and political processes. Under certain circumstances, however, this causal arrow is reversed. A policy's emergence and continued existence can affect the possibilities for future policymaking by altering the social and political environment. Public policies affect the possibilities for future policymaking by shaping the identities, interests, and incentives of key social actors (Skocpol 1992). The existing policy repertoire can influence the goals of important constituencies. For example, it can alter their attitudes toward governmental intervention and the form it should take (Gottschalk 2000; Morgan 2006).

One significant form of policy feedback is the empowerment of social groups with a stake in the status quo. The adoption of a policy can facilitate the organization of its beneficiaries. They might mobilize to protect the policy against political attack and to press for its extension. The participatory patterns of senior citizens in the United States are illustrative. Most interest groups representing the providers and recipients of government services to the elderly were formed after the adoption of Social Security, Medicare, and the Older Americans Act of 1965 (Walker 1991, 30). Several scholars detect a similar dynamic in health care policy, where stakeholder mobilization helped prevent the creation of national health insurance (Mayes 2004; Quadagno 2005). The establishment of new programs can restructure the long-term interests of politicians and interest groups (Hacker 2002; Pierson 1993).

The political clout of program beneficiaries can constrain the options that policymakers possess. Groups that reach a certain size are politically powerful, and elected officials who prefer another policy arrangement will feel pressure to accommodate them (Pierson 2004, 73). Reforms that do not mobilize a strong supporting coalition, in contrast, are not likely to have a long shelf life (Patashnik 2003, 2008). Furthermore, the fragmentation of political authority in the American political system provides certain advantages to groups hoping to preserve the status quo (Howard 2007, 136). Indeed, a recent study of lobbying concludes that "one of the best single predictors of success in the lobbying game is . . . simply whether [the group] is attempting to protect the policy that is already in place" (Baumgartner et al. 2009, 6). Understanding who is invested in a specific policy and how that investment is sustained over time makes it possible to explain programmatic durability (Thelen 1999, 391).

Stakeholder mobilization is an important element of education policymaking. Groups favored by the status quo often lobby successfully to protect their prerogatives, illustrating the potential impact of policy feedback. An early study of interest groups revealed that education associations possessed a "continuing interest in the administration of whatever programs are on the books" (Bailey 1975, 45). A more recent account concurs, describing the emergence of "an 'education-industrial complex' that fought hard to protect existing programs and to create new ones" (McGuinn 2006, 34). Policy feedback is an important determinant of programmatic durability, as new educational programs "were likely to persist if they produced *influential constituencies* interested in seeing them continue" (Tyack and Cuban 1995, 57; emphasis in original). Job generation contributes to persistence. Those employed by new education programs have a profound interest in their maintenance.

Policy feedback suggests that successful venue shopping can have long-term consequences. Reformers' success in a particular institutional setting may affect what is possible in other venues. Program beneficiaries may work to ensure that future decisions are also made in that venue, because shifting the locus of decision-making authority may introduce an element of uncertainty that puts their previous gains at risk. Groups that have been successful in court or at an executive agency may argue that subsequent decisions should be made in those institutional venues, and officials who favor an alternative policy arrangement may find their options constrained as a result.

In addition, government officials with jurisdiction over a program may work to preserve the status quo because it gives them an opportunity to cultivate the political loyalty of its beneficiaries. If a policy is perceived as successful, officials may engage in credit claiming, an effort to "generate a belief in a relevant political actor (or actors) that one is personally responsible for causing the government, or some unit thereof, to do something that the actor (or actors) considers desirable" (Mayhew 1974, 52–53). An electoral logic drives credit claiming, as those who believe that elected officials are responsible for positive outcomes will be more likely to support their reelection. Government officials with jurisdiction over an existing policy, especially if they are elected officials, may therefore resist attempts to move decision-making responsibility to actors in another institutional venue. Reformers therefore might face opposition from program beneficiaries and from the policymakers empowered by existing arrangements.

Government officials may also work to preserve the status quo because they simply want to protect their bureaucratic turf. Such a dynamic may emerge regardless of whether the policy is viewed as successful. The existence of programs in a particular venue may therefore cause the "filling up" or the "preemption" of a policy space (Pierson 1995). Officials with jurisdiction over a program may fight attempts to alter the status quo. This dynamic differs from the one surrounding program beneficiaries. Program beneficiaries, such as senior citizens defending Social Security (Campbell 2002, 2003), are constituencies to whom elected officials must respond if they wish to win reelection. Government officials may not always possess comparable electoral power, but American federalism gives state and local officials potential influence over their national counterparts. Members of Congress represent geographically defined districts, giving them an electoral incentive to take account of subnational officials' preferences. Frayed relations can lead to charges that legislators have lost touch with their district or state. State officials might challenge the incumbent in a future election or retaliate during the decennial redrawing of district lines.

In his seminal essay on policy feedback, Paul Pierson (1993) explains how policy initiatives can affect government elites' resources and incentives. Most research in this tradition focuses on the notion of bureaucratic capacity and the conditions under which policies generate the specialized knowledge and managerial experience that facilitate government intervention. The existing scholarly literature provides several compelling examples of elite-level feedback. It is often vague, however, about the precise factors that comprise bureaucratic capacity and the specific circumstances under which it will affect subsequent policymaking. As a result, Pierson (1993, 605) concludes that "work on this dimension of policy feedback clearly has a long way to go."

One potentially constructive direction for research on elite-level policy feedback is to emphasize the lobbying activities in which government officials engage. American federalism is an especially propitious arena in which to investigate this dynamic, which begins to explain why successful venue shopping can have significant consequences for long-term policy development. When policies are adopted at the subnational level, officials with jurisdiction over existing programs may defend their authority against encroachment by their colleagues at the national level. Professional associations whose primary constituencies include governors, state legislators, and other officials are active participants in the national policymaking process (Cammisa 1995; Haider 1974). Like program beneficiaries, subnational officials may defend the status quo and lobby for existing policies to be maintained and expanded. They value money and authority, and they "have an interest in maintaining or increasing their authority over federally funded programs" (Cammisa 1995, 21). Their lobbying may limit the possibility of major policy change. The evidence presented in this book suggests that preschool education generated multiple forms of policy feedback. Existing policies have been defended by both their beneficiaries and the officials with jurisdiction over them.

Explaining Preschool Politics in the United States

Understanding how and why early childhood policy in the United States took on its current form requires a developmental approach that is sensitive to processes that play out over considerable periods of time. Policymaking should not be depicted as a final policy result or outcome. Instead, it is best understood as an "unfolding historical process" (Patashnik 1997, 432). This book argues that the contemporary fragmentation of American preschool education can be traced to temporally distant events. The venue shopping that occurred after a critical juncture generated policy feedback, and the subsequent mobilization of program beneficiaries and government officials constrained the options of future generations of policymakers.

The critical juncture occurred when efforts to establish a national child development program fell short in the late 1960s and early 1970s. The absence of a comprehensive national policy contributed to the emergence of private-sector service providers, and preschool advocates engaged in venue shopping. Their successes created and expanded a mélange of public-sector programs at the national, state, and local levels, and these programs generated substantial policy feedback despite their limited breadth. Program beneficiaries and government officials with a stake in the status quo mobilized to oppose changes that would affect their prerogatives. When national lawmakers returned to the topic of preschool education in later years, they operated on more challenging political terrain because the constituencies that benefited from existing programs fought major policy change. This dynamic resonates with a central insight of the developmental approach, namely, that once a policy or an institution is in place, actors adjust their strategies in ways that reflect and reinforce the logic of the existing system (Thelen 1999, 392).

The remaining chapters of this book use archival material and statistical data to examine the changing terrain of American preschool politics. They combine congressional testimony, speeches, media accounts, and other public documents with private memoranda, strategy papers, and letters that illuminate actors' strategic calculations. The impact of federalism and venue shopping means that the analysis examines national episodes, developments at the state level, and their interaction. National policymakers have debated the appropriate national government role in preschool service provision on several occasions. These recurrent debates provide analytical leverage over questions of constituency organization and empowerment that are crucial to the developmental perspective. Changes over time in the identities and positions of key actors would suggest the impact of policy feedback, whereas stability along these dimensions would suggest its absence. Similar debates have occurred at the state level. Developments in the states provide an opportunity to examine the changing resources and incentives of various stakeholders, including officials with jurisdiction over existing programs.

Investigating preschool education makes a broader contribution to the study of social policy. It provides an opportunity to reassess the central claims of the policy development approach. Most existing scholarship focuses on "those prominent moments of contention and change about which so much is written" (Hacker 2005, 150). These studies emphasize certain eras like the 1930s and 1960s, key programs like Social Security and health care, and developments at the national level. Often embedded within these accounts, however, are general claims about the policymaking process. It is only possible for scholars to evaluate these claims by extending the frame of analysis across time periods, policy arenas, and institutional venues. By examining the evolution of preschool education at multiple governmental levels from the late 1960s to the present, this book represents such an extension. In addition to shedding light on the dynamics of a largely overlooked policy arena, it provides broader lessons about social policymaking.

2 | Historical Precedents and Forces for Change

Debates over the education and care of young children date back at least to the infant school movement of the early 1800s, and the contemporary rhetoric surrounding the issue resonates with the claims and counterclaims of earlier eras. After a brief review of developments in the nineteenth and early twentieth centuries, this chapter examines three national government endeavors that preceded the critical juncture of the late 1960s and early 1970s. These programs share two key characteristics. First, they were viewed as temporary initiatives to address emergency conditions. Second, they were targeted rather than universal. In sum, the national government provided services to specific subgroups in response to temporary crises (Beatty 1995; Lazerson 1972; Slobdin 1975).

In the language of the analytical framework outlined in chapter 1, the historical episodes profiled in this chapter represent the "antecedent conditions" that preceded a critical juncture (Collier and Collier 1991, 30). As such, they constitute the baseline against which its consequences must be assessed.[1] The philosophy underlying the emergency nursery schools of the Great Depression, the wartime child care centers of the 1940s, and Head Start illustrates how the debates of the late 1960s and early 1970s, with their emphasis on universal access and a permanent national government presence, broke sharply with the past. The concluding section of this chapter describes how several demographic, intellectual, and political forces in the 1960s reshaped the debate over early childhood policy. The large-scale entry of women into the labor force, pathbreaking research in cognitive psychology, and a changing political environment altered societal attitudes toward early childhood and placed the topic on the national political agenda.

Infant Schools, Day Nurseries, and Nursery Schools

In the early nineteenth century, the infant school movement was the focus of the debate over early childhood policy. This movement emphasized the education and care of young, poor children whose parents worked outside the home. Some supporters viewed the infant schools as a way to facilitate work among low-income parents. Others viewed character and religious education as infant schools' primary benefit, arguing that low-income children "would benefit from both early character training and an education in Christian dogma" (Cahan 1989, 6). A third group emphasized infant schools' potential developmental benefits, portraying them as a way to deliver child-centered enrichment programs that would prepare children for elementary school (Cahan 1989, 8).

The infant school movement was short-lived. Shifting societal attitudes toward maternal roles in child rearing and a backlash against efforts to universalize the schools contributed to its demise. There were concerns about the cost of universalization and the fit between infant schools and the public school system. In addition, the movement violated societal norms that regarded childhood "as a discrete stage that had to be prolonged in order for children to develop properly under the watchful eyes of their mothers" (Michel 1999, 40). In the 1830s and thereafter, there was a revival of the notion that young children should be educated at home. Support for infant schools fell as Americans came to view the family as the "ideal agent of childhood socialization" (Cahan 1989, 11–12). The infant school movement declined rapidly, and "by the mid-19th century there was considerable hostility to the sending of three- or four-year-olds to any school" (Kaestle and Vinovskis 1978, S41).[2]

In the late nineteenth century, the rapid industrialization and urbanization of the United States and a massive influx of immigrants contributed to the rapid growth of day nurseries. Day nurseries were viewed as philanthropic work that would foster family preservation and absorb immigrant and poor families into the American mainstream by teaching values like cleanliness and patriotism (E. Rose 1999, 35). They emphasized health and hygiene and were a "child care service more custodial than educational or developmental" (Steinfels 1973, 52). Day nurseries provided minimal care, "for the simple reason that they lacked sufficient resources to be anything more elaborate" (Cahan 1989, 18). Established for working mothers who needed child care, day nurseries were usually open from seven in the morning to six at night.[3]

Despite their custodial orientation, day nurseries reflected societal ambivalence toward maternal employment. Supporters, facing charges that the nurseries contributed to the breakdown of the American family, often invoked "the heroic figure of the struggling widow or deserted wife, who could not be blamed for working" (E. Rose 1999, 29). The preservation and maintenance of the home was adopted as a guiding principle, and some supporters argued that a day nursery would allow an impoverished mother "to keep her children near her, a better solution, it was argued, than institutionalization" (Steinfels 1973, 50). Day nurseries never became very popular, and the families that relied on them typically did so for short periods of time. Mothers found them unappealing because they carried the stigma of charity and generally offered rigid, institutional care (E. Rose 1999). Day nurseries "fell into increasing disrepute" after the turn of the twentieth century (Cahan 1989, 21).

Nursery schools emerged in the 1910s and 1920s. They stressed educational development, and their organizers were convinced that "some definite educational plan is necessary before the age of five."[4] Supporters argued that nursery school enrollment provided valuable intellectual and health benefits (Bradbury 1936; Gesell 1924). They also believed that the school could contribute to better parenting. Even so, they remained sensitive to prevailing societal norms about the preeminence of the family. One supporter insisted that the opportunities nursery schools provided should not come "at the expense of the family": "The nursery school in its zeal to serve the immediate needs of the child should serve them in such a way that the responsibility of the home is sharpened, not dulled" (Gesell 1924, 19).

After the First World War ended, nursery schools were "the major emphasis in early childhood education" (Lazerson 1972, 48). Lacking the stigma of day nurseries, they enrolled a mostly affluent clientele and were viewed as "not a matter of charity, but of privilege" (E. Rose 1999, 100). The early 1920s were a period of growth. According to one estimate, "There were perhaps 3 nursery schools at the beginning of the decade and at least 262 when it closed."[5] The science of child development was emerging, and nursery schools were viewed as laboratories for the study of "normal, active, healthy young children."[6] Educators experimented with pedagogical methods and hoped to acquire "empirical information about what environment and educational procedures were best for young children" (Beatty 1995, 133).[7]

Nursery school organizers hoped that their experiments would lead the schools to be incorporated into the public school system. Although the schools proliferated during the 1920s, organizers were unable to achieve their bolder goals. By the end of the decade, the movement seemed to be losing momentum. Supporters' hopes that nursery schools would be universalized went unfulfilled, due in part to concerns about the potential cost of a universal program. By the early 1930s, foundation support for nursery education was declining, and government support was virtually nonexistent. Private nursery schools generally shortened their hours, offering half-day programs that suited the needs of their middle- and upper-class clientele. It took a national emergency to "reverse the retreat to privatization of preschool education" (Beatty 1995, 168).

The Great Depression and Emergency Nursery Schools

The Great Depression spurred the national government to extend its role in early childhood policy, at least temporarily. Publicly funded emergency nursery schools emerged as one component of the New Deal and were portrayed as a temporary response to extraordinary economic conditions. One historian described the program as "a temporary measure whose first priority was to provide employment for teachers" (E. Rose 1999, 151). Another noted that it "intended first and foremost to function as an employment program" (Michel 1999, 120). The schools maintained the "twin goals of helping the economy and helping children, in that order" (Beatty 1995, 177). Despite its limited duration and impact, the Depression-era program nevertheless marks an important chapter in the development of early childhood policy.

In October 1933, the director of the Federal Emergency Relief Administration announced that federal work-relief funds and grants to state educational agencies would be used to fund emergency nursery schools. Sponsored by the Works Progress Administration (WPA), the schools were controlled by state and local educational agencies. This bureaucratic arrangement reflected the fact that "no one wanted [the schools] to be simply child-minding or babysitting centers" (Hymes 1979, 13).[8] Economic objectives trumped concerns about educational content, however. Government officials hoped to open as many nursery schools as possible, leading some nursery educators to worry about staff training and school quality.

The program grew rapidly during its early years. Supervisors were appointed in virtually every state, and the program received support from state educational, welfare, and health agencies. During its first four years of operation, approximately seventy-five thousand children between the ages of two and five attended approximately nineteen hundred nursery schools organized in forty-seven states and the District of Columbia.[9] Patterns in New York State are illustrative. In 1932, one year before the estab-lishment of the WPA program, there were thirty-four private nursery schools and no public nursery schools in the state. Four years later, there were "67 Federal nursery schools, four nursery schools publicly supported and a still further increase in private nursery schools over the 34 schools of 1932."[10] At its peak, according to one estimate, the WPA program en-rolled approximately five hundred thousand children in nearly three thou-sand schools nationwide (Beatty 1995, 184).[11]

While many early childhood educators hoped that the emergency nursery schools would become permanent, they recognized that the schools existed "primarily to provide employment for the women who worked at these child care centers."[12] The regulatory provisions of the WPA program reflect its aims as a jobs program. The Great Depression had forced many public schools to close their doors, causing massive lay-offs. The staff for the nursery schools was drawn from this pool of unem-ployed teachers and nurses, and 95 percent of the federal funds for the schools were earmarked for wages (E. Rose 1999, 145). These provisions suggest that the schools were only "a temporary expedient, a stopgap mea-sure until teachers could return to the school system" (Rothman 1973, 19).

In a similar vein, economic hardship was a prerequisite for enrollment. Children were eligible if they were between the ages of two and five and if their families were receiving relief (Beatty 1995, 179).[13] Federal regulations required that the nursery schools be free to the children of these needy and unemployed families (Hymes 1979, 15). In terms of both the teachers it employed and the children it enrolled, the emergency nursery schools targeted those in economic need.

While the program's educational objectives were superseded by its eco-nomic ones, the former did affect the operation of the emergency nursery schools. In June 1934, for example, each state commissioner of education was permitted to hire a trained nursery school specialist who did not have to be eligible for relief. More than one specialist could be hired if the num-ber of nursery schools in the state warranted it (Hymes 1979, 17). Admin-istrators consistently emphasized the educational benefits of the program. They also sought to identify it with the public schools in an effort to con-vince local school districts to adopt nursery schools on a permanent basis (E. Rose 1999, 146). Their efforts were largely unsuccessful, however, and the schools continued to be viewed as a jobs program.

By the 1940s, the size of the WPA program had started to decline. Based on the 1940 U.S. Census, one report estimated that 38,375 children were enrolled in the federally financed nursery schools.[14] Another estimated that 1,661 WPA schools enrolled 46,101 children as of October 31, 1942.[15] Both estimates suggested that fewer schools and students were involved in the program. As the economic crisis receded and the schools were threatened with extinction, however, a different emergency spurred the national government to extend its role in early childhood services.

The Second World War and the Lanham Act

The emergency nursery school program was discontinued in June 1943, yet the national government had already embarked on another foray into early childhood policy. This time, it resulted from the nation's mobilization for the Second World War. With many American men fighting overseas, the United States faced a labor shortage at home. Employing mothers of young children was viewed as something that should not be done until "all other sources of labor were exhausted and the employment of additional women was essential to the war effort."[16] The war effort soon necessitated their employment, however. When mothers entered the workforce, most observers agreed that the government should provide adequate care for their children, and there was "no debate about the need for federally aided day care" (Slobdin 1975, 22). The exigencies of wartime produced a consensus. Like the emergency nursery schools that preceded them, the wartime child care centers were viewed as a targeted temporary response to a national crisis. They were part of "a 'win-the-war,' not a 'save-the-child,' program" (Cahan 1989, 37). One administrator explained, "From the standpoint of government and from the standpoint of the shipyards, we were effective if we enabled mothers to work in the yards."[17]

Maternal employment was viewed as a necessary evil during the wartime mobilization.[18] Appearing before the Senate Committee on Education and Labor in June 1943, Dr. William F. Montavon of the National Catholic Welfare Conference argued that "the national interest is served best when the mother and the child remain in the home together," but he acknowledged that the war created a "temporary, abnormal condition" that necessitated large-scale female employment.[19] Hundreds of thousands of American men were serving overseas, creating a manpower shortage that, according to Senator Carl Hayden (D-AZ), made women "the only reservoir of workers in war industry."[20] The needs of the war effort superseded the conventional belief that mothers should care for their own children in their own homes.

As more mothers joined the workforce, the issue of day care rose to the fore. Supporters of government intervention argued that day care would enable women to accept employment and would make them more productive as workers. One advocate explained, "[T]he fact remains that many women will not consider employment until the community offers some program for the care of their children."[21] The Child Welfare League of America proclaimed more forcefully, "It is hardly American to leave a mother, too often poorly paid for her work, to shift for her child without some minimum guarantee of community service and some subsidy for the child's care."[22] Some observers felt that coaxing women into the workforce without providing day care would exact a terrible social cost in terms of disease, illiteracy, and juvenile delinquency. They also feared that women would be too preoccupied to perform their jobs effectively if their children received substandard care. Since the war was a national emergency, many observers felt that the national government should fund the care mothers viewed as essential. Hayden said, "We are responsible for the war and the consequences of war and therefore Congress should contribute liberally toward meeting a problem that is a war problem."[23] In short, the war created emergency conditions that necessitated publicly funded day care.

The Federal Works Agency provided grants for day care under Title II of the Lanham Act. Section 202(c) enabled the Federal Works Agency to provide financial assistance to schools in areas affected by the war effort, and the care of children of employed mothers was regarded as a "proper extension of the school service."[24] Grants were limited to "war impacted areas" and required a finding that "an acute shortage of facilities or services either exists or impends which would impede the war effort" and that those needs could not be met without national government assistance, an "excessive" tax increase, or an "unusual or excessive" increase in the debt limit of the locality in question.[25] Grant amounts were based on need, cost, and the availability of local revenues. It was estimated that "approximately two-thirds of total maintenance and operating costs of all Lanham child care projects [was] covered by Lanham funds."[26] The remainder came from parental fees and other local contributions.

The first Lanham Act grants for purposes of day care were issued on August 31, 1942. The program expanded rapidly and reversed the declining enrollments that characterized the emergency nursery schools.[27] By February 1943, 260 units had been approved for Lanham Act grants in 28 communities, providing for 9,600 children at a cost of $854,000. By June, 2,685 units with a capacity of 138,410 had been approved in 369 communities at a cost of $8,988,000.[28] Total enrollment also grew rapidly, from approximately 43,000 children in September 1943 to 108,157 children in 2,995 wartime centers by June 1944. At this later date, there were 1,700 nursery school units with an enrollment of 50,929 children.[29] By July 1945, the units devoted to younger children enrolled 73,660 youngsters.[30]

Some of the most famous wartime child care centers were financed and administered by the private sector. Edgar Kaiser, owner of a shipbuilding operation in Oregon with twenty-five thousand employees, feared that the low salary schedule stipulated by the Lanham Act would cause child care centers to lose teachers to higher-paying jobs in the shipyards. He therefore adjusted salaries at his centers so that they were in keeping with the shipyard as a whole. As a result, they attracted skilled professionals from across the country. By June 1945, the staff consisted of five child nutritionists, six group supervisors, ten nurses, one hundred professionally trained nursery school teachers, and two family consultants. The centers provided a wide range of services, and they were widely celebrated for their quality (Slobdin 1975).

Providing care for the young children of working mothers was viewed as a "grim, unsentimental necessity in a nation geared to the production of tanks and more tanks, bombs and more bombs, planes and more planes."[31] Yet the Lanham Act program, like the emergency nursery schools that preceded it, raised advocates' hopes for a permanent postwar program. They believed that high-quality programs like the Kaiser Child Service Centers demonstrated nursery schools' positive impact on child development. One observer argued that "nursery schools have demonstrated that they have a definite place in contributing to the wholesome development of young children."[32] As a result, the WPA and Lanham Act programs sparked a broader debate over early childhood policy.

The campaign to make nursery schools a permanent element of the educational system began during the war. In January 1940, the White House Conference on Children in a Democracy adopted a report that recommended, "School systems should provide nursery school, kindergarten, or similar educational opportunities for children between the ages of 3 and 6."[33] Supporters claimed, "The nursery school is not for problem children; it is for all children."[34] Despite their lobbying efforts, however, three proposals to extend the national government's role in early childhood policy suffered defeat in Congress during the Second World War (Lazerson 1972, 51). In 1943, a particularly heated debate occurred over the War Area Child Care Act, also known as the Thomas Bill. Its demise, which is sometimes portrayed as a defeat for the effort to provide universal access to preschool education, has been traced to infighting among children's agencies and advocates and to objections from women in labor unions and from African American groups (Beatty 1995, 188; E. Rose 1999, 169–70).

Although the Thomas Bill and similar proposals made limited headway, the WPA and Lanham Act programs contributed to an attitudinal shift toward female employment and day care. The wartime centers were especially important. They presented themselves as a public service rather than a private charity and contributed to "the growing conviction that [child care] was educational and thus benefited children, not just their mothers" (E. Rose 1999, 177). Many observers speculated that demand for child care would continue into the postwar period. Indeed, when working mothers were surveyed about their postwar employment plans, many of them answered that, societal norms against female employment notwithstanding, they planned to continue working. A survey of 2,778 working mothers in twenty-seven Ohio communities found that 47 percent of them planned to work indefinitely, 32 percent planned to work only for the duration of the war, 8 percent planned to work only for a short time, and 13 percent were undecided. Fifty-seven percent of the respondents indicated that they would need day care for their children after the war.[35] A survey conducted in the Los Angeles area found that 63.5 percent of working mothers planned to continue working in the postwar period, 17.4 percent of them did not plan to work, and 15.2 percent were undecided.[36] In Detroit, a survey of 1,448 working mothers found that 54.5 percent planned to continue working, 37.6 percent did not plan to continue working, and 6.8 percent were undecided.[37] The surveys were few in number, a fact that nursery school advocates lamented,[38] but they suggested that postwar demand for child care services would remain high.

Several prominent national organizations supported continued public funding of child care services. In a May 1945 memorandum, the Child Welfare League of America argued that "the time has come for such planning in the federal government as will facilitate the development of day care of a quality consistent with American standards of child welfare."[39] The president of the National Association for Nursery Education claimed that "generous federal aid will be needed" to close the gap between the need for nursery schools and their availability.[40] At a meeting in 1946, the United Auto Workers of the Congress of Industrial Organizations pledged to "work to make nursery schools a permanent part of our school structure, free to all parents in the community wishing to avail themselves of the opportunity."[41] Various organizations urged the federal government to provide permanent funds for early childhood services, and they continued their efforts after the war ended.[42]

Early Childhood Policy in the Immediate Postwar Period

As the Second World War drew to a close, President Harry S. Truman extended funding for the Lanham Act child care centers for six months. The subsequent termination of the program confirmed that national government support of child care centers had been a temporary response to emergency conditions.[43] Washington State, New York State, and several counties and cities allocated funds to extend the lives of the centers, and local industries, service clubs, and lay organizations in other communities made similar financial commitments.[44] Continued support from the national government, however, was not forthcoming. Representative Helen Gahagan Douglas (D-CA) introduced legislation during the Eightieth and Eighty-First Congresses that sought to "assist the States and Territories in providing more effective programs of public kindergarten or kindergarten and nursery-school education,"[45] but neither proposal received serious consideration.

Early childhood advocates nonetheless viewed the late 1940s as a moment of opportunity. They felt that the WPA and Lanham Act programs had generated unprecedented publicity for early childhood policy. In 1947, one advocate claimed, "Interest in nursery and kindergarten education is at a high point. . . . Public attention is beginning to recognize these schools for young children as an essential for parents and as an economic asset in terms of the conservation of childhood."[46] The National Association for Nursery Education launched a publicity campaign whose goal was to "attach amendments to state education laws which would make it possible for nursery education to be provided as part of the public educational system."[47] It offered interested parties a fact sheet, magazine articles, radio scripts of fifteen-minute dramatic sketches, a film, and pictures of small children to assist their lobbying efforts.

During the immediate postwar period, advocates experienced their greatest success in California. The state legislature allocated a one-year appropriation of $3.5 million for the child care program in 1946. Without these funds, the centers established during the war would have had to close. The bill enabled the state to retain a large proportion of its child care centers and laid the foundation for its postwar child care program.[48] Child care advocates won annual and biannual child care appropriations until 1957, when the program became a permanent part of the state budget. Their success has been attributed to a favorable political environment. A surplus existed in the state treasury, opponents never coalesced into an organized countermovement, and advocates cultivated an influential set of allies (Reese 1996). The California program remains the oldest continuous state child care program in the country. Supporters struggled to achieve their goals in other states.

The Midcentury White House Conference on Children and Youth in 1950 devoted some attention to nursery schools and kindergartens. At the time of the conference, states and municipalities funded only 10 percent of child care facilities across the country, and another 14 percent operated with funds from community chests. Commercial nursery schools constituted 43 percent of the total, and voluntary organizations, such as churches, philanthropies, and institutions of higher education, constituted another 23 percent (Michel 1999, 177–78). A conference report emphasized the "necessity for making nursery schools and kindergartens far more widely available, as well as for considerable flexibility in policies on age of admission."[49] Attendees adopted sixty-seven recommendations, including one stipulating "[t]hat as a desirable supplement to home life, nursery schools and kindergartens, provided they meet high professional standards, be included as a part of public educational opportunity for children."[50]

The overall landscape of early childhood programs changed very little during the 1950s.[51] In 1960, preschool attendance remained uncommon, and most parents relied on private nonprofit and commercial sources. During the 1960–61 academic year, only about 1 percent of the school districts in the United States operated public nursery schools. There was some minor regional variation, but the overall "distribution throughout the country [was] relatively even, though extremely low."[52] The slow growth of public programs meant that most children who attended preschools attended private nursery schools, and only about 6 percent of the first-grade children in public schools had attended either a public or a nonpublic nursery school.[53] Given this limited reach, it is not surprising that the Golden Anniversary White House Conference on Children and Youth in 1960 reiterated the 1950 conference's goal of expanding public programs. It called for the increased "provision of supplemental services for parents of preschool children, such as day care centers, nursery schools, kindergartens, and summer day camps."[54] Repeated calls for expanded public services did not have a major policy impact during the immediate postwar period.

The most noteworthy policy change occurred in 1954, when the federal income tax code was revised to allow a tax deduction for specific employment-related dependent care expenses. The tax deduction allowed working adults (widows, widowers, divorced persons, or married mothers) to deduct up to six hundred dollars a year for child care that enabled the taxpayer to work. The maximum deduction was available to individuals or couples earning less than forty-five hundred dollars per year. The tax deduction received broad support, but most members of Congress "made it clear that they did not condone maternal employment in general" (Michel 1999, 205). By allowing minimal expenditures and keeping the income cap relatively low, Congress "gave a nod to the employment of low-income women while maintaining its distance from child care in general" (Lombardi 2003, 35).

The tax deduction represented a sea change in attitudes toward poor women. Whereas mothers' pensions and Aid to Dependent Children supported them to remain at home with their children, the tax deduction underwrote the cost of child care to encourage them to join the workforce.[55] Despite its limited initial reach, the tax deduction "turned out to be the most significant breakthrough in child care policy of the 1950s" (Michel 1999, 209). In the 1970s, it was transformed into a tax credit, and its eligibility provisions were broadened considerably. The tax deduction played a significant role in the evolution of early childhood policy, but it differed sharply from the strategy of service provision that was embraced by the WPA and Lanham Act programs.

The War on Poverty and the Creation of Head Start

On March 16, 1964, the White House delivered a message to Congress that called for a "national war on poverty" and described several programs to assist low-income individuals and families. Its goal was "to allow [the poor] to develop and use their capacities, as we have been allowed to use ours, so that they can share, as others share, in the promise of this nation."[56] With the creation of Head Start in 1965, early childhood education became a key component of the War on Poverty. It was viewed as a way to address the long-term disadvantages that accompanied growing up in poverty and to prepare disadvantaged children for elementary school. The launch of Head Start had much in common with the emergency nursery schools and Lanham Act centers. It was a targeted, temporary response to an emergency situation (Beatty 1995; Lazerson 1972; Slobdin 1975).[57]

The creation of Head Start reflected growing interest in compensatory school programs. During the late 1950s and early 1960s, the Ford Foundation funded early childhood initiatives at several experimental sites as part of its Great Cities School Improvement Program (Vinovskis 2005, 26). Changing views of child development, with their emphasis on the importance of the first five years of life, encouraged many to view compensatory schooling programs as a way to address the root causes of poverty. By the early 1960s, leading politicians like Robert F. Kennedy viewed preschool education as a "normal and desirable component of comprehensive efforts to improve deteriorating inner cities" (Vinovskis 2005, 30).

Early childhood policy received considerable attention from the Johnson administration. In August 1964, consultant Harry Levin issued a brief assessment of preschool programs, concluding that "schooling must start on a preschool basis and include a broad range of more intensive services."[58] He predicted that the "present combination of circumstances . . . makes a large scale establishment of preschools inevitable."[59] Anticipating a landslide victory in the November election, President Johnson appointed several task forces to make legislative recommendations. His Task Force on Education assembled thirty-one papers, including two devoted specifically to preschool. It portrayed preschool as a resource for disadvantaged children, not as an opportunity that should be provided to all children (Vinovskis 2005, 54–57). After the election, lawmakers transformed this interest in early childhood policy into concrete proposals.[60]

In a special message to Congress in early 1965, Johnson announced his intention to locate a preschool program within the Office of Economic Opportunity's Community Action Program and called the initiative "Head Start" for the first time (Vinovskis 2005, 73). In February, the Head Start Planning Committee endorsed a comprehensive vision of child development and reached an "unofficial consensus" that Head Start should begin as a small pilot program. It did not object, however, when the administration decided to "proceed immediately with a nationwide Head Start program that would serve 100,000 children" (Zigler and Muenchow 1992, 22).

The ambitious decision to launch Head Start as a nationwide program offered several advantages. The availability of unused funds from the Community Action Program (CAP) facilitated its rapid expansion. The cost of the nationwide launch actually "represented a solution—a worthwhile way to allocate the remainder of the unused CAP funds before the end of the fiscal year" (Zigler and Muenchow 1992, 25). Nationwide implementation was also politically beneficial. It "made the program highly visible" and "created the grass-roots support—and a potential vote from every congressional district—that would protect Head Start later on" (Zigler and Muenchow 1992, 28).

The main drawback of the nationwide launch was inconsistent quality among Head Start centers. Many centers lacked the resources they needed to achieve their objectives. For example, there was a shortage of qualified teachers with training and experience in early childhood education. In addition, local school districts worried that Head Start would impose a national curriculum, so program supporters were reluctant to mandate a specific educational approach (Zigler and Muenchow 1992, 42). Head Start therefore allowed local communities to make many curricular choices, which fostered uneven program quality. Concerns about program quality led some critics to question whether Head Start would significantly help disadvantaged children, but the program nonetheless enjoyed strong public and bipartisan support at its inception in the summer of 1965.

A preschool panel at a White House conference in July is illustrative. The panel featured "an enthusiastic commitment to Head Start as a fresh breeze in American education" and "an all-pervading feeling that the momentum of Head Start should not be lost."[61] Head Start received especially effusive praise from consultant J. W. Getzels. Getzels wrote that Head Start "represents the awakening of the American conscience to the nation's most serious problem, and we can take pride that a generation hence no one will be able to say as we are about a generation ago that although the problem was recognized nothing courageous to solve it was attempted."[62] This support for Head Start was accompanied by a broader call for national government action, including a large-scale financial investment in early childhood programs. Panelists urged the president to support "a national commitment for a war on ignorance directed specifically at the preschool child."[63]

At the conference, Representative Albert Quie (R-MN) announced his intention to offer an amendment to the Elementary and Secondary Education Act (ESEA) "to incorporate within the traditional school structure programs like Head Start for preschool children."[64] Other participants objected to Quie's idea because they wanted the initiative to be affiliated with community action programs. When Quie offered his amendment to the ESEA, it provoked an extended debate on the House floor. Democrats complained that the proposal was too prescriptive and too narrowly focused on early childhood programs, whereas Quie and his Republican colleagues argued that the Democratic alternatives devoted insufficient attention to preschool and would not facilitate a close relationship between early childhood education and the public schools (Vinovskis 2005, 82–85). The Republican congressman's proposal nonetheless reflected the bipartisan appeal of Head Start and preschool education. In a 1966 memorandum, in fact, Republicans claimed credit for the idea behind Head Start and described it as "the most successful of the new poverty programs."[65]

The enthusiasm surrounding the nationwide launch of Head Start caused some supporters to worry that "too much was being promised too soon" (Zigler and Muenchow 1992, 27). Head Start provided several social services, but it was eventually evaluated primarily along the dimension of cognitive gains. The notion that children's intelligence could be affected by their environment led to speculation, much of it by program supporters, that Head Start would raise enrollees' IQ scores. Supporters who worried about the overselling of the program argued that evaluations relying primarily on cognitive gains were "unrealistic and unfair."[66] One observer explained "[T]hey tried taking kids for six weeks in the summer, giving them a razzmatazz program, and some injections, and a little feeding up, and then expecting to go back five years later and find that these children had I.Q.s that were twenty points higher than the ones who hadn't been subjected to this. . . . What could be more patently ridiculous?"[67] Cognitive gains and IQ scores nevertheless continued to be the primary dimensions along which Head Start was evaluated.

Early evaluations of Head Start led to setbacks for the program. A March 1967 report on the first summer and winter Head Start programs was inconclusive. It found that program attendees experienced significant gains in some contexts but not in others. Furthermore, follow-up studies suggested that just six months "after the end of the experience differences between Head Start and non-Head Start children had been reduced."[68] This "fade-out" problem, which had been recognized as early as 1965,[69] led to the launch of the Follow Through pilot program in June 1967. Follow Through attempted "to capitalize upon and supplement the gains children make in preschool experiences through continuing their participation in a program" of comprehensive social services.[70]

Head Start received a fundamental challenge in April 1969, when the Westinghouse Learning Corporation released its preliminary report on the long-term impact of Head Start enrollment. It focused on the attitudes and academic achievements of former Head Start enrollees in first, second, and third grade and concluded, "Head Start children could not be said to be *appreciably* different from their peers in the elementary grades who did not attend Head Start in most aspects of cognitive and affective development measured in this study."[71] Although the data in the report could be interpreted in several ways, the report was widely viewed as evidence of Head Start's limited effectiveness. One historian describes the Westinghouse report as "damning criticism . . . which suggested that the intellectual gains of preschool compensatory education evaporated after a few years in elementary school" (Cravens 1993, 257). The report placed Head Start supporters on the defensive, yet the program survived these initial difficulties due to its strong political constituency and widespread public support (E. Rose 2010, 29; Vinovskis 1999a, 74–75).[72] There were calls for the outright elimination of Head Start, but by 1969, the program "had become too popular among the public and politicians to be abandoned" (Vinovskis 2005, 143).

Supporters also defended Head Start against several efforts to transfer it to the Office of Education in the Department of Health, Education, and Welfare (HEW). HEW secretary Robert Finch argued that the transfer would improve Head Start by facilitating greater program length and continuity and increased technical assistance and evaluation efforts.[73] He suggested that the transfer would benefit Head Start financially, allowing it to draw on departmental resources "without necessarily going up for a higher appropriation for Head Start as such."[74] He wanted to reassure Head Start supporters who feared that the program would get lost in a large department and that its community action component would evaporate. In June, the Nixon administration announced that Head Start would be placed under the jurisdiction of the Office of Child Development, a special agency within HEW that was set apart from the Office of Education (Vinovskis 2005, chap. 8).

Due to their long-term political impact, two features of Head Start deserve further attention. The first is the program's comprehensive approach. The Head Start Planning Committee's decision to endorse a comprehensive program has been characterized as "one of its most important recommendations" (Hymes 1979, 34). Head Start is premised on the assumption that child development is a "multifaceted process" involving children, their parents, other family members, and the community at large.[75] In addition to its educational goals, it strives to improve physical health and nutritional outcomes. It is a child development program that attempts to "integrate all services needed by young children into a unified program to influence their total development."[76] The comprehensive nature of Head Start foreshadowed the debates of the late 1960s and early 1970s in which supporters of a permanent, national, universal early childhood program insisted that it should emulate the Head Start model.

A second attribute of Head Start that had an important long-term political impact is its emphasis on parental involvement, which ultimately became a source of both controversy and political support (Zigler and Muenchow 1992). Active parental involvement was an "absolute requirement of an acceptable Head Start program," and every grantee was required to establish a policy advisory committee with at least half of its membership made up of parents or parent representatives.[77] A Head Start program manual published in September 1967 outlined four major kinds of parental participation: (1) participating in the process of making decisions about the nature and operation of the program; (2) participating in the classroom as paid employees, volunteers, and observers; (3) welcoming center staff into their homes for discussions of how parents can contribute to child development in the home; and (4) participating in educational activities developed for and with help from the parents.[78] Parental input on program operation and the possibility of paid employment had an especially profound long-term impact. Parents and families who have participated in Head Start have been heavily involved in its planning and governance and, as subsequent chapters of this book will show, have often defended these prerogatives.

Head Start's generation of jobs for adults was a source of both national and local controversy in 1969. When the program was delegated to the Office of Child Development, HEW insisted that the transfer would lead to no job losses, and it emphasized its commitment "not only to the hiring of non-professionals in Head Start programs, but the development of career ladders for them."[79] Around the same time, a controversy erupted over whether Minneapolis public schools administering Head Start programs were giving parents sufficient input in program decisions and preference for classroom positions. School system leaders argued that the "vast majority of Head Start aides" had always been Head Start parents or residents of poverty-area neighborhoods.[80] Parental involvement in Head Start had long-term implications because it gave Head Start parents and their advocates a stake in the existing policy repertoire and caused them to resist proposed changes.

Demographic, Intellectual, and Political Forces for Change

Until the 1960s, the national government role in early childhood policy could be classified as a "series of crisis interventions" (Cahan 1989, 37) that reflected "a lack of comprehensive social policy and the formation of temporary policy in times of crisis" (Takanishi 1977, 158). Government intervention was "reluctantly funded by the public and only in extraordinary historical times" (McGill-Franzen 1993, 175). As one observer explained in 1946, "WPA had the tendency to make us think of nursery schools only as a means of employing teachers. Lanham Funds forced our thinking somewhat into a groove where we saw the nursery school only as a means of freeing mothers for work. These were not children's purposes; they were 'secondary purposes' which nursery schools can serve."[81] The programs of the 1930s and 1940s had been temporary targeted responses to national crises. Head Start was similar along those dimensions.

In the late 1960s and early 1970s, government officials turned their attention to programs serving a broader constituency, moving away from targeted programs and toward universal ones. The importance of this shift cannot be overstated in light of the precedent set in earlier decades. Supporters had long argued that early childhood services should be available to all children. Only in the late 1960s and early 1970s, however, did lawmakers seriously consider establishing a permanent national framework for the universal provision of educational, nutritional, and health services. Why did this shift occur?

In his influential model of the agenda-setting process, John Kingdon (1995, 165) argues that "policy windows" open only when a "problem is recognized, a solution is developed and available in the policy community, a political change makes it the right time for policy change, and potential constraints are not severe." The merger of these streams provides policy entrepreneurs with the opportunity to push their preferred policy solution. Kingdon's model helps explain why the debate over early childhood policy shifted from an emphasis on targeted, temporary programs to the serious consideration of a permanent, universal program. A combination of demographic, intellectual, and political forces placed early childhood policy on the national political agenda and contributed to a decisive break with the past.

Demographic Change: Trends in Female Employment

Changing societal conditions can draw officials' attention to new issues or cause them to revisit old ones. In the context of early childhood policy, the most crucial demographic shift was the transformation of the American workforce between the Second World War and 1969. During this period, mothers of young children entered the labor force in large numbers, and a debate ensued about whether and how the government should respond to this change. Among mothers with children under age eighteen, rates of participation in the labor force increased from less than 10 percent in 1940 to 30 percent in 1960 and about 40 percent in March 1969.[82] The employment rate of married women with children under age six increased from less than 12 percent in 1950 to more than 30 percent in 1970 (E. Rose 1999, 213). This trend has been called a "historic substitution [that] transformed the demographics of the twentieth-century American economy and affected all classes" (Sealander 2003, 13). Many families could not rely on grandparents or other relatives to provide care for their young children, because "the traditional extended family structure [had] been fractured."[83] As a result, many more American children were cared for outside their homes.

Scholars trace this demographic shift to various sources. Gornick and Meyers (2003, 28) attribute it to the Second World War, which caused a "temporary employment shock [that] set in motion irreversible changes in attitudes toward the employment of married women." Others describe it as part of a larger economic and social transformation, as families headed by a breadwinner and a homemaker became less common. David Frum (2000, 68–69) argues that the entry of women into the workforce was part of a larger trend toward "expressive work [that] was caused at least as much by new ideas about the meaning of work as by the need for more family income." Economic necessity was another potential cause. Supporters of government intervention often claimed that women entered the labor force in order to make ends meet. The Policy Council of the National Women's Political Caucus, for example, attempted to legitimize governmental support by arguing, "The vast majority of women work not by choice but because they must."[84]

Regardless of its ultimate source, there is no disputing the political significance of this demographic shift. The widespread participation of mothers of young children in the labor market fomented controversy about whether and how the government should respond. Supporters of government intervention pointed to demographic changes to justify policy change. In 1967, one advocate noted that other countries had taken action because "[they] are realists and they reason that if you take the mother away from the home and employ her, something must be done about the children who are left without supervision and without the love and attention that only a mother could give."[85] Congressional Republicans were especially struck by the fact that these trends in the labor market affected many families in the lower-middle and middle income ranges. According to one staffer, "From the simple day-care question we very soon spilled over into the whole area of child development."[86] This transition reflected broader intellectual changes.

Intellectual Change: Developments in Cognitive Psychology

The fact that the mothers of young children entered the workforce in unprecedented numbers did not require a specific course of action. The split between day nurseries and nursery schools in the early twentieth century, for example, illustrates how one could adopt a custodial approach to early childhood and care or place a stronger emphasis on educational content.[87] The debates of the late 1960s and early 1970s emphasized educational programs and focused on the notion of child development. Supporters often justified this focus by referring to an intellectual shift in cognitive psychology.

The mid- to late 1950s were "a transition point in American psychology in general, and in child psychology in particular."[88] Many psychologists rethought the process of cognitive development and characterized intelligence as something affected by environmental forces. In doing so, they broke with the "Gesellian era, with its emphasis on maturation and the implicit notion of the fixed I.Q."[89] In short, many cognitive psychologists rejected the long-standing idea that intelligence was fixed at birth. They argued that early childhood experiences had profound implications for subsequent development. This paradigmatic shift led to "rapid growth in interest in early childhood education . . . by suggesting that certain kinds of experiences may affect the rate of early cognitive development" (Cahan 1989, 48). It heightened the perceived importance of children's experiences during the first five years of life.

Several psychologists contributed to this intellectual shift, but the work of J. McVicker Hunt and Benjamin Bloom was especially influential.[90] Developmental psychologist Sheldon H. White explained, "The papers by Bloom and Hunt must easily have been the most frequently cited publications in discussion of preschools."[91] Hunt and Bloom "produced some of the earliest and most effective arguments for early childhood education in the late 1950s and early 1960s" (Vinovskis 2005, 11). Advocates of increased investment in early childhood education often invoked their research.

Hunt's *Intelligence and Experience* was published in 1961. Hunt argued that intelligence was modifiable and could be affected by environmental forces. He proposed that a "substantially higher adult level of intellectual capacity [can] be achieved by providing quality encounters with the environment in the early years."[92] He emphasized the interaction between an organism and its environment: "Much of the evidence reviewed in this work is concerned with showing that experience, and especially early experience, is of importance" (335). Hunt was optimistic about the potential long-term impact of early childhood experiences. Arguing that additional research might make it "feasible to raise the average level of intelligence as now measured by a substantial degree," he speculated, "In order to be explicit, it is conceivable that this 'substantial degree' might be of the order of 30 points of I.Q." (267). This optimistic speculation helps explain why Hunt's book sparked such widespread interest in early childhood policy.

Published in 1964, Bloom's *Stability and Change in Human Characteristics* examined data from about one thousand longitudinal studies. It questioned the notion of a fixed IQ and described intelligence as a developmental concept. Bloom noted increased stability in intelligence measurements with time and pointed out that about 50 percent of the variation in intelligence at age seventeen was accounted for by age four. This pattern, he concluded, "would suggest the very rapid growth of intelligence in the early years and the possible great influence of the early environment on this development" (68). He hypothesized that the impact of environmental factors and deprivation were most pronounced during the first few years of life. He concluded that "the increased ability to predict long-term consequences of environmental forces and developmental characteristics places new responsibilities on the home, the school, and the society" (231). He argued that these responsibilities must be met early in life, when it is easiest to bring about desirable changes. Bloom's book was very influential. It "[threw] the spotlight on the tremendous importance of the early years of life, and [showed] how hard it was to bring about changes later in life. It added up to a strong plug for early childhood education" (Hymes 1979, 33).

Some psychologists and other scholars questioned whether appropriate conclusions were being drawn from the research described in the preceding paragraphs. They worried that the potential benefits of early experiences were being overstated. Scholars such as Edward Zigler felt that the "environmental mystique" was a valuable corrective to the Gesellian era but had been oversold and that "scientists and lay people alike were displaying an almost magical faith in the power to increase mental capacity" (Zigler and Muenchow 1992, 13).[93] Others focused on the lessons that educators and legislators drew from this research in cognitive psychology. One pair of critics complained, for example, that the advocates of early schooling "make unfortunate twin assumptions: that a child's intelligence can be nurtured by organizing it, and that brightness means readiness for school."[94] They argued that early schooling might be damaging over the long term if it occurred in a setting that failed to provide warmth and security, and they asserted that "one of a child's primary needs in these formative years is for an environment free of tasks that will tax his brain."[95]

Despite these and other critiques, cognitive psychology research provided a scientific justification for increased interest in early childhood policy. Scholars like J. McVicker Hunt and Benjamin Bloom questioned the notion of fixed intelligence and emphasized the impact of the first five years of life on cognitive development. This intellectual transition was especially important because it provided a rationale for focusing on child development rather than on custodial child care. At around the same time, the political environment offered opportunities for elected officials to propose a major expansion of the national government's role in this policy arena.

Political Change: The War on Poverty and the Shifting Contours of Education Policy

Several political developments raised the profile of early childhood policy in the late 1960s and early 1970s, a period of social reform and national government activism. In a 1972 speech, S. P. Marland Jr., the U.S. commissioner of education, described the 1960s as a time of "almost unparalleled idealism" during which Americans "turned our sense of social justice into massive federal funding and corresponding law."[96] The size and scope of national government activity expanded dramatically in this period, fueled by an activist president and, after the 1964 election, an overwhelmingly Democratic Congress. This activism reflected public opinion. James Stimson (1991, 64) argues that "the liberal winds of the 1960s were blowing in the latter part of the previous decade, a gradual run-up that was gone soon after it was generally recognized to be in place." This bundle of domestic policy preferences meant that Americans were willing to countenance major expansions of national government activity.

State and local government authorities had traditionally exercised control over educational programming. As late as 1959, one scholar wrote, "The desirability of *local* control of the public schools is an article of faith among most trained educators and many other Americans" (Eliot 1959, 1032; emphasis in original). Local control was justified on several grounds. It allowed educational programs to be adapted to social and economic conditions and the unique needs of local communities. It permitted experimentation, which resonated with the popular portrayal of the states as "laboratories of democracy."[97] Localities could try out new ideas, and if their experiments led to improved educational outcomes, they could be emulated elsewhere. Finally, local control encouraged political participation, serving as "an indispensable laboratory for training an intelligent and competent citizenry for larger civic affairs and more responsible positions" (Hales 1954, 7).

National government aid to the public schools had been debated in the 1930s and 1940s, and both major party platforms endorsed it during the 1948 presidential campaign (Vinovskis 2005, 13). Three interrelated issues, however, made it "impossible to shape a winning coalition in Congress" (Thomas 1983, 273). One issue was financial aid for parochial schools, which was seen as a deal breaker by those who viewed it as a violation of the separation of church and state. A second issue was financial aid for segregated public schools, especially after the landmark *Brown* decision in 1954. The civil rights issue resonated especially strongly with policymakers from southern states. A third issue was the possibility that national government aid to the public schools would lead to "federal control" of education policy. Fears of centralization and totalitarianism were especially important in the context of the Cold War. Multiple historians have described the issues as the "three R's" of race, religion, and reds (Bailey and Mosher 1968, 21; Thomas 1975, 3). Several education bills failed to clear these political hurdles. By the late 1950s, one of the "most distinctive attributes [of American politics was] the tenacity with which the United States, unlike most nations, had resisted a national education policy" (Graham 1984, xvii).

Observers disagreed about what the future held. The ongoing controversy surrounding aid to parochial and segregated schools led one scholar to predict that "general federal aid is still far off" (Eliot 1959, 1043). Another argued that "education appears to be on the threshold of an appreciable increase in federal control" (Hales 1954, 54). The period from 1960 through 1964 laid the foundation for the passage of legislation. Supporters altered their legislative strategy by "thinking of education in terms of social welfare and economic growth and presenting the program in an omnibus bill and messages."[98] Francis Keppel, the U.S. commissioner of education from 1962 to 1965, eventually developed a compromise that satisfied both the teachers unions and Catholic leaders, "finding a legislative formula that would permit massive federal assistance of a kind that would at the same time strengthen state and local initiative" (Bailey and Mosher 1968, 35). These powerful constituencies recognized that an insistence on ideological purity would prevent them from receiving tangible benefits (Sundquist 1968,

206). As a result, the "customary fragmentation of the education lobby was displaced by a rare demonstration of unity."[99] The leadership of President Lyndon B. Johnson was crucial. Johnson "placed his substantial influence behind federal policies aimed at federal support of American education" (Bailey 1975, 36). A skilled legislative tactician, he "made education his highest domestic policy concern after civil rights" (Thomas 1983, 277).

Johnson signed the Elementary and Secondary Education Act into law in 1965.[100] A delicate balancing act was necessary for its passage, and the ESEA "was a closely woven tapestry of educational objectives and program proposals that Congress could not greatly alter without a serious impairment of substance or political appeal" (Bailey and Mosher 1968, 48). The core of the statute was Title I, which was devoted to the schooling of economically deprived children. Although Title I did not provide general aid, "[w]ide geographical funds and a semblance of 'general aid' were ensured by counting all school age children in poverty, and by requiring that a school district only have three percent eligible children to qualify for a grant" (Bailey and Mosher 1968, 49). The ESEA expanded the national government's role through several categorical programs, but its passage "was celebrated . . . as a historic breakthrough for general aid" (Graham 1984, 79). Historians and politicians described its passage in dramatic terms, focusing on its implications for federalism and education policy. They called the ESEA "a radical departure for the federal government" (McDonnell 2005, 36) and "a clean break with earlier models" (Bailey and Mosher 1968, 60). States and localities now shared control over education policy with the national government.

Passage of the ESEA fundamentally reshaped the debate over education policy. Public attitudes toward the national government and its role "changed rather dramatically and rather fast."[101] In 1968, Representative John Brademas (D-IN) noted that "the politics of education in the United States has altered very sharply in the last several years."[102] The commissioner of education described national education funding as one of "those formerly controversial issues that once threatened to topple the Republic but that now have gained widespread acceptance."[103] Historians used similar language. By the late 1960s, there "was no longer serious debate over the propriety of a major federal role in education" (Thomas 1975, 34). According to one scholar, "The question would be, henceforth, not *whether* the national government should give aid but *how much* it should give, for what purposes—and with how much federal control" (Sundquist 1968, 216; emphasis in original). Passage of the ESEA represented a major policy shift, altering the role of the national government in education policy.

In sum, the 1960s were a period during which lawmakers expanded the scope of national government activity in education policy. Passage of the ESEA in 1965 was the culmination of a decades-long struggle over the issue of education funding. The ESEA legitimatized national government involvement in a policy arena that had previously been dominated by states and localities. When advocates later pressed for the national and universal provision of early childhood services, the ESEA constituted a precedent on which they could build.

Summary: Forces for Change in Early Childhood Policy

A combination of demographic, intellectual, and political forces placed early childhood policy on the national political agenda in the late 1960s and early 1970s. Mothers with young children entered the labor force in unprecedented numbers, which meant that more American children were being cared for outside their homes. Research in cognitive psychology affected parents' and policymakers' ideas about the type of care that was best for these children. By heightening the perceived importance of the first five years of life, this research suggested that any care young children received outside their homes should have a prominent educational component. Politically, the decade of the 1960s was an era of increased national governmental intervention. One of the legislative landmarks of this era was the Elementary and Secondary Education Act, which expanded the role of the national government in a policy arena that had previously been dominated by states and localities. This confluence of forces raised the profile of early childhood policy and caused lawmakers to debate the national government's role in its provision.

Conclusion: Changing Attitudes toward Early Childhood Education

During the 1960s, a fundamental shift occurred in how politicians and the American public thought about early childhood policy. Historically, the national government had been limited to administering targeted policies under crisis conditions, but by the end of the decade, several organizations and politicians endorsed the creation of a universal national framework. The National Education Association and the American Association of School Administrators argued that "the opportunity for early education at public expense should . . . be universal" for all children over the age of four (Educational Policies Commission 1966, 5). Using governmental re-sources to expand access to early childhood programs possessed biparti-san appeal. Some Republicans acknowledged the cost of a universal pro-gram but cited its potential long-term benefits: "The cost to institute such a program would be high, but would more than pay for itself by savings in law enforcement, manpower, job retraining, welfare payments and mental health services."[104] Perhaps the most important change of the decade was a shift in how Americans viewed the role of the national government. The idea that early childhood programs should be run by the national govern-ment received significant public support. A July 1969 Gallup poll sug-gested that "two-thirds of the American public favored the establishment of federally funded day care centers."[105] These results suggest a remarkable willingness to countenance governmental intervention in a realm that had traditionally been considered the private domain of the family.

In sum, the 1960s were a period of dramatic change in the politics of early childhood. By 1965, "[t]he number and diversity of compensatory preschool projects [were] growing so rapidly that it [was] hazardous to say anything about *the* nature of the program with risk of oversimplifying and being out of date almost at once."[106] In an April 1968 speech, Harold Howe II, the commissioner of education, predicted, "If I read the signals cor-rectly, this whole area of early education will be a major emphasis for the next several decades."[107] Howe would soon be proven correct, as the con-fluence of several demographic, intellectual, and political forces led to the introduction of many major legislative proposals, foremost among them the Comprehensive Child Development Act of 1971.

3 | A Watershed Episode: The Comprehensive Child Development Act

Interest in early childhood policy remained high after the inauguration of President Richard Nixon, thanks in part to the widespread attention Head Start received. A March 1969 memo to the Advisory Committee on Head Start argued that the program helped produce "an unprecedented amount of national interest in the importance of early childhood development."[1] Some accounts in the popular press touched on similar themes. An article in *Business Week* explained, "The concept of widespread day care for preschool children, developed during the Johnson years, is generating more interest and enthusiasm during the Nixon Administration than ever before."[2] In Congress, the central debate surrounded the appropriate role of the national government in this policy sector.

As the congressional debate crystallized, it shifted in two directions that had important long-term consequences. The first shift was the widespread embrace of a comprehensive approach to child development. Programs for young children were viewed as part of a multifaceted effort to improve children's overall well-being. Head Start epitomized this more encompassing approach. It offered educational, nutritional, and other services and sought to reach children, parents, and the larger community. The April 1969 creation of the Office of Child Development within the Department of Health, Education, and Welfare also reflected this shift. HEW secretary Robert Finch alluded to this new way of thinking as he announced the creation of the new office: "Today, our nation's schools and child care programs are in the process of changing toward a more comprehensive approach to the physical, social and intellectual development of children and their families."[3]

The second shift represented an even sharper break with the past. Whereas previous governmental initiatives were targeted and crisis-oriented, the late 1960s and early 1970s witnessed a turn toward universal programs. By April 1967, the National Education Association (NEA) had proposed universal schooling beginning at age four, a recommendation that one observer attributed to Head Start and early childhood research.[4] In a March 1971 statement, the Research and Policy Committee of the Committee for Economic Development endorsed a "massive effort to establish both public and private preschool educational programs."[5] The turn toward universal programs "represented an abrupt departure from previous government policy" (E. Rose 2010, 43), and it reshaped the politics of early childhood policy.

The combined impact of these two shifts took some observers by surprise. One explained, "As I reflect on the past decade, I also am struck by the fact that I never thought in the early '60s there would be a nationwide program, a nationwide emphasis on the needs of young children."[6] Perhaps the most remarkable development of all was the 1971 passage of the Comprehensive Child Development Act, which both supporters and opponents viewed as a step toward a permanent national framework for the universal provision of preschool services. Even though Congress proved unable to override a presidential veto, its passage was noteworthy. After a brief overview of the policymaking context of the late 1960s and the legislative and executive branch activity that preceded the passage of this landmark bill, this chapter describes the politics of the Comprehensive Child Development Act. The significance of this critical juncture cannot be overstated. The veto sparked a series of reactions and counterreactions that help explain the fragmentation and decentralization of early childhood policy in the contemporary United States.

A Changing Context

The late 1960s were a time of considerable ferment in early childhood policy. Passage of the Elementary and Secondary Education Act facilitated some of this activity. In fiscal year 1967, over $1 million in Title I funds were expended for services for prekindergarten and kindergarten children.[7] Title III of the ESEA authorized spending on supplementary educational centers and services, and in the same fiscal year, there were sixty-one projects serving an estimated forty thousand preschool children at a cost of $3.1 million.[8] These funding levels rose rapidly in the late 1960s. In fiscal year 1969, the Office of Education spent approximately $50 million in Title I funds and $12 million in Title III funds. It also spent about $30 million on the Follow Through program that supplemented Head Start, and it issued $100,000 in grants to state education agencies for early child-hood education projects. The agency's total allocation for early childhood education in fiscal year 1969 was approximately $115 million.[9]

The national government also allocated funds to several day care pro-grams. By September 1969, three major programs existed within HEW. Head Start funds could be used for day care, state welfare departments could receive grants-in-aid for child welfare services including day care services, and Aid to Families with Dependent Children (AFDC) funds could be used for day care under certain conditions. The Department of Labor usually included day care funds as part of its manpower training grants, and the Department of Housing and Urban Development (HUD) provided matching funds (on the basis of two-thirds to one-third) for the construction of neighborhood centers that usually included day care.[10] Multiple task forces and panels on child development provide further evi-dence of heightened national government interest in early childhood pol-icy. The Federal Panel on Early Childhood was created in 1968 "as a first step to improve and expand all early childhood programs financed by fed-eral funds."[11]

The income tax deduction for child care expenses, which had been es-tablished in 1954, remained in effect. As of May 1970, it permitted a deduc-tion of up to six hundred dollars for the care of one child and up to nine hundred dollars for the care of two or more children under age thirteen so long as the care enabled a working woman or another specified person to be gainfully employed. These limits applied to all widows, widowers, and separated and divorced persons, regardless of income. To claim the de-duction, a married woman or a husband whose wife was incapacitated had to file a joint return with the spouse. The deduction would be reduced by one dollar for each dollar of the combined adjusted gross income ex-ceeding six thousand dollars.[12]

State and local government activity also occurred. More states and lo-calities supported kindergarten programming or made kindergarten at-tendance compulsory rather than voluntary. Before the late 1960s, kinder-garten had generally been viewed as "advanced nursery school" or as the "stepchild of the elementary school";[13] it was not well integrated into the public school system. Things changed significantly and rapidly. A fall 1968 survey of sixty-four communities found that 69.8 percent of the children who were eligible to attend kindergarten were doing so, with 58.1 percent enrolled in public kindergartens.[14] A report on the survey attributed these changes to Head Start, which, the authors claimed, made kindergarten "more respectable and more fundable."[15]

Despite this government activity, the supply of early childhood services paled in comparison to the demand for them. A March 1969 Library of Congress report noted that the aforementioned government programs would meet only a small proportion of this demand because they focused on low-income families. It concluded, "As far as the non-needy general public is concerned, there are at present no federal programs or proposals which could be expected to provide it with day care facilities and services on any significant scale."[16] Over the next decade, this claim would frequently appear in debates over government involvement. Supporters of increased national government involvement argued that the needs of the American family were not being met.

The late 1960s and early 1970s also witnessed growing interest in early childhood programs among private nonprofit and for-profit organizations. A May 1970 report by the Department of Labor summarized several innovative programs created by corporations, labor unions, women's groups, and others. It noted, "The widespread shortage of day care has brought many businessmen into the field. Numerous companies are setting up chains of day care centers under the franchise system."[17] In October 1970, *Business Week* profiled the growth of the private sector and concluded, "The future may hold a billion-dollar bonanza for the fledgling industry."[18] Two former educators described this development as a "hustle" and questioned the ability of profit-making corporations to provide high-quality care.[19] They noted that private-sector programs tended to be expensive and custodial, and they argued that those with an educational component tended to neglect thinking processes and social development.[20]

During the late 1960s, in sum, the general contours of early childhood policy were changing. Young children were increasingly being cared for outside their homes, and more public funds were being spent on preschool, kindergarten, and day care. These governmental efforts, even when combined with those of nonprofit and for-profit organizations who entered the day care market, seemed incapable of meeting the growing demand for early childhood programs. In the words of the executive director of the National Committee for the Day Care of Children, "This relatively slow rate of growth bears absolutely no relation to the nation's need for more day care facilities."[21] Many observers concluded that the national government should try to fill the growing gap between supply and demand. Both the Nixon administration and Congress took action in the late 1960s.

Precursors to the Comprehensive Child Development Act of 1971

On October 20, 1968, just weeks before he was elected president, Richard Nixon gave a radio address in which he argued that the national government had a vital role to play in education policy. He pledged to "maintain our national commitment to preschool education, expanding as necessary such programs as Head Start and Follow Through."[22] Nixon attempted to make good on this pledge upon taking office. A year later, the administration claimed it had taken five "significant actions" on early childhood policy. The first was rhetorical, a presidential "commitment to assure that every child would have adequate developmental opportunities in the first five years of life."[23] The second significant action was the creation of the Office of Child Development. Developmental psychologist Urie Bronfenbrenner hailed this action as a major step forward because it reflected "a broad-gauged and realistic grasp of the critical importance to the nation of a far-reaching, coordinated, comprehensive approach to child development."[24] The third significant action occurred in July 1969, when the administration sent a representative to testify on the Headstart Child Development Act. This bill was one of several early childhood measures introduced during the Ninety-First Congress.

The final two actions illustrated the administration's belief that day care was inextricably linked to welfare reform. President Nixon's welfare reform proposal, the Family Assistance Plan (FAP), was listed as the fourth significant action. It included a major day care authorization whose goal was to allow previously unemployed welfare recipients to work. The administration insisted that the authorized care "would be developmental and comprehensive in nature."[25] FAP's existence and demise would influence the debate over the Comprehensive Child Development Act. The Department of Health, Education, and Welfare encouraged wider use of AFDC funds for day care, which was the fifth significant action listed in the memo. The national government provided three dollars for every state dollar spent on the "development and operation of day care programs for the children of welfare recipients who were participating in work and training programs, and also for the children in families which are former or potential recipients of public welfare."[26] HEW also promoted coordinated early childhood planning and action through the Community Coordinated Child Care (4-C) program. The 4-C program was "a structure of community organizations brought together to coordinate, plan and mobilize *all* of that community's resources for children."[27] This effort had attracted the interest of several states and about one hundred communities by October 1969.[28]

Day care and child development were also prominent topics at the White House Conference on Children and Youth in 1970. In a 1973 interview, the presidential appointee who directed the conference noted that the administration did not have a "great commitment" to these issues and that "it would have been embarrassing not to have one."[29] The conference nonetheless illustrated the continued interest in early childhood policy. Its forum on developmental child care included a task force on delivery services that said programs should be "universally available at parental option, offering a diversity of choices."[30] It also emphasized programs that were developmental, rather than custodial, in nature. One participant explained, "Day care must be . . . more than baby-sitting. It must build on what we know about child growth and development, about the developmental tasks of children. It is education, health, nutrition, socialization, and more."[31] Conference delegates were asked to rank sixteen issues, and "comprehensive family-oriented child development programs" including "health services, day care and early childhood education" ranked first in a weighted average of the 1,912 ballots cast.[32] The president of the Day Care and Child Development Council of America called day care "the star of the conference show"[33] and argued that the success of the developmental day care forum meant that "we have now the potential of becoming a national force."[34]

Several early childhood measures were introduced by Democrats and Republicans during the Ninety-First Congress. Representative Patsy T. Mink (D-HI) reintroduced the Preschool Centers Supplementary Education Act.[35] The bill provided funds for day care centers to expand, upgrade, supplement, and increase the educational content of their programs. Mink called her bill "an extension of the Head Start opportunity to children not now eligible for it, though nonetheless needful of it."[36] She also joined forces with Representatives John Brademas (D-IN) and Ogden Reid (R-NY) to sponsor the Comprehensive Preschool Education and Child Day Care Act of 1969, which attempted to open up "comprehensive programs of child development . . . to all children, not just the disadvantaged."[37] In the Senate, Walter Mondale (D-MN) and twenty-one Democratic cosponsors introduced similar legislation, the Headstart Child Development Act of 1969. While similar in their focus on universal access to comprehensive services, the House and Senate bills offered contrasting approaches to the question of service delivery.[38]

Jule Sugarman, the acting director of the Office of Child Development, urged the Nixon administration to respond to this congressional activity. In June 1969, he wrote, "Our objective should be to develop legislation which makes possible financial support to public agencies or private agencies with a long-term commitment to providing children's services."[39] Sugarman argued that such a proposal should give priority to communities who were seeking to coordinate their preschool and day care programs and to programs serving the disadvantaged. In October, he argued that the president was losing control of the issue to Congress and that it was "highly desirable for the president to regain the initiative by proposing a comprehensive early childhood bill."[40] He even described the possible parameters and authorization levels of a presidential initiative.

Sugarman was something of a freelancer within the administration. He did "a great deal of negotiating with [Congress] without checking out what was considered appropriate by the administration."[41] The direct negotiations led others in the administration to conclude that he was "working with [Congress] a good deal more closely than is considered appropriate for a bureaucrat in the executive branch of the opposite party to do."[42] In December 1969, Sugarman testified before a House subcommittee on the Preschool Education and Child Day Care Act of 1969. He had been sent "with instruction to say little, very little, about this bill and to appear somewhat negative, which under orders he did do. But that was simply stalling around."[43] Despite Sugarman's efforts and increasing congressional momentum behind early childhood legislation, the administration's position on these initiatives remained ambiguous.

Lacking a clear signal from their nominal party leader, congressional Republicans offered their own early childhood legislation. Representative Ogden Reid and Senator Charles Goodell (R-NY) introduced the Federal-State Education Act of 1969. Developed by New York governor Nelson Rockefeller, it provided "substantial block grants to each of the states for use at the preschool, elementary, secondary, vocational, junior college, higher and adult education levels."[44] States could spend as much as 55 percent of their grant monies on early childhood programs.

Congressional Republicans also worked on early childhood legislation that modified the bill that their Democratic House colleagues had developed. Before introducing legislation in the spring of 1970, they met with several different members of the Nixon administration in an attempt to generate support. The meetings did not lead anywhere, and it became "gradually and increasingly evident . . . that there wasn't going to be very much action," due to the administration's "previous commitment to welfare reform."[45] Undaunted by a lack of presidential support, congressional Republicans introduced the bill. A subcommittee held hearings on it and reported it to the full committee. Nothing further was done, but Republicans were optimistic about what the future held for early childhood legislation. One participant explained, "We went away feeling rather good that we had aired the subject. We had complete, full, legislative hearings on it, built a real framework, a real foundation for action in the beginning of the 92nd Congress. We'd come in, we'd be all ready, everybody would be all steamed up."[46] Subsequent developments demonstrated that several distinct constituencies were indeed "all steamed up" but that the real legislative battle was only about to begin.

The Comprehensive Child Development Act of 1971

When the Ninety-Second Congress convened in 1971, advocates of an expanded national government role in early childhood policy were optimistic about their prospects.[47] In an April 1971 speech, Senator Mondale, who had been appointed chairman of the newly created Subcommittee on Children and Youth of the Senate Labor and Public Welfare Committee in February, stated, "The prospects have improved for expanded government support of early childhood efforts. We will have some kind of legislation shortly, and along with it more money."[48] Mondale's prediction matched the feeling of congressional Republicans who felt that legislative action was imminent. The debate over early childhood legislation proved more controversial than Mondale and others anticipated, however, and advocates' inability to clear all of the necessary legislative hurdles would have profound long-term implications.

The Child Development Coalition and Its Proposal

On January 15, 1971, Senator Mondale sent a letter to Marian Wright Edelman of the Washington Research Project. Noting congressional interest in child development and the organization's expertise, he wrote, "I would welcome your judgments on the essential components of such legislation, and would also like to ask your assistance in bringing together the ideas and opinions of similar groups who would make useful inputs at this stage in the development of a national program."[49] The organization was very receptive to this request. The bills debated during the preceding Congress caused some labor and civil rights groups to fear that "a very successful, community-based Head Start program [would be turned] over to state government, with inadequate standards and inadequate funding and with a tremendous risk of losing parent and community involvement."[50] Edelman and others felt that the most effective response would be to convene a broad coalition of groups with an interest in children. The coalition would debate the main issues, make its policy decisions, draw up legislation, and ask members of Congress to introduce the bill.

The Washington Research Project called a meeting and invited representatives from the "liberal day-care establishment," labor groups, women's groups, and civil rights groups.[51] They were pleasantly surprised by the positive response they received. Diverse constituencies attended the meeting for distinct reasons. According to Edelman, "The women were there, in part, for their children, but in part because they wanted to have options. Labor was there for the political reasons of needing to help its constituency who had child care problems. The civil rights movement was there because it had a stake in these Head Start programs in the South."[52] The National Welfare Rights Organization, whose interest grew out of the day care provisions of President Nixon's Family Assistance Plan, joined the coalition.[53] The American Federation of Teachers and the NEA also participated, even though "there was a real emphasis away from early childhood education programs in the public schools."[54] The National Association for the Education of Young Children was an active coalition member, while some other early childhood groups were not actively involved.[55] Though the coalition was criticized as only involving "the usual people who anybody normally would expect to speak up for [child development legislation],"[56] it successfully brought together diverse constituencies who shared an interest in early childhood policy.[57]

The coalition worked for months before agreeing on a proposal. It prioritized developmental child care, socioeconomic diversity, parent-controlled programs, a substantial investment of new money, and local flexibility and control.[58] The group brought its proposal to Senator Mondale and Representative Brademas and asked them to introduce it in bipartisan fashion. Mondale was receptive and "basically introduced the bill the way the coalition felt it should be enacted."[59] Brademas, hoping to garner Republican support and bowing to the political realities of the House, made several changes. The House version of the bill provided for less parent participation and lower authorizations than the Senate version. The House version was also silent on the "very crucial question [of] whether states or localities would be responsible for the administration of the program."[60] It provided that only localities with populations in excess of "blank" would be eligible to do so. No figure was filled in when the bill was introduced.[61] Despite their differences, both versions of the legislation reflected the main goals of Edelman's coalition.

The proposal called for a comprehensive approach to child development that incorporated educational, nutritional, health, and remedial services.[62] This feature of the proposal reflected the intellectual shifts described in chapter 2 of this book. Supporters explained that a custodial approach to day care would not serve children's interests. Mondale argued, "The one non-negotiable criterion is that these early childhood programs enhance the child's development rather than simply enabling the mother to work."[63] This focus also implied, however, that the coalition and its supporters did not favor a purely educational program. In the context of Head Start, Representative Albert Quie (R-MN), a key congressional player in early childhood policy, had referred to the danger of "permitting the public school educational establishment to place undue emphasis on the educational aspects and so little on the other aspects of training [children]."[64] Similarly, the coalition believed that only multifaceted early intervention programs would have lasting effects. They used Head Start as their model and called for "health services, nutrition services, educational services of some undefined kind but some educational help, and whatever else kind of help that family needed."[65]

Socioeconomic diversity represented the second key element of the legislation. Neither the Senate nor the House version made comprehensive services available to all children, but both versions laid the foundation for a universal program. The original Senate language stated that programs "should be available as a matter of right to all children regardless of economic, social and family background."[66] Mondale said that he hoped to "build on the successful experience of Head Start and deliver educational, health, and nutritional day care services to *all* children."[67] In the words of one opponent of the bill, "The time frame for making the program universal was never clearly set forth, but the intention of universality was clear."[68] Creating the framework for a universal program was "perhaps [the] most revolutionary" element of the proposal (Zigler and Muenchow 1992, 123).

The universal approach was justified on both policy and political grounds. In policy terms, supporters pointed to the potential educational benefits of economically integrated programs. In an April speech, Mondale quoted Dr. Edward Zigler, director of the Office of Child Development: "The middle-class child does have a number of attributes that the poor child could profitably model. By the same token we often find in poor children particular strengths and characteristics worthy of emulation by the middle class child."[69] Brademas referred to the famous Coleman Report to make a similar point about the ability of young children from distinctive backgrounds to learn from one another. He argued that "poor children develop much more rapidly, at least in cognitive terms, when they participate in programs with children of middle income backgrounds than when segregated by family income."[70] As Congress debated the legislation, the National Organization for Women described the ethnic and socioeconomic integration as critical and concluded, "We cannot support programs that further separate the poor from the rest of the population."[71] Civil rights leaders made a similar point in a letter to President Nixon, claiming, "By bringing together children of different racial, social, and economic backgrounds, the program would provide them with an invaluable opportunity to grow up knowing each other as individuals."[72]

In addition to lauding the policy impact of a universal program, supporters described it as a political strategy. In the United States, antipoverty policies targeted on the poor alone "have not been politically sustainable, and they have stigmatized and demeaned the poor" (Skocpol 1991, 414). Coalition members alluded to this history in pressing for a universal program. One explained, "We don't have a very good history in this country of programs that are available only to the poor. The history of successful social programs has been programs that are universally available."[73] According to Marian Wright Edelman, the legislation consciously sought to include "middle-class folk" to avoid being called a "poor people's program."[74] Coalition leaders worried that "poor people's programs were not going to be able to command the constituencies that were needed for long-term survival."[75] The debate over universality influenced the rhetoric that proponents used to justify the legislation, as they emphasized its benefits for all children. It also led to a heated debate about the income level at which eligibility should be set. Eligibility levels became a key point of contention between congressional leaders and the Nixon administration.

Parent-controlled programs represented a third component of the coalition proposal. Conceding that social scientists would offer competing interpretations of the child development literature, Edelman claimed, "What we do know will make a difference . . . is that families have to be involved with children if there's going to be any long-range effect. . . . There is just a limit to what government can do."[76] As a result, she felt that "the key decision-making power should rest with parents and families."[77] Parental involvement would serve two objectives. First, it would lead to better outcomes for children, as the education they received and the other lessons they learned would be reinforced in the home. According to developmental psychologist Urie Bronfenbrenner, "If [early intervention] programs are to have lasting effects they must concentrate not only on the child himself, but equally, if not more, on the environment in which he lives, especially the members of his family."[78] Second, parental involvement would aid community empowerment, a primary objective of the Community Action Program. Many coalition members had been involved in that program.

The legislation also called for a substantial investment of new money in early childhood programs. Edelman argued that a strong financial commitment from the national government was necessary to reach children and families who would not otherwise have access to the kind of help that they needed.[79] The House version set a lower authorization level than did the Senate version, but the cost of the program over the short and long term was a key issue. Civil rights leaders argued, "We do not know exactly what the program will cost in the years ahead. We *do* know, however, that the cost of *not* having a program is already too high."[80] Some supporters portrayed government spending on early childhood programs as an investment that would pay for itself over the long term.

Others argued that the financial impact of the legislation would not be that large. Brademas, for example, pointed out that it required the creation of a child development council and the approval of a comprehensive child development plan. These requirements, he argued, would limit financial outlays over the short term.[81] Despite various attempts to downplay the cost issue, some opponents possessed "a very real fear that it's going to cost too much."[82] For a Republican administration that wanted to reform welfare and cut program costs, the potential price tag of the legislation seemed "horrendous."[83]

The last major component of the proposal was local flexibility and control. Indeed, the issue of program administration provoked considerable controversy. Some members of the coalition, especially civil rights groups, rejected any legislation that granted state governments a prominent role. Their views grew out of their experiences in southern states, especially in Mississippi. The state of Mississippi declined to apply for Head Start funds in 1965, leading a group of private, public, and church organizations to form the Child Development Group of Mississippi (CDGM). After CDGM's first year of operation, the Office of Economic Opportunity (OEO) accused CDGM of mismanaging funds and cut off its funding. The grant was given to another group viewed as less threatening to whites. Edelman, an influential CDGM board member, helped save the program by finding a new director and persuading local leaders to work within the system to regain funds. The Mississippi experience nonetheless made her a strong foe of state administration (Zigler and Muenchow 1992). She argued that "anybody who was southern, who had been working with community-based programs, saw [state administration] as the end of all these very good southern programs."[84] In both its initial proposal and its lobbying efforts, the coalition fought to preserve local control. Critics viewed its position as an overreaction and argued that "you cannot build every piece of legislation around what you think might happen in Mississippi."[85]

In both its House and Senate forms, the Comprehensive Child Development Act of 1971 represented a fundamental change in how the national government approached early childhood policy. Its ten bipartisan cosponsors in the House described it as "the most significant proposal on child care ever introduced in Congress."[86] Brademas noted that it offered stability and, "for the first time," a "permanent commitment by the federal government to better the lives of all children."[87] Its key features—comprehensive services, socioeconomic diversity, parent-controlled programs, a substantial investment of new money, and local flexibility and control—represented a "radical departure from previous government attitudes toward early childhood services" (Steinfels 1973, 18). There was no precedent for its extension of national government assistance to nonpoor families, and it was not linked to the traditional justifications that characterized the emergency nursery schools, wartime day care centers, and Head Start (Nelson 1982, 278). Supporters of the bill did not frame it as a temporary response to crisis conditions. Instead, they advanced several claims that reflected the diverse objectives of the child development coalition, each of which was challenged by opponents of the legislation.

The Cases for and against the Comprehensive Child Development Act

As members of Congress considered the legislation, they generally focused on its eligibility requirements, the nature of the services it would provide, and the question of prime sponsorship. Even among its supporters, there was "a considerable difference of opinion as to the population to be served, the content of the program, and the delivery system."[88] By emphasizing issues of program structure, Congress arguably neglected the fundamental philosophical question of whether national government involvement in early childhood policy was appropriate (McCathren 1981,

111).[89] Significant public attention to that broader question did not emerge until President Nixon vetoed the bill in December 1971, and I will discuss it in that context. This section profiles four prominent rationales for national government involvement and explains how opponents responded to each of them.

The relationship between day care and welfare reform was the first rationale for national government intervention. The child development coalition did not emphasize this potential link, but the Nixon administration was especially interested in it. Several program indicators suggested the existence of a "welfare crisis" in the 1960s. Welfare caseloads, participation or take-up rates (the percentage of eligible persons that received benefits), and program outlays all grew explosively. Congress made several changes to welfare policy during the 1960s, but none of them had the desired effect. The expansion of day care availability was viewed as a potential solution because it would help "welfare mothers to be able to take jobs or obtain training in order to get off the welfare rolls—thus cutting welfare rolls in the short run."[90]

Critics questioned this connection and pointed to the limited ability of earlier reforms either to move welfare mothers into the labor market or to provide high-quality child care for their children. For example, one essay on the history of day care centers in the United States questioned whether they had ever successfully moved women into the labor force. It concluded that the historical record was "filled with cautionary tales that scarcely legitimate the kind of inflated rhetoric that we are now hearing" (Rothman 1973, 13).

Cognitive development was a second justification for national government intervention. Supporters believed that all children would benefit from child development programs, but they emphasized its potential impact on disadvantaged children. Mondale cited recent research finding that "ghetto youngsters lose on the average of 17 I.Q. points between 15 months and three years of age if they receive no preschool education or tutoring."[91] Supporters also claimed that child development spending would pay for itself over the long term due to its impact on cognitive development and other outcomes, because it would help produce effective members of society, reducing future spending on various social programs. For example, they claimed that "providing developmental opportunities for disadvantaged children [could reduce] the likelihood that they will enter welfare rolls in the future."[92] Brademas cited the congressional testimony of Sheldon H. White: "It may turn out to be more sensible to invest heavily in the first years of a child's life and spend less as he moves through elementary and secondary education."[93]

Critics of the child development legislation, citing the Westinghouse study of Head Start and other sources, doubted that early childhood programs would be a positive experience. Questioning whether the developmental impact of the programs would be lasting, they contended that young children would be better served by remaining at home. In sum, they argued that "sending four-year-olds off to school results in far more harm than good."[94] They also claimed that supporters were overselling the potential benefits of early childhood programs while neglecting their potential drawbacks.

The third rationale for national government intervention was the transformation of the American workforce. The proposal would "provide adequate day care for the increasing number of children in families where both parents work."[95] Supporters of government action argued that the day care needs of the American family were not being met. Senator Fred Harris (D-OK), for example, referred to a "crisis in the availability of child care services."[96] Supporters of the legislation often described a discrepancy between the demand for day care services and the number of available slots. A June 1971 press release argued that there were "five million preschool children in the United States whose mothers work, yet day care services are available for only 641,000 of these children."[97] With the number of working mothers projected to continue on its upward trajectory, supporters pressed for government action. Changes in patterns of participation in the labor force and their accompanying impact on the American family, they argued, required greater public investment in early childhood programs.

The transformation of the American labor force was due largely to increased participation among women, including the mothers of young children. Women's equality therefore represented a fourth rationale for government intervention. Supporters argued that the legislation gave "all women, not just the poor, a genuine choice between child care and work outside the home."[98] This justification was frequently associated with the broader movement for women's liberation, which included child care availability among its major objectives. According to one report, "Twenty-four hour community controlled day care was a major cry around which women across the country rallied on Women's Liberation Day, August 26, [1970]."[99] The movement argued that child care should be available to all women regardless of their employment status, run by the people who use it, viewed as an educational and social experience, and voluntary. Supporters claimed that "there are many mothers who would like to work but cannot find adequate day care."[100] Women's equality was an especially controversial rationale for national government intervention, due to its association with the women's liberation movement. One observer called this connection the political factor "that's doing [the most] to weaken the chances of getting legislation."[101]

Opponents of the Comprehensive Child Development Act reacted especially strongly to the child care shortage and women's equality justifications. They denounced the measure in strong terms, bemoaning its implications for American family life. They argued that day care enrollment would weaken the mother-child bond, with harmful consequences for children and their families. For example, one letter to House Speaker Carl Albert (D-OK) attributed the most serious social problems of the day to the breakdown of the family unit, noting, "You must realize that removing children from their mothers' influence for extended periods of time during their formative years could prove disastrous."[102] Other critics questioned the underlying premises of the women's liberation movement, arguing that most women "find spiritual and emotional satisfaction in being the hand that, through rocking the cradle, as the timeworn synecdoche has it, comes to rule the world."[103]

For some opponents, the notion of government-supported child care was especially threatening to their values. The mayor of Belle Glade, Florida, argued that the bill was "designed to destroy the family and the home, place our children in government institutions, and lead us into a totalitarian state."[104] A conservative publication complained that the child development legislation would "destroy the nation's economy, the nation's morality, the family unit, law and order, and ALL individual incentives and resourcefulness."[105] The strident and alarmist tone of these critiques is striking.

Intense rhetorical attacks on the Comprehensive Child Development Act were commonplace by the late summer. The legislation was repeatedly denounced in harsh terms in *Human Events,* a publication of the John Birch Society. A group of conservative professors from around the country formed the Committee on Children and produced a report documenting the faults of the legislation.[106] This elite activity was supplemented by the efforts of "independent parents' groups across the country [that were] united in their concern over the diminishing cohesiveness of the family unit."[107] Trying to derail the legislation, opponents repeatedly stressed themes of parental autonomy and individualism, claiming that American homes should remain "inviolable retreats from busybodies—especially federal busybodies."[108]

In sum, the child development coalition and its allies claimed that their proposal would help welfare mothers in entering the labor force, enhance the cognitive development of (disadvantaged) children, meet the growing day care needs of the changing American family, and contribute to the achievement of women's equality. The diverse members of the coalition privileged these goals to varying degrees but were united by their support of the proposal. Opponents disputed all of these claims, deriding the bill as "parent replacement" legislation that regarded children "almost as wards of the state."[109] They argued that it was fiscally irresponsible, administratively unworkable, and loaded with family-weakening implications. As these battle lines were drawn, however, neither side knew for certain whether it could claim the Nixon administration as an ally.

The Nixon Administration and Child Development Legislation

Supporters and opponents spent months attempting to divine the administration's position on the Comprehensive Child Development Act. Advocates repeatedly referred to Nixon's 1969 message to Congress in which he promised to "make a national commitment to providing all American children an opportunity for healthful and stimulating development during the first five years of life."[110] They claimed that endorsing the child development bill would enable the president to fulfill his pledge. In developing and lobbying for its proposal, however, the child development coalition made limited contact with the Nixon administration. A lawyer with the Washington Research Project conceded that this inattention to the executive branch was "probably the one place where we didn't do the job we should have done."[111] In June, the administration issued a statement "indicating interest in some form of a child development bill."[112] This tepid endorsement papered over a divide within the executive branch. As the legislation continued to wind through Congress, however, "the administration pulled more and more away from any interest in and support for child development."[113] Consequently, neither supporters nor opponents felt confident about presidential support.

According to historian Sonya Michel (1999, 248), the Comprehensive Child Development Act "initially caught the Nixon Administration somewhat off guard," because the administration had been focused on welfare reform. Certainly, key players like Daniel Patrick Moynihan and Richard Nathan placed a higher priority on welfare reform than on child development.[114] The amount of bipartisan activity on the latter topic during the Ninety-First Congress, however, drew notice from at least some members of the administration. In February 1971, HEW secretary Elliot Richardson decided to back the House bill from the previous session as long as some modifications were made. A departmental work group drafted substitute language, submitting its initial recommendations to the secretary just after the new House legislation had been introduced in March.

In a memo, the departmental work group highlighted several differences between its proposal and the new House legislation. Even with the changes made by Brademas, the new proposal placed a higher priority on local and parental control and was "much more community-dominated."[115] Prime sponsorship was a key area of disagreement. The departmental proposal limited prime sponsorship to states, cities with populations of at least five hundred thousand, and Indian reservations. The House bill had a more expansive definition, allowing smaller units of local government and public or private nonprofit groups to qualify as prime sponsors. The composition and role of child development councils and local policy councils was another area of disagreement, and it reflected the broader debate over parent and community control. Income eligibility standards, the provision of services for national government employees, and the role of the Office of Child Development were addressed. The departmental work group also discussed potential legislative strategies, but it did not make a definitive recommendation about how Richardson should proceed.[116]

Although the work group's memo indicates that HEW was giving serious thought to child development legislation, it would be a mistake to interpret this stance as the administration's position. There was a battle within the administration between HEW and the Office of Management and Budget (OMB). In fact, the HEW memo mentioned that "OMB is disinclined to recommend that the administration support child care legislation."[117] OMB believed that publicly funded day care should be "strictly limited to families who fell under the provisions of the Family Assistance Plan" (Steinfels 1973, 189). This division was crucial, because Richardson could not testify on behalf of the administration or enter good faith negotiations with Congress until OMB cleared his position. A House subcommittee held hearings on the legislation in late May and early June. Richardson and Edward Zigler, director of the Office of Child Development, were invited to testify on behalf of the administration, but "they had nothing to say [because OMB] had still not come forward with an acceptable position."[118] The Senate extended a similar invitation to the HEW secretary, and Richardson postponed his testimony three times as he waited for clearance.

On June 8, Richardson finally sent Brademas a statement explaining that the administration favored a "workable, unified system for administering the various child care programs now in place and soon to be enacted by the Congress."[119] A Democratic insider summarized this position as "indicating interest in some form of a child development bill, controlled by the states, no authorizations listed, and considerably less parental participation."[120] The statement was widely interpreted as a victory for Richardson and an unexpected breakthrough, but significant differences remained between what the administration had endorsed and the amended legislation moving through Congress. Zigler and another official were not well received when they finally testified before a Senate subcommittee, even though their testimony "seemed to provide a 'green light' for child development legislation" (Zigler and Muenchow 1992, 142).

The primary problem was that the administration was unresponsive to what had occurred on Capitol Hill. The original bill had been substantially rewritten, and positions on such issues as prime sponsorship had begun to harden, but the administration failed to provide "the kind of testimony that could be given directly in reference to the bills being proposed; it was as though you were speaking into a vacuum. If one were to contemplate the ideal child development legislation that the administration would support, this is what it would comprise."[121] Observers continued to describe the administration's position as "unclear"[122] and "hazy"[123] because it had not engaged the revisions that had already been made. Months had passed in which the Office of Child Development's "hands were tied," with "no way to negotiate seriously and to make any kind of promises on behalf of the administration."[124] In a sense, Richardson's breakthrough was too little, too late.

The Child Development Bill Moves through Congress

In attempting to move its proposal through Congress, the child development coalition and its congressional allies made two crucial tactical choices. The first one, which set them up for significant second-guessing, was to conduct a stealth lobbying campaign with limited input from and attention to the American public at large. It brought together dozens of organizations and sought to line up the necessary congressional support. Its campaign "was not an effort to educate the country. It was undertaken deliberately that way, because it was thought [to be] best and the quickest way to get it through the Congress."[125] Edelman described this strategy as a calculated gamble but a tactical necessity: "It was our judgment that . . . if we had any chance of getting it through we were going to have to be very quiet, just do our work, line up our support, and move it."[126] This stealth approach led one observer to claim that the legislation "was not a popular act, it was a lobby of lobbyists."[127] The coalition's decision not to engage the public seemed to affect only the late stages of the congressional policy-making process.

The second tactical choice made by the coalition and its allies was to attach the child development program to a bill extending the life of the Office of Economic Opportunity. The OEO was scheduled to expire on June 30, 1971, and they assumed that Congress and the president would not allow that to happen. They believed that this tactic would permit consideration of the child development program at the earliest possible date and enhance its chances of becoming law. This tactical decision facilitated the proposal's movement through Congress, but it was insufficient to prevent a presidential veto.

Several major controversies arose as Congress considered the Comprehensive Child Development Act. Program eligibility was a major sticking point. Supporters generally viewed a universal program as their long-term goal, but the legislation would not serve all children in the short term. Services would be free for children living in families with incomes up to a certain level, and higher-income families would be able to participate by paying a fee. The chief policy issue was where the line should be set. The House and Senate versions of the legislation initially drew the line at $6,960 for a family of four, a figure the Bureau of Labor Standards (BLS) had determined as the cost of family consumption.

Critics, including the Nixon administration, argued that a high cutoff would increase the cost of the program. After the Senate passed legislation with the BLS provision, Richardson sent a letter to House minority leader Gerald Ford (R-MI). Noting there that the legislation was inconsistent with the administration's welfare reform proposal, Richardson estimated that a program using the BLS standard would cost twenty billion dollars.[128] He warned that an unfunded program would lead to a "tragically unfulfilled promise to the American people of the kind that has already undermined their confidence in the government."[129] Although the figure of $6,960 had received strong bipartisan support in committee, the legislation was amended on the House floor to reflect the administration's preference. Eligibility for free services would be limited to families making under $4,320 per year. The child development coalition and its allies viewed this change as "a very serious problem because it would permit targeting so carefully on the poor that there would never be broad enough involvement in the program to increase it to meet even a fraction of the needs that existed."[130] The discrepancy between the House and Senate versions of the bill would eventually be reconciled by a conference committee, with the House prevailing on the eligibility issue.

Another sticking point was the issue of prime sponsorship, which became "the principal item of debate during [the legislation's] journey through Congress" (McCathren 1981, 106). The Nixon administration felt that prime sponsorship should be limited to state governments for reasons of administrative feasibility. It would mean that there would be no more than fifty administrative bodies to monitor, regulate, and fund (Steinfels 1973, 205). Richardson relented slightly on this stance in his June statement, outlining a program in which "for cities with a population of 500,000 or more an option for self-designation as prime sponsor is available if the chief elected official requests such a designation through the governor."[131] As has already been discussed, many members of the child development coalition were skeptical of a state-based approach and felt that local boards would be more sensitive to the needs of poor and minority children. Mondale expressed similar reservations. He argued that any grant to the states "gets to be pretty thin by the time it reaches the end of the pipeline. It is terribly important that we make money available directly to community groups and directly to local governments."[132]

The issue of prime sponsorship came to a head in the House, where Brademas battled his own committee chair, Representative Carl Perkins (D-KY), over the population cutoff. Brademas and Republicans on his subcommittee had agreed on a figure of one hundred thousand. Republicans pledged to support the bill if this major feature, which they perceived as providing a "positive role for the states," was retained.[133] Perkins, in contrast, wanted to lower the figure to ten thousand. Republicans joined forces with a few Democrats to defeat the chair's amendment in committee, but Perkins was successful on the House floor. This amendment increased the number of eligible localities and "had the effect of stripping the bill of almost the entire Republican support it had in the House."[134] State officials were alarmed by this change. Even before it was made, the National Governors' Conference sent a letter to Albert Quie (R-MN) in which it complained that the House proposal "would, in effect, bypass state governments." The conference pressed for "a strong state role with related federal safeguards."[135] Congress essentially ignored this entreaty. One Republican congressional staffer claimed that the governors "really didn't get organized" and were "totally lost in the process."[136] Their limited impact on the Comprehensive Child Development Act stands in sharp contrast to the prominent state government role during later debates over early childhood policy.

As Congress considered the legislation, insiders predicted an especially tough fight on the Senate floor. One staffer foresaw "some tough, close votes that could go either way on several issues like local vs. state control, parental involvement, and eligibility for other than poor children."[137] Indeed, the first real opposition became evident as the Senate debated the bill in September. Senator James Buckley (Conservative-NY) "launched a whole attack on the concept of child development" and "denounced [the bill] as an effort to impose federal control over all American children."[138] With administration backing, Senator Robert Taft Jr. (R-OH) introduced six amendments to narrow the scope of the child development program. The amendments would have, among other things, lowered the income eligibility threshold for free services and limited the role of child development councils. The floor managers of the bill successfully defeated all six amendments, which received support from conservative Republicans and several southern Democrats.[139]

The climax of the Senate debate occurred when Taft introduced a motion to recommit the bill to the Labor and Public Welfare Committee with instructions to delete the child development program. The motion was defeated, 17–46. On September 9, the Senate passed the bill by a 49–12 roll-call vote. The House followed suit three weeks later, adding the comprehensive child development program to the OEO bill on the floor. The House passed the OEO extension by a 251–115 roll-call vote on September 30.

The House and Senate bills differed significantly on prime sponsorship, parental control, and other features of the child development program. As a result, the bill went to a conference committee. The conflict between Perkins and Brademas persisted. Perkins, using his prerogatives as committee chair, took the unusual step of not appointing the sponsor of the bill to the conference committee. Perkins feared that the legislation would negatively affect his rural district, a concern shared by others who represented similar areas, but his decision to exclude Brademas from the conference committee was also described as "petty" and "personality oriented."[140] Conferees adopted a provision permitting localities with a population of five thousand or more to be designated as prime sponsors if they met certain requirements. This provision "infuriated House Republicans because they felt that the conference committee had ignored their views" (Zigler and Muenchow 1992, 145). Five of the six House Republican conferees refused to sign the conference report because they objected to the proposed delivery system. The provisions for prime sponsorship also generated staunch opposition from both Democratic and Republican governors (Cohen 2001).

The conference committee spent significant time debating who would receive free child development services and what type of fee scale would be established for those above the cutoff. The Senate version made free services available for families of four with annual incomes below $6,960, while the comparable figure in the House version was $4,320. Mondale and Quie attempted to negotiate a compromise, but Richardson insisted on the lower figure. Eventually, Richardson endorsed a compromise on the fee schedule. It adopted the House cutoff for free services, incorporated a "very modest fee" for those making less than $6,960, and gave the HEW secretary the authority to set a sliding fee scale for families above that level.[141] As the conference concluded and House Republicans expressed their qualms about the delivery system, however, Richardson "wrote a strange letter which in essence removed his initial support."[142]

The child development coalition and its congressional allies generally praised the conference report. The American Academy of Pediatrics urged its adoption and described its emphasis on the community level as "responsive to the needs of individual children and communities."[143] The League of Women Voters concurred, stating, "Those who see in this legislation threats of federal control over the minds of children should recognize that it is precisely the requirements for local prime sponsorship and parental participation that protect against just that danger."[144] Alluding to the difficult conference negotiations and a possible presidential veto, Mondale praised the conference report and expressed his hope that "the compromise [on free services] would prevent a threatened Administration veto."[145] Opponents of the child development section argued that it would be expensive and impossible to administer and that it intruded on parental autonomy. On December 2, the Senate adopted the conference report by a 63–17 roll-call vote. The vote in the House took place five days later and was much closer, due in part to administration lobbying and a concerted effort by minority leader Gerald Ford to defeat the conference report. The House adopted the report by a 211–187 roll-call vote, with 135 of the opposition votes coming from Republicans. The Comprehensive Child Development Act of 1971 was then sent to the president as part of the OEO bill.

The Veto

The Nixon administration's position on the Comprehensive Child Development Act remained unclear and puzzling to conference committee participants. Supporters hoped for a favorable outcome because the proposal responded to the president's call for a national commitment to the first five years of life, reflected the top priority of the 1970 White House Conference on Children and Youth, and enjoyed bipartisan support in both houses of Congress.[146] After the measure finally cleared Congress, "the signals came very clearly that the president was probably going to veto the bill."[147] The president returned the measure without his approval shortly after the House approved the conference report. By that point, the occurrence of the veto was not as surprising as its tone. Written by Patrick Buchanan, the president's veto message harshly denounced the child development program and "offered a sweeping indictment of the whole concept" (Zigler and Muenchow 1992, 147).

The veto message criticized other aspects of the OEO legislation but described the child development section as its "most deeply flawed provision."[148] It acknowledged the need for additional day care services in the United States but criticized the measure for its "fiscal irresponsibility, administrative unworkability, and family-weakening implications."[149] The proposed cost of the program was one hundred million dollars for planning and program development in fiscal 1972 and two billion dollars in fiscal 1973. Nixon argued, "[T]he expenditure of two billions of dollars [sic] in a program whose effectiveness has yet to be demonstrated cannot be justified. And the prospect of costs which could eventually reach $20 billion annually is even more unreasonable."[150] In terms of program administration, the president criticized the child development program for relegating the states to an "insignificant role" and "creating a new army of bureaucrats."[151] He claimed that the low population cutoff "actively [invited] the participation of as many as 7,000 prime sponsors—each with its own plan, its own council, its own version of all the other machinery that has made Head Start, with fewer than 1,200 grantees, so difficult a management problem."[152]

Supporters of the child development program were especially offended by the language the president used to describe its negative implications for the American family. Nixon closed his veto message by asserting, "For the federal government to plunge headlong financially into supporting child development would commit the vast moral authority of the national government to the side of communal approaches to child rearing over against the family-centered approach."[153] This portrayal of the child development program struck a chord with many Americans, tapping into their strong distrust of the national government and appealing to the ideal of parental autonomy. Conservative columnist James J. Kirkpatrick argued that the veto "ranks among [President Nixon's] finest state papers of recent months."[154] Supporters of the bill denounced the tone of the veto message. Brademas later called it "one of the most inaccurate and demagogic messages ever penned by an American president."[155] An attorney with the Washington Research Project said, "It was just a cruel and very deceiving veto message."[156]

Observers attributed Nixon's rhetoric to several factors. Some pointed to the president's standing with the conservative wing of the Republican Party. During the summer, the John Birch Society, the American Conservative Union, the Mormon Church, and several other conservative organizations had launched a letter-writing campaign against the child development proposal. By the time Nixon issued his veto, he faced increasing pressure from this constituency after announcing his intention to visit China. In addition, conservative representative John Ashbrook (R-OH) had recently announced that he would run against Nixon in the 1972 Republican primary. The child development program therefore "offered the president an opportunity to regain some of the support he might be losing with the trip to China. That is, he couldn't cancel his trip to China, but he could veto this and echo some of the concerns about communal upbringing and governmental control that the right wing had been offering."[157] One observer stated simply, "I personally think the president made a very practical political decision that he had more to gain from vetoing it than from signing it."[158]

The coordinated conservative lobbying campaign was especially noteworthy in the absence of anything comparable among the bill's supporters. One insider claimed, "It was the right wing that mobilized, and the liberal coalition supporting child development did not. No public outcry ensued. One lesson certainly to be learned from all of this, is that [supporters spent] too much time talking to each other and not enough time in finding ways to mobilize and inform public opinion."[159] This observation indicts the coalition's tactical choice to attempt to move the bill through Congress without a grassroots campaign. Conservative organizations produced an avalanche of letters against the proposal, but supporters could not generate a comparable wave of public support.

Several observers questioned the political skill and effectiveness of the child development coalition, while others argued that it ultimately failed to achieve its objectives due to its unwillingness to compromise.[160] One Republican Senate staffer said of the coalition, "They felt it was an all or nothing ballgame, or at least that was the impression that they gave; and I still feel that we would have had something had they been willing to bargain more."[161] Coalition leaders rejected the charge that they had not been sufficiently flexible. Edelman said, "It's very clear to me in retrospect, and looking at the president's message, that whatever bill we'd done would still have resulted in his vetoing that bill. He had *no* intention of signing it."[162]

Other observers attributed the veto message to the declining fortunes of the administration's welfare reform proposal. Historian Elizabeth Rose (1999, 215) explains, "When it became clear that his larger welfare reform measure was unlikely to pass, however, [the president] decided he had little use for a large-scale day care program and vetoed the bill." Indeed, the presidential veto message made multiple references to the Family Assistance Plan, noting that it had been before Congress for over two years and characterizing the child development provisions as duplicative.[163] The conflict between welfare reform and child development legislation highlights the difficulty of adopting innovative policy changes if they are not a high presidential priority (Thomas 1975, 174). In a 1975 interview, Quie noted that "major legislation has tended to come from an administration" during the Johnson and Nixon presidencies.[164] The Comprehensive Child Development Act was a congressional initiative that was developed with minimal input from the executive branch. One staffer argued that a prominent source of the veto was the fact that the bill was being compared to Medicare even though it was not a presidential initiative: "I think it would be difficult for any president . . . to stand up and sign a bill which he had not requested, a bill of this magnitude."[165] Signing such a bill, he argued, would implicitly acknowledge that the administration had failed to recognize an important societal problem and that Congress had made up for the shortcomings of the executive branch.

Conclusion: The End of the Beginning

The strident tone of the veto message had its intended effect. On December 10, the Senate failed to override the veto. The vote was 51–36, with twenty-nine Republicans and seven southern Democrats backing the president. Thirteen Republican senators who had previously voted for the conference report switched positions and voted to sustain the veto. Thus the remarkable story of the Comprehensive Child Development Act came to an end.

Many child development advocates were disheartened by this turn of events. One member of the Office of Child Development said that a "post-partum depression" swept over the agency and was shared by many individuals on Capitol Hill.[166] The veto squelched any enthusiasm in the House of Representatives for a child development bill, as Perkins and others concluded that developing new legislation would ultimately be an exercise in futility.[167] With the benefit of hindsight, several scholars have pointed to the veto as a crucial turning point in the evolution of early childhood education and care in the United States. David Kirp (2004) characterized it as the moment when "the national movement for universal preschool came heart-breakingly close to success." Joan Lombardi (2003, 4) used similar language, claiming that the veto "set the child-care agenda back for decades: While other countries moved ahead, the United States stood still."

Such assessments overlook that the debate over the appropriate governmental role in child development never really ended. As will be described in chapter 5 of this book, the Senate pressed ahead with revised legislation in 1972, even though supporters recognized that they faced an uphill battle. For Edelman and other leaders of the child development coalition, the veto simply was not a reason to halt their campaign. She explained, "You go back year after year until you get it. It's going to be harder to get it now, there's going to be more debate. But it seems to me if you're committed to a thing you go back."[168] The decentralized institutional structure of the American political system meant that child development supporters did not necessarily have to go back to Congress to achieve their policy goals. They could and did turn to other institutional venues, most notably the states. This tactical choice produced some political successes but also contributed to the long-term fragmentation of early childhood policy.

4 | Venue Shopping, Federalism, and the Role of the States

One of the distinctive features of the American political system is the extent to which it decentralizes political authority. This institutional fragmentation can impede the adoption of expansive policies, but it also provides multiple access points for reformers. Frustrated in one institutional context, reformers can try to achieve their goals in another setting, a phenomenon known as venue shopping. Child development advocates were disappointed by Nixon's veto of the Comprehensive Child Development Act and their failure to override it, and many of them concluded that developing new congressional legislation would be an exercise in futility. The implausibility of success at the national level did not, however, eliminate the possibility of policy change. Instead, it simply meant that advocates would have to turn to another institutional venue to achieve their goals.

Congress continued to consider comprehensive child development legislation, but federalism allowed advocates to shift their focus to the state level. Supporters of a more expansive government role in early childhood education concluded that they needed "to pay a lot more attention to state governments than we have in the past."[1] The states were favorable terrain for their efforts, because state lawmakers were frustrated by their relatively limited role in the debate at the national level. Governors and other state leaders felt that the Comprehensive Child Development Act, with its controversial provisions for prime sponsorship, had essentially ignored the states. Some of them attributed this outcome to "the ineffectiveness of the representation of state interests and capabilities to Congress."[2] The Education Commission of the States (ECS) used a grant from the Office of Education to launch its Early Childhood Project. The project aimed to facilitate better communication between Congress and the states and to disseminate policy-relevant information to interested state-level actors.

The combined efforts of child development advocates and professional associations like the ECS bore substantial fruit in the early to mid-1970s. States across the country established offices of child development to improve the administration and coordination of programs for the very young, funded social services for children who were too young to attend primary school, and established preschool projects. By the middle of the decade, the ECS could reasonably claim that the state-level momentum in early childhood education "has become increasingly purposeful and sophisticated. The capacity of the states to plan and provide services for young children and their families is clearly on the rise."[3] This state-level activity in the aftermath of Nixon's veto did not result in the creation of a comprehensive child development program, but it reshaped the structure and politics of early childhood education over both the short term and the long term.

Early State-Level Activity and the Education Commission of the States

At a December 1972 conference, former South Carolina governor Robert McNair described his experience testifying before Congress on the Comprehensive Child Development Act. When McNair claimed that its provisions for prime sponsorship would lead to overlap and waste, the "response from several of the more vocal members of the House Select Subcommittee on Education was 'But what have the states done in the early childhood field? Do you come to us with clean hands?'" McNair recalled, "Misplaced as I thought their emphasis was, it was difficult to answer—then."[4] The former governor's reflections summarize one of the major themes of this chapter: the pace of state-level activity in early childhood policy picked up considerably in the early 1970s.

State governments were involved in early childhood policy before the debate over the Comprehensive Child Development Act, but their efforts were limited. Fueled by the National Kindergarten Association (NKA), a national umbrella organization, one arena of state-level activity was the provision of state funds for kindergarten. The NKA was structured as a national umbrella organization and included "broad representation from academia, elite society, and educational organizations" (Beatty 2001, 170). Its lobbying effort exemplified successful venue shopping. Thwarted in its effort to pass a national kindergarten bill, the group lobbied for universal public kindergarten in states and localities. In 1967, an ECS survey revealed that thirty-three states provided public funds to school districts that instituted kindergarten programs. Several states mandated kindergarten as an integral part of their public schools. A 1967 Colorado law, for example, required schools to establish kindergarten by September 1970 to maintain accreditation, and a Massachusetts law passed that same year required kindergartens in every school district in the state by 1973.[5] The movement toward universal kindergarten continued into the mid-1970s. At that point, it was an established public responsibility in most parts of the country, and the NKA board of directors "decided it had fulfilled its mission and dissolved the organization" (Beatty 2001, 175).

In the late 1960s, there were also hints of increased interest in child development more broadly. For example, in 1969, West Virginia received a small planning grant from the Appalachian Regional Commission. It used the grant to develop plans for seven regional demonstration centers in early childhood education, an important development in a state "with no specific planning being done in early education, no existing public supported early education programs to serve as models, a serious lack of certified early education teachers, and limited experience in interagency coordination and cooperation in the delivery of services to children."[6] The following year, two of the centers were funded by the same commission. Their successful operation led the legislature to fund the remaining five demonstration centers in 1971. On November 1, 1971, Governor Arch Moore issued an executive order that created the Interagency Council for Child Development Services.[7] Even though these developments possessed limited reach, the speed with which they occurred in a state that had demonstrated limited prior interest in early childhood policy is striking.

The Education Commission of the States took several steps that highlighted its growing interest in early childhood education.[8] In 1967, one year after its founding, the ECS "endorsed Early Childhood Education as a top priority education need in practically all the states."[9] Working with nine Washington-based professional associations, the organization put together a packet of materials that it mailed to key legislators and other select figures in each of the states.[10] The packet included a cover letter announcing that "the staff of the Education Commission of the States stands ready to assist you" in developing early childhood programs.[11] At the organization's annual meeting in 1968, ECS commissioners adopted the following resolution: "The value of and need for early childhood education has been established to such a degree that there is no longer any basis for questioning 'whether' early childhood education should be provided, only 'how' and 'when.'"[12] They called on Congress to "increase early childhood education funds for disadvantaged pupils, provide incentives for more state and local financial effort, and consolidate federal programs in this area."[13] ECS commissioners expressed similar concerns at a September 1968 meeting with the secretary of health, education, and welfare and the commissioner of education. They lobbied for a "functional block grant for early childhood education or some other effective means . . . to provide strong incentive for the inclusion of this level of education in all school systems."[14] By the late 1960s, the ECS viewed early childhood education as one of its top programmatic priorities.

ECS continued to work on early childhood education into the next decade. In 1970, ECS chairman and Utah governor Calvin Rampton formed a twenty-four-member Early Childhood Task Force. It published a report on program alternatives in child development in June 1971.[15] In addition to providing state policymakers with basic data "on the most important alternatives for state-supported child development services," the report contained several recommendations.[16] It recommended using a comprehensive approach including children younger than three and their parents; instituting training programs for children and parents in their homes; and developing classroom programs for three-, four-, and five-year-olds through an expansion of Head Start. It also recommended that states establish credentials in early childhood education or provide for a specialization in early childhood education. Finally, it suggested that states develop sound principles of financing for their early childhood programs, so that "early childhood education is treated as an integral part of the state's overall education program."[17]

The second phase of the task force was known as the Early Childhood Project. Its purpose was to "provide assistance to the states to initiate or expand services for young children and their families through improved state coordination of delivery systems."[18] The project received an initial grant of $92,814 from the U.S. Office of Education,[19] and its activities included reviews of statewide activities, expert testimony, assistance in drafting legislation and executive orders, consulting and technical assistance, and the dissemination of policy-relevant information.[20] A related goal of the project was to serve as an "organized mechanism to express state concerns to the federal government."[21] The project had a horizontal component, facilitating information exchanges among state officials, and a vertical component, representing state officials at the national level.

The priorities of the Early Childhood Project shifted subtly in the aftermath of Nixon's veto. One of its first endeavors was to develop a list of "target states" and assist them in initiating or expanding their early childhood programs.[22] In August 1972, the task force reviewed the project's first few months and recommended priorities for its second fiscal year. It decided to move away from venue shopping and reduce its emphasis on target states. The thirty-three states that had asked to participate in the project faced similar challenges, so the task force concluded that it should focus on these common concerns and complete "draft model legislation for state use in setting up an appropriate structure for administering early childhood programs."[23]

The ECS also hosted conferences that facilitated information exchange among the states. The conferences "[brought] together people with decision-making responsibilities to analyze the issues which they all face and to evaluate the techniques which they are utilizing."[24] They complemented the documents published by the commission and enabled state leaders to learn from one another's experiences. The Early Childhood Project hosted its first conference on implementing state early childhood programs in December 1972. More than two hundred persons from thirty-seven states attended the conference, which featured several nationally known experts in child development.[25] A speaker from California who described a bill that had recently been signed into law by Governor Ronald Reagan explained, "[S]ome preschool and Head Start teachers were threatened by [our] approach. Although they worked for the program, they began to back away. . . . People sometimes have stakes in what is the status quo. They may vocalize on change, but they may be afraid."[26] The feedback dynamic he described, in which reformers needed to accommodate actors with a stake in the status quo, foreshadowed future developments at the state and national levels.

The Early Childhood Project received a continuation grant from the U.S. Office of Child Development in 1973. It added "several new emphases to its ongoing program of assisting the states in improving their services to young children and their families."[27] The project's focus shifted to strengthening the family, early screening of handicapping conditions, child abuse prevention, day care licensing codes, and revenue sharing.[28] After receiving a fourth year of funding from the U.S. Office of Child Development, the Early Childhood Project sponsored three regional conferences in 1975.[29] Each conference lasted three days and was devoted to needs assessments, child abuse prevention, and day care issues. The conferences "were designed to provide technical assistance to state decision-makers."[30] The commission retained its interest in early childhood education policy, but the conferences represented the last major undertaking of the Early Childhood Project, which disbanded in October 1975.[31] Thereafter, the commission would pursue its goals without the formal institutional apparatus that the project represented.

Forces for and Obstacles to Change at the State Level

The presidential veto provoked responses in other institutional venues that provided the basic framework within which American early childhood policy subsequently evolved. It spurred a series of reactions and counterreactions that had a profound effect over both the short term and the long term. Increased activity at the state level was especially significant. This activity was driven by two forces whose convergence produced various policy changes across the country. Child development advocates represented the first force. Their desire for a departure from the status quo and their pessimism about the prospects for change at the national level led them to search for more-favorable political terrain in the states. State officials represented the second force. Frustrated by their inability to influence the national debate, state-level actors, working through such organizations as the ECS, devoted considerable time and attention to the issue of child development.

In the early 1970s, Milton J. E. Senn conducted dozens of interviews with the individuals involved in what he called the "child development movement." A common topic in these interviews was the role of the states in early childhood policy. Several interviewees described increased state activity as desirable. A former Republican staffer called for "voluntary efforts" at the state level and argued that a state-based strategy was more likely to be successful: "It's quicker than having to wait for federal legislation, which is always then going to have the same specter of socialism about it, and . . . that's going to turn off more people who need persuading."[32] Another Republican staffer added, "I'm pretty much convinced that the only way that we're really going to see a nationwide network of the kinds of services that children need is probably to come at it . . . through the localities and through the states [and] through the local school systems."[33] These points of view reflected the emerging Republican consensus that the states should have a prominent role in any child development bill.

Others agreed about the role of the states. A staff scientist at the Foundation for Child Development stated bluntly, "I think the state situation has to be taken into account. If there is a child development bill, the states cannot be left out completely."[34] An attorney working with the Children's Defense Fund, which had been founded by Marian Wright Edelman in

1973, predicted, "The day is coming when we are going to accomplish at least as much, if not more, at the state level, because the federal government has in so many areas done such a miserable job and wasted so much money; at least that's the way people feel."[35] Similarly, Provost Nicholas Hobbs of Vanderbilt University, a child psychologist, claimed, "[The states] are becoming increasingly important, and they should become important—money will flow through state governments."[36] Thus actors with diverse backgrounds and political perspectives viewed the states as an increasingly viable institutional venue for the development of child development policies.

Importantly, many state officials were open to the idea of expanding early childhood education programs. Several forces contributed to their openness. The debate over the Comprehensive Child Development Act brought heightened attention to the issue, raising its political profile at the state level. Marian Wright Edelman explained the political ramifications of these congressional developments, "It made the states aware there really was a constituency out there, which is one of the things you shouldn't forget. . . . It showed them there's gold in their mines in terms of money for them . . . [and] they now want to talk to us more and more and are inviting us to more and more of their meetings."[37] The ECS Early Childhood Task Force, made possible by financial support from the Carnegie Foundation, institutionalized this state-level interest. Through its contribution and "perhaps unknowingly," the foundation "set up a group that has become very important in the state interest in early childhood development."[38]

The congressional debate was also significant due to the content of the bill that the president vetoed. As has already been mentioned, many state officials were frustrated with their lack of input. They believed, with some justification, that the Comprehensive Child Development Act had privileged local governments and community organizations over the states. Many state officials were interested in early childhood policy as a way both to improve the lives of young children and to defend state prerogatives against national encroachment. The states therefore provided favorable political terrain for those who were frustrated with developments at the national level and wanted to find a new institutional venue in which to pursue their goals.

The fifty states did not offer equally favorable political terrain for the proponents of expanded governmental activity, however. Advocates seemed more likely to succeed in some states than in others. For this reason, one component of the venue shopping of the early 1970s was an assessment of potential target states. A major goal of the ECS Early Childhood Project, as has already been described, was "providing assistance to selected target states in initiating or expanding their early childhood programs."[39] For the ECS to become involved in a state, its governor had to request such assistance with the backing of the chief state agencies administering early childhood programs. By April 1972, twenty-nine states had asked to be considered for selection as target states, an enthusiastic response that illustrated the state-level interest in this issue. The commission relied on several criteria in making its final determination, but the first criterion listed in one newsletter, "state commitment to early childhood services," was revealing. With its goal of beginning intensive activity in no more than four states by October, the organization sought to build on existing state-level activity.[40] This strategy was later employed by universal preschool advocates in the 1990s and early 2000s.

In addition to recognizing that their probability of success depended on the specific states in which they pursued their goals, child development advocates realized that they would need to clear many of the same hurdles they had confronted in Congress. First, government programs designed to assist families with young children were likely to be characterized as intrusive. An ECS report explained, "Attempts to support and guide the direction of family efforts in childrearing can quickly raise fears for the sanctity of the family. Some persons and groups feel such efforts to be an intrusion into private life, bordering on socialism."[41] One consultant attributed resistance to day care licensing standards in Massachusetts to Americans' "strong strain of 'rugged individualism' that makes [them] uncomfortable with authority."[42] As a result, advocates often described government programs as a "supplement to the family that does not try to replace the family."[43]

Supporters of an expanded governmental role in early childhood policy believed that they could overcome this cultural predisposition by framing their proposals as maintaining or even expanding parental choice. They therefore prioritized flexibility and the availability of diverse options. One advocate argued, "We can no longer allow the myth to continue that developmental goals can be achieved only through center arrangements."[44] The availability of center-based and home-based care was the subject of much discussion, and the appropriate role of the public school system further complicated this issue. Many child development advocates agreed with commissioner of education Terrel Bell, who argued that "the neighborhood elementary school ought to assume a new role as a source for delivery of services for children in the neighborhood."[45] Indeed, the appropriate locus of control over child development programs became a central element of the congressional debate of the mid- to late 1970s.

The cost of child development programs represented a second hurdle to their enactment. At a December 1972 conference, Edward Zigler, who had served as the first director of the Office of Child Development and had been involved in the administration of Head Start, described preschool programs as expensive and concluded, "If this society had all of the money in the world, a universal preschool program would be to my liking. . . . When I think of all the problems of children in this country and all the problems of the schools, one more year of early education does not seem terribly important. It should not be a high priority."[46] The cost of early childhood education and care was also an issue for targeted and less-comprehensive state programs. A December 1975 ECS report noted, "Day care is perhaps the service most in demand and most expensive to provide."[47] It proposed several ways to fund this service, including giving tax credits to industry, providing small business loans for persons wishing to start new centers, setting up centers as part of the high school curriculum, making creative use of federal funds, and adding day care to a kindergarten program. Program cost had been a pressing issue during the congressional debate, and it also bedeviled lawmakers at the state level.

The issue of parental involvement generated considerable controversy. Reformers hoped state programs would enable parents to become more involved in their children's lives. They feared that a lack of continuity between program and home would prevent the programs from reaching their potential. Some advocates called for state programs modeled on Head Start and community action projects.[48] Most advocates agreed about integrating parents into any child development program, but they disagreed on the amount of authority parents should exercise. Should parents have jurisdiction over such issues as budgeting, staffing, and program design? How should the membership and administrative responsibilities of key decision-making committees be determined? Some educators argued that parental involvement required a partnership between parents and professionals. One program administrator explained, "To me, the problem is not that parents don't care or want to work with us. Too often, I'm afraid, they are stiff-armed by school administrators; they aren't welcomed or wanted. We educators must take the initiative in reaching out a hand to bring parents in to share in significant policy decision making."[49] Generating a desirable level of parental involvement preoccupied policymakers and professionals alike as they debated how to proceed.

Another area of concern was overlap and duplication among existing federal and state programs. The director of Florida's new Office of Early Childhood Development explained, "[W]ithin the many federal and state programs, there is much overlapping and much duplication of effort; confusion, frustration, and reduction of benefits have resulted."[50] He was due to leave his post after only one year, and he said that one of his biggest challenges was to "draw in enough state agency people and people from the private and public sector so that . . . they will pick up the ball and run with it."[51] His experience illustrates how supporters of policy change must often generate "buy-in" from existing stakeholders if they are going to be successful. The challenge of program fragmentation would become more difficult over time and represented both an administrative obstacle and a political obstacle to major change.

In sum, the institutional structure of the American political system enabled advocates to turn to the fifty states. Nevertheless, this shift in venue did not guarantee success, and advocates had to think carefully about both the objectives they would pursue and the terrain on which they would pursue them. Several states took action in early childhood policy in the years immediately following Nixon's veto, but the policy shifts that resulted did not create state-level programs that were as ambitious as the Comprehensive Child Development Act. One widespread policy change, in fact, was a bureaucratic reform whose goal was simply to improve the coordination and delivery of services to young children and their families.

Offices of Child Development

The heightened interest in the education and care of young children led dozens of states to establish offices of child development in the early and mid-1970s. This administrative reform addressed the programmatic fragmentation that scattered services for children and their families among five or six different agencies. The relevant agencies included health departments responsible for immunizations, education departments offering special education, and welfare departments administering a range of child and family services. Advocates of expanded governmental activity viewed the creation of state offices of child development as an indication of "an increasing awareness of the need to coordinate services to children and families, and to allocate public funds in ways that will enhance family viability and ensure the maximum development of human potential."[52]

Several factors contributed to the creation of state offices of child development. The congressional debate over the Comprehensive Child Development Act played a crucial role. In a 1973 interview, Marian Wright Edelman explained, "Since [the veto], the states have understood that there is going to be child development one way or another and they ought to get in it. And you have a lot of states now beginning to open up their offices of child development. I think it's more style than substance."[53] Another advocate was more sanguine about the benefits of these administrative changes, calling the offices "one of the good things that's come out of the veto."[54] He claimed that even if states did not establish the comprehensive programs advocates preferred, the mere existence of the offices meant they would be prepared if the national government became willing to send them money for child development programs. A September 1973 ECS report mentioned that very possibility and suggested that state lawmakers designate the office as the state's prime sponsor for any child development programs authorized by Congress. Such a designation, it argued, "provides a way for a state to be ready to take advantage of federal legislation which may be enacted at some future date, if a state wishes to be in that position."[55]

Other national developments contributed to the creation of state offices of child development. In the mid-1970s, an ECS report claimed that this activity could be attributed to "a combination of ideas, forces and events." Contributing factors included the creation of Head Start and other programs in the mid-1960s, a continuing increase in the number of working mothers in the United States, the 1970 White House Conference on Children and Youth, and the initiation of the federal Community Coordinated Child Care program.[56] In addition, the Nixon administration had established the Office of Child Development within the Department of Health, Education, and Welfare in 1969. The creation of state offices of child development mimicked administrative developments at the national level.

While the national debate brought heightened attention to the need for a coordinating agency at the state level, some of the earliest state activity occurred in the period leading up to Nixon's veto. A 1969 amendment to the Appalachian Act enabled the Appalachian Regional Commission to fund child development programs. Several states took advantage of these funds to create interagency committees for child development. The Arkansas Governor's Council on Early Childhood Development was created through an executive order in 1969,[57] and a December 1971 executive order established the Mississippi Child Development Council.[58] Other interagency committees were created legislatively. In 1971, the state legislature in North Carolina passed a bill establishing that state's Governor's Advisory Commission on Children and Youth.[59] These and other agencies "helped to create interest in other states, provided the impetus for action by serving as specific examples of the need for planning and coordination and served as models from which the [office of child development] concept evolved."[60]

State-level interest in the coordination of early childhood services soon became national in scope. It took on a standardized form as more states referred to the agencies as offices of child development. One of the first states to do so was Idaho, where Governor Cecil Andrus established the state's Office of Child Development by executive order in November 1971. It was located in the Office of the Governor, which gave it the "clout, rights, and privileges" associated with the state chief executive, as well as "the necessary interdepartmental support for reorganization and coordination of children's services."[61] In Colorado, an executive order created the Governor's Commission on Children and Youth, in a state where "until recently there were no efforts to coordinate existing early childhood programs or develop a comprehensive state plan."[62] In 1972, Massachusetts established its Office for Children within the Executive Agency of Human Services. One of that office's goals was to assure "the sound and coordinated development of all services to children."[63] In Minnesota, a planning group began to develop recommendations for the governor about how to "create a mechanism within state government for coordination of child development and child care programs, research, training, and technical assistance."[64]

The movement to establish state offices of child development gained additional momentum in 1973. By January, the ECS had published a booklet containing model legislation that had been drafted by the commission's Early Childhood Task Force. A separate newsletter described the bureaucratic reform as an administratively desirable way for the states "to demonstrate their willingness to take the initiative in child development programs, rather than being put in the position of reacting to federal legislation."[65] This portrayal, combined with the commission's advice to designate the office as a prime sponsor for any congressional child development programs, illustrates how state officials had become more assertive about their role in early childhood policy. This assertiveness had not been evident during the debate over the Comprehensive Child Development Act. Only two years later, state officials viewed themselves as key stakeholders in this policy arena and mobilized to protect their prerogatives.

By February 1973, twelve states, in every region of the country, had created offices of child development. They included Alaska, Arkansas, Florida, Idaho, Massachusetts, Mississippi, North Carolina, South Carolina, Tennessee, Texas, Vermont, and West Virginia.[66] In May, Louisiana governor Edwin Edwards signed an executive order establishing an office of early childhood development within the department of education. Similar executive orders were being considered in Washington and Utah.[67] Several states considered the administrative reform during their 1973 legislative sessions. Legislators in Colorado introduced a measure that "closely followed the model legislation drafted by the ECS Early Childhood Project."[68] Similar bills were introduced in Hawaii, Kansas, Maine, Missouri, and New York, and the Hawaiian legislation was enacted into law in June. Supporters attributed this outcome to the obvious need for reform, the involvement and support of key administrators, and "a policy commitment on the part of the governor to the basic concept incorporated in the legislation."[69] State-level activity continued into the summer, as conferences on child development were held in Arkansas and Louisiana.[70]

Fourteen state offices of child development existed by July 1973, with all but one of them established in the previous two years.[71] That year, administrators in twelve states voted to create the National Association of State Directors of Child Development. The newly elected president of the professional association explained that its two primary objectives "would be to exchange information and promote child development programs and related services in all states, and to strengthen the voice of the states in setting national policies in those areas."[72] The group soon began to pursue its second objective. Its members unanimously endorsed a resolution calling on President Nixon to name a permanent director of the Office of Child Development; the post had been vacant for over a year. The directors also "voted to develop legislative criteria to be used to measure the acceptability of federal child development legislation," agreeing to meet in December to adopt guidelines.[73] The creation of the professional association and its early activities illustrate the increased assertiveness of state officials in this policy arena.

State activity continued in 1974. That year's volume of the Council of State Governments *Suggested State Legislation* included the model legislation developed by the ECS.[74] A law establishing an office of child development gained enactment in Tennessee, and similar legislation was considered in Arizona, Maryland, Minnesota, New York, North Carolina, Ohio, Oklahoma, and West Virginia. The Tennessee statute granted the new office "broad authority for comprehensive child development programs for children under six."[75] In Massachusetts, the legislature endorsed the Children's Budget, which provided eighteen million dollars in new state monies for children's services throughout the state. It funded an expanded preschool program for the physically handicapped and included five hundred thousand dollars to "finance the first year of new demonstration day care projects designed for children from all families . . . on a sliding scale basis."[76] The governor of Idaho broadened the scope of that state's Office of Child Development to include all human services programs.[77] Child development advocates suffered a setback in Florida, however. The legislature refused to appropriate any funds to that state's Office of Early Childhood Development, effectively terminating its operations.[78]

The widespread establishment of state offices of child development was important for both policy and political reasons. In policy terms, the offices were viewed as a way to coordinate the planning and delivery of services for young children and their families and to ameliorate the programmatic fragmentation and duplication that characterized existing arrangements. The goal of this administrative reform was to "use the existing governmental structure more effectively and to control increasing expenditures by reducing the duplication of services and directing state planning toward a preventive orientation."[79] Proponents believed that the offices would help coordinate the work of state and local agencies and the public and private sectors, enabling states to use their manpower and financial resources as effectively as possible.

The political impact of the state offices was equally significant. They signaled heightened state interest in early childhood policy and gave state officials an institutional foothold through which they could attempt to defend their perceived interests. The founding of the National Association of State Directors of Child Development was important, as was the establishment of the Association of Early Childhood Specialists in State Departments of Education in April 1974. These professional associations promoted the exchange of policy-relevant information among interested parties and lobbied for programs at the state and national level. A September 1975 letter illustrates the latter dynamic. Writing to one of the congressional champions of child development legislation, the former president of the National Association of State Directors of Child Development argued that the states deserved a more prominent role in such legislation. Focusing on the state offices, he claimed, "[W]hile much of the movement in the states is of recent vintage, it is significant. I respectfully urge you to give every consideration to encouraging these efforts by providing support . . . for those states that have shown their good faith and capability to do statewide planning and coordination."[80] State lawmakers could also point to several other steps that gave them a stronger stake in this policy arena.

Other Policy Changes at the State Level

The establishment of state offices of child development illustrated how more states needed a bureaucratic apparatus to coordinate early childhood services. State governments were increasingly active. Both the number and size of state early childhood programs grew considerably during the early to mid-1970s. States conducted "needs assessments" to determine the ideal and present levels of services available. They provided public support for various forms of prekindergarten services and developed certification requirements for prekindergarten teachers, paraprofessionals, and administrators. These policy shifts did not establish comprehensive child development programs, but they nevertheless gave state officials an expanded stake in this policy arena.

Demographic changes spurred state officials to conduct "needs assessments" in their jurisdictions. Rising numbers of working mothers demanding day care for their children, in combination with troubling trends in nationwide infant mortality and poverty rates, led some observers to conclude that American children faced increasingly problematic conditions. The goal of a needs assessment was to generate practical knowledge about what children needed in a particular jurisdiction. More than a simple service inventory, a needs assessment typically began with a statement of such broad goals as the ability of all children to realize their cognitive potential. It then discussed a potential service that would contribute to the achievement of the goal and compared its availability to the number of children in the state who would benefit from it. This process was intended to assess the desirability of expanding existing programs and establishing new ones. Those conducting a needs assessment were encouraged to think about how they were going to implement its results. Coalition building and convincing the broader public that the needs merited a governmental response were crucial elements of a successful assessment. In addition, a needs assessment would only become a viable plan of action if it ranked the needs it identified and accounted for the political and fiscal realities of the state in which it was conducted.[81]

Needs assessments, in sum, combined a statement of goals with data on the status of children and families. Their goal was to give "state policymakers and the public . . . a clearer idea of what services and programs exist, what further resources are needed and what kinds of services are desired."[82] At its 1967 annual meeting, the ECS adopted a resolution calling on the states to conduct something like a needs assessment. It stated, "Each state is urged to set up a broadly-based task force to study the available resources and recommend the commitments necessary to establish a comprehensive program of educational experiences for all preschoolers in the state."[83] Needs assessments were supposed to be comprehensive, incorporating health care and other issues in addition to education. Many states conducted needs assessments over the next decade, often under the auspices of the councils and offices of child development described in the previous section. The assessments were especially common in the aftermath of the debate over the Comprehensive Child Development Act. A May 1976 report stated, "The majority of the states indicate that they have initiated or completed some type of assessment procedures within the last three years."[84] Many of the assessments focused on services for young children and their families.

A few examples illustrate the wide range of social services examined by needs assessments. In Alabama, the Interdepartment Coordinating Committee for Early Childhood Development conducted a study in approximately half of the state's counties on the need for health, nutrition, educational, and social services for children between the ages of one and six. In Arkansas, the Office of Early Childhood Planning conducted a statewide needs assessment of services for children from birth to age eight in such areas as early education, child care, and health care. Indiana's state committee for the Community Coordinated Child Care program conducted a statewide survey to assess the status of licensed day care centers for children between the ages of three and five. The Child Development Planning Project in Minnesota carried out a statewide analysis of the full range of services available to children from birth to age six. In Utah, the Office of Child Development conducted a statewide needs assessment survey of day care services, preschool and kindergarten education services, and child welfare services for children from birth to age eight.[85]

The widespread performance of needs assessments illustrates the heightened state-level interest in early childhood policy. In the early to mid-1970s, many states also funded social services for children who were too young to attend primary school or established preschool projects. Needs assessments were significant not only in and of themselves. They also reflected a broader interest in policy change and, in some states, helped bring about such change. The ECS, because it viewed early childhood policy as a top programmatic priority, carefully tracked these changes through various reports and surveys that provide a useful lens through which to view state-level activity.

A 1972 survey examined state spending patterns and certification requirements. It asked about kindergarten and preschool programs and concluded that "public support for kindergarten and other early childhood services is growing."[86] It found that forty-two states provided some form of state aid for kindergarten. State aid for prekindergarten was limited; only twelve states offered some form of public support. It was more common for states to provide "pre-first graders" such state-supported services as medical and dental care, nutritional programs, or special programs for the handicapped. At least thirty states offered such services, which were typically targeted at the economically disadvantaged or the handicapped. Certification requirements for preschool teachers and administrators, which existed in twenty-four states, also signaled increased interest in early childhood policy. The survey tracked the number of colleges with degree programs in early childhood education and the number of junior or community colleges with associate degree programs.[87] In terms of public funding, services, and certification requirements, state involvement in early childhood policy was widespread.

The ECS conducted a follow-up survey two years later. Its results suggested additional movement between 1972 and 1974, and a report on the survey concluded that "public support for kindergarten and other early childhood services continues to grow."[88] This growth was more evident along some dimensions than others. Even by 1974, for example, state funding for prekindergarten programs was "still the exception rather than the rule."[89] Only eleven states (California, Georgia, Maine, Massachusetts, Missouri, Pennsylvania, South Carolina, Tennessee, Vermont, Washington, and West Virginia) provided public support, which represented a slight decline. However, the number of states offering "pre-first graders" other state-supported services, such as medical and dental care, nutritional programs, or special programs for the handicapped, rose from thirty in 1972 to thirty-eight in 1974. The certification of professionals working in early childhood was also slightly more common. Half of the states required certification for prekindergarten teachers and administrators by 1974, while the number of states requiring certification for prekindergarten paraprofessionals rose from two to six.[90]

The certification of paraprofessionals garnered significant interest in the early 1970s and led to the creation of the child development associate (CDA) credential. The U.S. Office of Child Development and three early childhood organizations developed the credential. Motivated by "the growing need for skilled child care workers to provide quality programs for young children in the United States" (Hinitz 1998, 88), they assumed that the skills needed to work with children were not related to a specific number of credit hours in formal college-level courses but could be ac-

quired through a properly structured training program.[91] A consensus on
the original competency standards was reached in 1974, even though critics argued that it was "too oriented toward the needs of educational programs such as Head Start and preschools, and shortchange[d] the personal, affective requirements of a round-the-clock day care center."[92]

In May 1975, the ECS Early Childhood Project distributed a report
tracking state-level policy shifts in early childhood policy. Based on various sources, the report listed legislation on "the very young and education" that passed in 1974. Seventeen states established preschool projects
or began preschool activity that year. This count provides a conservative
estimate of state-level activity, because it does not include bills that were
vetoed, failed, or were carried over or bills that fell into related categories.
Even this conservative estimate indicates the breadth of state action in the
aftermath of the presidential veto. Most of the projects were compensatory
in nature and served disadvantaged populations. They did not provide
universal access to preschool or related services. For example, the primary
purpose of a Connecticut project was to provide a learning experience for
preschool children with learning disabilities. A project in Illinois provided
an early intervention program for three- and four-year-old children who
exhibited sensorimotor, language, or conceptualization delays or disorders or social affective disorders. Maryland provided early childhood services to the hearing impaired and the visually impaired. A North Dakota
project supplemented the minimal services available to preschool children in the rural northwestern region of the state, with a special emphasis
on serving the learning disabled.[93] These projects illustrate the widespread
interest in early childhood programs but suggest that most policy initiatives were targeted rather than universal.

In the fall of 1975, the ECS conducted a telephone survey whose goal
was to "determine what the priorities for young children were, some of the
major barriers to meeting those priorities and predictions of future
trends."[94] One to three persons were interviewed in each of the states
about their top priorities. Day care, cited as a priority in thirty-nine states,
ranked as the third-highest priority overall. A report on the survey mentioned that one obstacle to increased day care funding was the "reluctance
of some legislators to authorize programs that might 'take the child away
from the home,'" explaining that some state legislators did not accept "a
mother's right to work."[95] It suggests that the state-level debate over day
care funding echoed the themes that were prevalent during congressional
discussions of child development.

Respondents identified several areas of concern with respect to existing programs. They worried about the efficiency and cost-effectiveness of their service delivery systems and about fragmentation and duplication of services. Worried about not having sufficient staff to administer the expanding state programs, they advocated additional training programs for in-house staff. Many respondents also cited such barriers to implementation as insufficient capabilities for data collection and a lack of public awareness. The activities described in this chapter, such as the creation of state offices of child development and the performance of needs assessments, sought to address some of these concerns.

The foreword of the report touched on the states' relationship with the national government. It acknowledged that "the federal government is setting the top priorities for children in the United States," but it was highly critical of national policymaking.[96] According to the foreword, national government activity and funding helped set state political agendas, but these national priorities "are not arrived at systematically" and "are far from comprehensive."[97] Furthermore, the foreword noted that the tendency of national agencies to bypass state governments and work directly with localities promoted additional fragmentation, duplication, and inefficiency. Combined with the examples cited elsewhere in this chapter, the tone of the foreword suggests a new assertiveness among state officials in early childhood policy.

Conclusion: The States as Stakeholders

By the mid-1970s, the states had become a major locus of policymaking activity. Some supporters of the early childhood movement nevertheless remained frustrated with the pace of policy change. At the annual conference of the National Association for the Education of Young Children in November 1975, the ECS Early Childhood Project arranged a symposium for educators and state leaders. Many members of the three-hundred-person audience "expressed great frustration in trying to accomplish concrete gains in early childhood programs."[98] Their efforts had not led to the development of the kind of widespread, comprehensive programs they felt were necessary in order to serve the needs of young children and their families, and one panelist even suggested that the early childhood movement may have passed its peak. There were legitimate reasons for this frustration. By December 1975, services like early health screening, family counseling, preschool, and day care were "available in only a limited number of communities and usually only to families on welfare or otherwise deemed likely to require welfare assistance in the future."[99] Those who felt that most American families needed access to these services were dismayed by their limited availability.

Focusing solely on the limited reach of state-level early childhood programs, however, fails to recognize their short- and long-term significance. Offices of child development and preschool projects gave state officials an increased stake in this policy arena, and some observers speculated that these tentative initial steps were a sign of things to come. One observer predicted that "the trend over the last four, five years toward looking more to the states is probably . . . going to go further."[100] Indeed, that was the goal of many of the state lawmakers who worked through such organizations as the ECS in their efforts to expand the governmental role in early childhood policy. They hoped heightened state activity would demonstrate to doubters in Congress and elsewhere "that the states have not only the will but the capacity to play a major role."[101] The Comprehensive Child Development Act had largely bypassed the states, and state officials were determined not to be overlooked in future legislation. Thus the venue shopping of the early 1970s altered the political contours of the broader debate over early childhood policy, establishing an increasingly powerful stakeholder whose preferences would have to be taken into account.

5 | Congressional Activity and the Dissolving Early Childhood Coalition

As state officials established early childhood programs in the early and mid-1970s, Congress continued to debate the appropriate role for the national government in this policy arena. The demise of the Comprehensive Child Development Act did not settle the issue, even though the measure's supporters recognized that major policy changes were unlikely. This chapter examines the congressional aftermath of Nixon's veto, during which comprehensive initiatives like the Child and Family Services Act of 1975 and narrower proposals like the Child Care Act of 1979 faltered. Preschool advocates scored important victories, however, by establishing and defending more-limited government interventions. The treatment of dependent care expenses in the Internal Revenue Code evolved, with important changes that broadened the reach of tax relief and facilitated the proliferation of many different types of child care (Michel 1999, 237). Enrollment in and spending on the Head Start program grew, and its beneficiaries and defenders acquired additional political clout.

By the end of the decade, preschool education in the United States looked considerably different than it had at the beginning of the 1970s, in terms of both its general features and its political dynamics. This chapter explains how the congressional developments of the 1970s fragmented early childhood policy while simultaneously giving disparate actors a stake in existing arrangements. The absence of a comprehensive national approach, paired with the state-level developments described in chapter 4, helped solidify the decentralized nature of this policy realm as enrollment in private-sector preschool programs, generally serving a more affluent clientele, rose dramatically. This multifaceted evolution transformed the politics of early childhood by restructuring the preferences of various actors, making it more difficult for them to coalesce around a single policy prescription. Perhaps the most striking development of the 1970s was the dissolution of the coalition supporting a comprehensive child development program. Members embraced the idea of government involvement in this policy realm, but they disagreed on the form that such involvement should take. The increased political activity of such groups as the American Federation of Teachers brought this disagreement to the fore.

Action in the Senate, Inaction in the House

The sweeping language of Nixon's veto convinced many supporters of child development legislation that, in the words of one official, "[i]t was pretty clear that nothing much was going to happen."[1] The bipartisan consensus on the need for government action had evaporated, especially in the House of Representatives. The controversial actions taken by the conference committee in 1971 and the opposition of the Nixon administration caused many House Republicans to shy away from the issue. A bipartisan group of senators was undaunted, however. When Congress reconvened in 1972, Senators Gaylord Nelson (D-WI), Jacob Javits (R-NY), and Robert Taft Jr. (R-OH) joined Walter Mondale (D-MN) in sponsoring the Comprehensive Headstart, Child Development, and Family Services Act. The bill proposed "a network of preschool educational services for low-income children and developmental day care programs for youngsters whose parents are working."[2] Participation in all programs would be voluntary.

Supporters claimed that the bill demonstrated their desire to resolve all "reasonable differences between the Administration and Congress."[3] Addressing the controversy over prime sponsorship, the bill raised the population requirement from five thousand to twenty-five thousand, a shift that reduced, by more than two-thirds, the number of localities eligible to serve as prime sponsors. Other features of the revised legislation, including the increased powers of mayors and governors serving as prime sponsors, caused supporters to argue that it was more administratively workable than the vetoed legislation had been. It also retained the fee schedule from the vetoed legislation, included an increased authorization for staff training and planning, and reduced authorizations for the first operational year by 40 percent, from $2 billion to $1.2 billion. In a May press release after the bill cleared the Senate Labor and Public Welfare Committee, Mondale asserted that "these and other changes adequately meet the concerns expressed by the president when he vetoed the original bill."[4]

The revised legislation also gave the states a more prominent role in program administration. It "reserved ten percent of the funds for use by the states to encourage comprehensive state cooperation and planning" and allowed five states to be funded on a demonstration basis as the sole prime sponsor of programs.[5] These concessions did not satisfy state officials. Governor Winfield Dunn of Tennessee, chair of the Education Commission of the States, claimed, "[T]hese alterations do not go far enough to meet the objectives of our established policy. There are still major flaws." He criticized the measure's provisions for prime sponsorship, argued that its local policy councils would "dilute the responsibility" of state and local officials, and said that the bill would "complicate the planning and coordination of comprehensive state child development programs and services."[6] In June, Senator Peter Dominick (R-CO) introduced an amendment that gave the secretary of the Department of Health, Education, and Welfare the authority to choose between competing state and local prime sponsors on the basis of their effectiveness. The successful passage of the Dominick amendment substantially increased the opportunities for states to serve as prime sponsors. The Senate eventually passed the Comprehensive Headstart, Child Development, and Family Services Act by a 73–12 vote.

The bill received an unfavorable response outside the Senate chamber. Many liberals felt that its Democratic sponsors made too many concessions. The Dominick amendment was a source of particular concern. One supporter argued that Nelson and Mondale "pretty much gave the other side everything they wanted."[7] These concessions were insufficient to generate any enthusiasm among conservatives. According to the Emergency Committee for Children, "While the rhetoric of the new bill has been made less offensive to the traditions of the family, the substance of the program remains the same."[8] It criticized the bill's cost and administrative provisions and argued that it would cause irreparable harm to children and families by undermining parental authority. Furthermore, the involvement of the national government "in the hitherto private area of family life" was labeled a "precedent to totalitarianism."[9] The new Senate bill did not win over its most conservative critics.

Perhaps more important, the proposal generated minimal support in the House of Representatives. According to one observer, "There was simply nobody to pick up the ball in the House. . . . and there was no way to get people together again on the bill."[10] Several factors worked against House action, foremost among them the opposition of Republicans who claimed that the revised proposal simply substituted a vast expansion of Head Start for the child development title in the previous bill.[11] They argued that any "expansion of Head Start or any other child development program must come through the public school systems."[12] This critique indicated that House Republicans envisioned an educational approach.

In addition to several substantive differences of opinion, political factors were also at work. Senate opponents had not defeated the bill, but they slowed down its consideration through various procedural maneuvers. By the time the House took up the new bill, the looming election cast doubt on its prospects. Many southern Democrats hoped to avoid votes on social issues that might identify them with the presidential campaign of Senator George McGovern (D-SD); they preferred to spend the rest of the term campaigning in their districts. Some observers speculated that House Republicans were reluctant to compromise because they anticipated a landslide victory that would give them a House majority.[13] A combination of policy and political factors prevented House action on the Senate bill.

After the 1972 elections, child development returned to the congressional agenda. Several House members introduced bills that would have used a system of prime sponsors at the community level to provide child care services, with priority given to economically disadvantaged children and to the children of working mothers or single parents. The proposals differed in their authorization levels, provisions for prime sponsorship, child care standards, and fee schedules. None of them, however, earned the same prominence or came as close to passing as did the Comprehensive Child Development Act.

The Ninety-Third Congress (1973–74) took three actions with regard to child care. First, it enacted the Social Services Amendments of 1974, which affected the child care services provided under Title IV-A of the Social Security Act. Second, it passed the Headstart, Economic Opportunity, and Community Partnership Act of 1974, which extended the authorization for that program and made some changes. The passage of these two laws illustrates the early fragmentation of government programs. The national government provided child care funds through multiple sources. Third, Congress held hearings on the pressures facing the modern American family.[14] These hearings highlighted the "tremendous increase in the number of mothers who are working" and the "virtual disappearance of the extended family" (Mondale 1975, 14). They also laid the foundation for another congressional effort at comprehensive child development legislation.

The Child and Family Services Act of 1975

In some ways, the congressional debate over the Child and Family Services Act of 1975 resembled the earlier debate over the Comprehensive Child Development Act. Advocates of increasing the national government's role in early childhood policy introduced an ambitious measure that preserved the core features of the bill Nixon vetoed. Many of its supporters had been members of the original coalition that Marian Wright Edelman assembled, and they used similar rhetoric to illustrate the "need" for legislation. Likewise, many of their opponents had been involved in the 1971 debate, and the highly charged rhetoric on which they relied was even more intense than it had been four years earlier. Like its predecessor, the Child and Family Services Act did not become law.

In other ways, however, the 1975 congressional debate illustrated subtle shifts in the politics of early childhood policy. Not much time had passed since the veto, but a different constellation of actors had an interest in the topic. For example, developments in the intervening years gave the states a more pronounced role in this policy arena. Similarly, the American Federation of Teachers, which played a peripheral role in 1971, became "actively involved in negotiations over the form and substance of new initiatives" (McGill-Franzen 1993, 70). Its involvement ignited a debate among supporters about the appropriate role of the public schools. The coalition began to dissolve as its members advanced competing visions based on their self-interest.

The Lessons of 1971

Reflecting their earlier experiences, backers of the Child and Family Services Act adjusted the content of their bill and their political strategy. In the fall of 1973, the day care coalition presented a proposal to congressional leaders that resembled the vetoed legislation but included some language from the 1972 Senate bill. Its major changes included a first-year authorization of two hundred million dollars for training and planning, with an authorization of "such funds as necessary" to follow in subsequent years. The proposal favored localities, but it made greater state involvement possible by eliminating the population threshold for prime sponsorship and imposing a requirement that potential prime sponsors demonstrate their ability to coordinate programs.[15] Child development advocates viewed their greater openness toward state involvement as essential. In February 1973, one supporter argued that state governments would have to be incorporated into any child development bill.[16] Their proposal also returned full administrative and policy control to the child development councils and made changes to the fee structure.[17]

The coalition delivered its proposal to Mondale and Javits in the Senate and to Brademas in the House. Although Brademas took a more skeptical view than his Senate colleagues, the coalition proposal provided the template for bills that were introduced in 1974 and 1975. Brademas described the 1974 House version of the bill as "somewhat more modest" than the bill Nixon vetoed in 1971. He noted that it placed a stronger emphasis on "the planning and development of programs prior to their actual implementation."[18] Even so, the Child and Family Services Act remained ambitious legislation.

In terms of political strategy, supporters made a concerted effort "to avoid the anti-family image Nixon had tagged on the 1971 bill" (McCathren 1981, 122). The bill's title reflected this objective. It included the word *family* to reflect advocates' belief that one could not help children without assisting their families. They hoped that framing the proposal as a family support program would "make politicians feel better" and give it "much more political appeal."[19] The coalition had redrafted the bill line by line with that goal in mind, and its congressional allies tried to convince their colleagues that the child development program would not infringe on parental prerogatives. Mondale claimed that the bill would "strengthen the role of the family as the primary and fundamental influence on the development of the child," by giving parents "the opportunity to choose among the greatest possible variety of child and family services" (Mondale 1975, 15).

Advocates portrayed the Child and Family Services Act as family-strengthening legislation. They stressed that participation would be voluntary and that children would be eligible "only after a written request from the parents or guardians has been received."[20] Brademas noted that the bill "requires parental involvement at every stage in the planning, development, and implementation of programs."[21] By emphasizing deference to parental prerogatives, supporters attempted to combat the charge that the bill was incompatible with mainstream American values. Supporters frequently mentioned that the bill was supported by many respected organizations, such as the American Academy of Pediatrics, the United States Catholic Conference, the League of Women Voters, the National Council of Churches, the Education Commission of the States, the United Auto Workers, and the American Association of University Women.[22] They argued that this broad support indicated that the bill was not radical proposal that its critics described. They also emphasized that it possessed broad bipartisan support and was "similar to provisions recently advocated by a Republican congressional task force and by both parties in their platforms at their 1972 national conventions."[23]

Supporters of the bill nevertheless acknowledged that they faced an uphill battle. The political and economic context had changed since the veto. Some of these changes were specific to the issue of early childhood. In March 1975, political scientist Gilbert Steiner described "an increasing fracturization of the children's cause" and worried that supporters would find themselves "cutting each other up and making no advances whatsoever."[24] The increasing prominence of the states and the American Federation of Teachers, which will be described in more detail shortly, exacerbated this fragmentation. In addition, resistance to national government involvement was stronger than it had been in 1971, when more participants "had sort of a benign view of Head Start and thought it was kind of like nursery school and, well, nursery school's okay."[25] These benign views changed as policymakers and the public became more familiar with the stakes involved in early childhood policy.

The limited political prospects of the Child and Family Services Act also reflected broader changes in American society and politics. Historian Edward Berkowitz (2006) describes 1974 as the dividing line between postwar and modern America. As the country experienced a slumping economy, a growing national debt, and galloping inflation, the creation of major new domestic programs became increasingly difficult. In addition, the Watergate scandal led to the inauguration of a new president. Gerald Ford was more conservative than his predecessor, and in keeping with his efforts to "whip inflation," he sought to reduce government spending on education, child development, and many other social programs. The Watergate scandal also affected public opinion, leading Americans to be more skeptical and less trusting of their government. The scandal contributed to a Democratic landslide in the 1974 elections, but the victors operated in a new policymaking environment in which "ambitious federal social programs were off the table" (Berkowitz 2006, 232). The combination of "economic malaise and political crisis sent the welfare state into retreat" (Schulman 2001, xv).

Most supporters of the legislation acknowledged that it was unlikely to pass. The coalition did not "expect passage or enactment of a major bill in the next year or two" and viewed it "more as a vehicle on which to keep the issue alive and on which to hold hearings."[26] In a 1977 speech, Brademas isolated two crucial obstacles: "In the first place, we knew that President Ford would have vetoed the bill and that we simply would not have had the votes to override such a veto. Secondly, we knew that such were the strains upon the budget for the immediate fiscal year that we would not have had the money to authorize the amounts contained in our original bill."[27] Knowing that success was unlikely, however, did not stop advocates from pressing their case.

The Rationale for the Child and Family Services Act

In addition to portraying the Child and Family Services Act as family-strengthening legislation, advocates relied on many of the same arguments they had advanced in 1971. They described the bill as a cost-effective response to demographic changes. Women, including mothers with young children, continued to join the workforce in record numbers. This trend created a "revolution in labor-force expectations," as "it became the norm for women to work outside of the home during the seventies" (Berkowitz 2006, 68). In a November 1974 speech, the director of the Women's Bureau claimed that "the availability of child care is often the pivot upon which a woman's decision to work or remain at home turns."[28] The rising number of preschools and kindergartens that served American children offered mostly part-day programs.

Day care centers generally offered schedules that were a better fit for working mothers, but proponents argued that there were too few slots to meet the "increasingly urgent need" for day care.[29] For example, Brademas claimed that "six million children under the age of six have mothers who work, while there are only one million places in licensed day-care centers for these children."[30] In December 1974, a Congressional Research Service report concluded that day care as an institution was insufficiently responsive to important societal changes.[31] Trends in women's participation in the labor force, increases in the number of single-parent families, and declines in average family size led developmental psychologist Urie Bronfenbrenner to conclude, "It's clear that something has got to be done, and enough people are going to become involved that they'll make that fact known."[32]

Supporters of the bill also argued that it was a wise long-term investment. For example, Mondale lamented that many children were "placed in understaffed day care centers that destroy the mind and spirit."[33] Throughout his 1972 reelection campaign, Mondale argued that these "cheated children . . . often turn up in institutions for the retarded . . . in unemployment lines . . . and in prisons. And the American taxpayer picks up the tab in the increasing cost of welfare, unemployment compensation, crime and other programs that symbolize our failure."[34] Proponents argued that spending money on child development programs would reduce future spending on various social services. Their claims about the "need" for child development legislation and its cost-effectiveness were not new, and a loud chorus of critics rejected their arguments.

The Opposition Campaign and the Anonymous Flyer

Like their adversaries, opponents of a more expansive role for the national government in early childhood policy relied on familiar arguments. They seemed to be in a strong political position in 1975. Resistance to a child development program had increased, and economic and political changes made the creation of major new domestic programs increasingly difficult. The political battle over child development had been a formative moment for the "New Right, whose remarkable growth, beginning in the early 1970s, derived in part from its opposition to universal child care" (Michel 1999, 238). Opponents of the Child and Family Services Act were well organized, forming the National Coalition for Children to combat the proposal. The coalition represented parents' groups in forty states and the American Conservative Union. It described itself as a "veritable army of parents, church-goers, and other citizens comprising a genuine grassroots movement which has arisen in opposition to a decade of federal imposition of programs and values to which the Judeo-Christian tradition is mostly opposed."[35] The emergence of this grassroots network, which was joined by other opponents, helps explain why the opposition campaign was especially intense.

Some critics questioned the need and desirability of a child development program. One essayist argued that "the day-care 'emergency' we are being told about doesn't exist, and didn't exist in 1971 when the revolutionaries began telling us about it."[36] Other opponents contended that the national supply of day care was "approximately equal" to the demand for early childhood programs.[37] They presented data purporting to show that there was no overall shortage of services, and they pointed to surveys suggesting that American families of all racial backgrounds and at all income levels preferred to "have their preschool children cared for in their own homes by friends and relatives or in conveniently located family group care situations provided by relatives or neighbors—not in publicly subsidized centers."[38] Critics also argued that child development programs would not deliver educational benefits, especially over the long term. Existing research, they claimed, demonstrated that "most preschool education projects appear to have little or no effect on the long-range cognitive abilities of participating children."[39]

Other critics objected to the specific provisions of the Child and Family Services Act. In congressional testimony, HEW secretary Caspar Weinberger expressed "extreme dissatisfaction with the bill,"[40] claiming that it was administratively unwieldy and duplicative. Speaking on behalf of the administration, he explained, "We strongly disagree with the idea behind this bill that we must build a wholly new delivery system for child care services which would bypass, even ignore altogether, the existing array of publicly funded services now directly and indirectly benefiting our children."[41] He criticized the bill for lacking direct linkages to existing programs like Head Start, the Work Incentives program, or the programs operating under various titles of the Social Security Act.[42] Weinberger also claimed that the bill gave the national government a "far too pervasive role in the organization and delivery of social services at the local level" and "push[ed] state governments to the sidelines, thereby overriding the traditional federal-state relationship."[43] This arrangement was administratively unworkable because it required the national government to work directly with thousands of local governments and voluntary organizations serving as prime sponsors. Weinberger's testimony resonated with the objections expressed in Nixon's veto message.

Cost was a prominent issue during the congressional debate. Weinberger argued that the "enormous strain [the bill] would ultimately place on the federal budget" was especially unwelcome during a period in which the United States confronted a large national deficit.[44] An editorial in the *Norman (OK) Transcript* acknowledged the bill's "admirable goals" but concluded that "it is probably an idea whose time has not yet come," because "with the state of the economy we just can't afford it at this time."[45]

Other critics used melodramatic language to describe the stakes of this legislative battle. They characterized the Child and Family Services Act as an affront to American values. Calling it a "grandiose, federally funded, social planning scheme,"[46] the National Coalition for Children claimed that the bill represented "the last power grab for children by the unwanted hand of the social planner."[47] An editorial in the *Indianapolis Star* labeled the bill "socialistic" and a "fantastic monstrosity,"[48] and one in the *Wall Street Journal* claimed that the child development lobby wanted "to substitute government professionals for the family."[49] Another critic said that the bill would create "special centers for propagandizing America's children, very much in the style and manner of the Hitler Youth,"[50] and concluded that it "would change Uncle Sam into Big Mama."[51] Although advocates portrayed the proposal as family-strengthening legislation, critics continued to describe it as a threat to parental autonomy.

In his memoir, Brademas described how members of Congress received a "rivulet, then a Niagara, of letters" attacking the measure (Brademas 1986, 42). One constituent wrote to Speaker of the House Carl Albert (D-OK), "I think this is about the most absurd piece of legislation I have ever seen."[52] Another letter writer asserted, "This is a communistic act and is against the people's constitutional rights. It is also against the will of God and should never have been printed. We are supposed to be a free people in a free and democratic society. If this bill is passed, all is lost."[53] Another critic claimed that the bill opened the door "to federal control of the divine institution of the family which is the center of American life."[54] Using apocalyptic language, one constituent asked the Speaker, "Are you voting for this measure or against it? This bill is a struggle of forces. In a very real sense, it is a vote for God or Satan. Where does your soul fall?"[55] The volume and tone of these letters illustrate the enormous outcry over the measure and the passionate terms on which it was denounced.[56]

Supporters attributed most of the allegations against the bill to an anonymous flyer that began circulating during the fall of 1975.[57] Its origins were murky, as media accounts and observers traced it to various regions of the country. According to the *Washington Post,* the campaign "began in the area of Oklahoma and Texas but soon moved to points North and East,"[58] while the *Kansas City Star* noted that "much of the distribution has been in the Middle West."[59] In February 1976, Brademas voiced suspicions that the flyer had originated in McLean, Virginia, or Washington, DC.[60] His guess seemed to implicate the Emergency Committee for Children and the National Coalition for Children, but both groups strongly denied this charge.[61]

Regardless of its origins, the anonymous flyer effectively galvanized opposition to the Child and Family Services Act. It claimed, "If passed [the bill] would take the responsibility of the parents to raise their children and give it to the government. . . . This all smacks of communism. This is what in fact has been and is being done in Soviet Russia."[62] The flyer included quotations from the *Congressional Record* suggesting that the bill would even give children the right to "sue [their] parents if they required [them] to go to Sunday school."[63] Its claims were repeated in editorials, television reports, and the flood of letters that constituents mailed to Congress. The flyer also led opponents to claim "that parents who are not doing a good job will have their children taken away from them, that parents cannot teach their children about God, that a charter of children's rights is being added to the act, and that parents would lose the right to form their children's characters."[64]

The language and impact of the flyer infuriated supporters of the legislation. Brademas decried its "false and totally outrageous allegations."[65] He argued, "It is high time to put a halt to these Watergate tactics of reckless smear and deception."[66] Mondale characterized it as "one of the most vicious and inaccurate propaganda campaigns I have witnessed in my fifteen years of service" and claimed that "there is not a shred of truth in any of these charges."[67] Opinion writers across the country, including opponents of the bill, denounced the flyer. One editorial blasted its "wild and completely false allegations."[68] Another characterized the flyer as a "parade of imaginary horribles" and "a circular made up of patent untruths and wild distortions."[69] A third argued that the attacks sink "to new lows of irresponsibility and falsehood."[70] The flyer's emphasis on religious instruction led a group of religious organizations to issue an "interreligious statement" that read, "These charges are totally inaccurate. There is nothing in this legislation that relates to religious preferences or religious instruction; nothing that relates to or alters the existing legal relationship between parents and their children; and nothing that provides for compulsory service of any kind."[71] Even two strong opponents of the legislation, the American Conservative Union and the National Coalition for Children, disavowed the charges leveled in the flyer.[72]

Some observers attributed the ultimate demise of the Child and Family Services Act to the anonymous flyer. Media accounts quoted supporters who claimed that the attacks "substantially hindered" its likelihood of passage.[73] Neither the House nor the Senate endorsed the proposal, a decisive defeat that another observer attributed to the vociferous opposition campaign: "Never in the history of American politics has a grassroots campaign based on distortion and blatant falsehood been so widespread, so virulent, and so successful" (McCathren 1981, 120). The truth, however, was more complex. Even before the smear campaign began, Brademas and Mondale "had in fact already decided, for other reasons, to set [their] proposals aside" (Brademas 1987, 41). In the summer, the two congressmen "agreed that if we pressed ahead with the bill in that session, President Ford would veto it and thereby seriously set back our effort. So we quietly decided to postpone action in 1975 in the hope that a Democrat would be elected to the White House in 1976" (Brademas 1986, 42). In October, Mondale acknowledged that the proposal would "certainly be vetoed" and that it lacked sufficient support for an override.[74] The two congressmen decided to postpone action before the anonymous flyer began to circulate, and Mondale's acknowledgment occurred before the opposition campaign received widespread publicity. By early 1976, observers asserted that the bill "has no realistic chance of adoption" and that "the furor is a false alarm."[75] The flyer and the reaction it spawned demonstrated the intensity of the opposition to the Child and Family Services Act, but they were not solely responsible for its defeat.

The Dissolving Preschool Coalition: The Role of the States and the American Federation of Teachers

Several areas of disagreement arose during congressional testimony on the bill. The appropriate role of the private sector was a contentious issue. Between 1970 and 1974, enrollment in private nursery schools had increased from 763,000 to 1,184,000 (55.2 percent), while enrollment in public nursery schools had grown from only 333,000 to 423,000 (29.7 percent).[76] Several witnesses urged that for-profit centers be excluded from public funding, citing past abuses and "arguing that the profit motive itself is a disincentive to providing the highest quality care for children."[77] Others argued that it was logical to rely on the private sector "in areas where no other child care facilities exist or where existing public facilities are overcrowded."[78]

The authorization levels in the measure were also controversial. Some witnesses expressed concern about the new emphasis on planning and training during the program's first year. They wanted immediate authorizations for program operation, claiming that "good programs could die out for lack of funds, leaving parents with no alternative care arrangements for a year while the system is being planned and personnel trained."[79] Others argued that these funds were insufficient to provide comprehensive services to children and their parents. Defenders of the bill argued that the authorization provisions refuted the charge that the child development program was unaffordable.

The topic of parental participation sparked disagreement over the composition and authority of parent policy committees and other groups. Eligibility requirements and the establishment of fee schedules also divided supporters of the legislation. Some witnesses favored the requirements and schedules proposed in the bill, others proposed slight modifications, and a third group argued that the child development program should be free and universal. Witnesses also debated the question of minimum standards and provisions for training personnel during the hearings.[80]

While several issues caused divisions within the child development coalition, none caused as much angst as the issue of prime sponsorship. Section 104 of the Child and Family Services Act revisited the designation of prime sponsors, and several witnesses "based their entire testimony on the crucial issue of the best delivery system for the services to be offered."[81] The appropriate role of state governments was a common point of contention. Some witnesses claimed that state governments would be effective prime sponsors because of their resources and oversight capabilities, but others argued that they were "too large and too remote to bring flexibility and quality to local programs serving communities with highly individual needs."[82] By September 1975, thirty-seven states had either a functioning office of child development, a grant to plan and establish an office, or an office functioning in part of the state.[83] In a letter describing this recent activity, a West Virginia official urged Brademas to "encourage these efforts by providing support through the Child and Family Services Act for those states that have shown their good faith and capability to do statewide planning and coordination."[84] In addition, the number of states providing public aid to kindergartens and to preschools had also increased since 1971. The states were firmly entrenched stakeholders, and state officials defended their existing prerogatives.

The increased assertiveness of state government representatives illustrated the broader fragmentation of early childhood policy. Press accounts noted that the national government "is providing an estimated $2 billion for child-care services through a confused welter of about 60 programs designed for disadvantaged families."[85] The Emergency Committee for Children called for greater "public discussion of the duplicative statutes on day care."[86] Government officials like Weinberger "sharply criticized the present system's fragmentation among over 200 agencies."[87] When Joseph A. Califano Jr. prepared a report on family policy for aspiring presidential candidate Jimmy Carter, he said that the United States offered an "inconsistent patchwork of policies affecting families."[88] The role of the states in this policy hodgepodge is especially important because it illustrates a subtle shift in the congressional debate. State governments played a minor role as Congress considered the Comprehensive Child Development Act, but their representatives were a much stronger lobbying presence four years later. This increased activity reflected both lessons drawn from the previous debate and the immediate impact of the venue shopping described in chapter 4 of this book.

National policymakers were also forced to grapple with a new candidate for prime sponsorship, namely, the public schools. On September 8, 1974, Albert Shanker penned a union-paid advertisement in the *New York Times* with the title "Early Childhood Education Is a Job for the Public

Schools." Shanker, who had become president of the American Federation of Teachers (AFT) in August after defeating David Selden in a bruising campaign,[89] argued that the Comprehensive Child Development Act and the Child and Family Services Act would lead to conflicting responsibilities, duplication and overlap, gaps and unevenness of access, and wide variation in service quality, because they allowed a broad range of sponsoring agencies.[90] He wrote, "The demands of special interests must give way to coherent public policy. As we expand the education of our children, the responsibility for the enlarged program must be borne by the public schools."[91] While admitting that the public schools were not perfect, Shanker argued that they were well suited to administering a universal system of early childhood education and care.

The campaign to expand the role of the public schools did not end with Shanker's essay. The AFT worked fervently on the issue and was actively involved in negotiations over the substance and form of new initiatives. It was a strong political force. A 1975 study of education interest groups described the AFT as one of the only "Washington-based associations . . . at the top of the heap of 'representational effectiveness' in the field of education policy" (Bailey 1975, 28–29). The AFT also affected the stance that organized labor writ large would take on the legislation. Because the bill did not urge public school responsibility for the child development program, the AFT threatened to block labor support (McGill-Franzen 1993, 70). In October 1975, a staffer on the House Subcommittee on Select Education wrote an internal memorandum in which he confided, "One thing that scares me is . . . our bill's lack of emphasis on the local public school as prime sponsors. . . . If we want blue collar support we must assess the power of Al Shanker."[92] The stance taken by the AFT strained the child development coalition, sparking a debate over "the political necessity of bargaining for AFT support in order to move any bill" (McCathren 1981, 94).

In January 1976, the AFT joined seven other education organizations to announce "a new, unified thrust" in early childhood development programs. Labeling itself the U.S. OECD Forum of Education Organization Leaders, the coalition called for an expanded national program of early childhood education and argued that the "public school system should have a major responsibility in the delivery of this service."[93] At the news conference announcing its objectives, the coalition issued a statement arguing that the schools were well suited to carry out a program that was developmental, rather than custodial, in nature. The statement concluded, "We recognize that this growing need demands a response from educators at every level. Given our understanding of the problem and our knowledge of what the schools can do, the members of the Forum call upon Congress to authorize the necessary funds to enable schools to begin the job."[94]

What caused the AFT to propose a child development system that would be administered by the public schools? In April 1975, education commissioner Terrel Bell had described early childhood education as a source of jobs for unemployed teachers: "We ought to utilize many of our trained teachers that the taxpayers have helped to train and now don't have jobs in this field. If they need some more training . . . and I suspect that is the case . . . we ought to provide it."[95] Political scientist Gilbert Steiner observed that the program Shanker endorsed would enable him "to find jobs for the large number of primary school teachers who are and will soon find themselves superfluous in a declining birthrate situation."[96] Other observers expressed similar sentiments. They argued that whatever the merits of the AFT's position, the union was "frankly motivated by the desire to find jobs for its members."[97] Critics like the Emergency Committee for Children blasted the AFT proposal as the "first step toward a scheme of universal early childhood education perhaps from age 3, a program which is openly advocated by certain teacher organizations as a means—to put it bluntly—of creating jobs."[98]

The AFT proposal contributed to the dissolution of the child development coalition.[99] A *New York Times* article described a "struggle for power between the teachers and the supporters of the Mondale-Brademas bills."[100] Another account claimed that "the fragile coalition of 1975 was quickly torn apart" by the disagreement over the appropriate role of the public schools (McCathren 1981, 124). Critics charged that the AFT presented a simplistic view of the public schools: "The image of the public school as a rational organization, the center of the community, flexible in programming, and accessible to parents, although certainly desirable, is, to say the least, questionable" (Fishhaut and Pastor 1977, 40). They argued that the school system would overemphasize educational development, undermining the more comprehensive objectives of a child development program.

Critics also contended that public schools often failed to achieve real parent participation or develop program continuity. As a result, they concluded that a uniform approach was less desirable than a more localized and diversified one. Some critics conceded that public school systems would occasionally be appropriate prime sponsors, but they argued that each individual community should make that determination for itself.[101]

Other critics claimed that a system administered by a single prime sponsor would deprive communities of the richness provided by a more pluralistic approach. They portrayed the fragmentation of existing programs as desirable because it offered greater parental choice. One set of critics wrote, "Parents will want different things for their children, and options should be available to enable them to make meaningful choices" (Fishhaut and Pastor 1977, 47).

Various actors had a stake in the status quo, which helps explain why the AFT proposal earned a mixed reception. Early childhood programs had changed significantly in a short period of time. The rapid growth in private-sector nursery school enrollment and the rise of for-profit day care centers, in combination with a mélange of state-level programs, meant that the AFT proposal would potentially harm several constituencies. One observer noted, "Perhaps the most immediate issue is the control and future of some 100,000 licensed day-care and child development facilities that serve about one million children outside the established school system."[102] The AFT may have viewed a child development program as a potential source of jobs for its members, but other stakeholders resisted its proposal for precisely that reason. An official of the Salvation Army explained, "It appears that the American Federation of Teachers is pushing to have day care turned over to boards of education so that the jobs day care teachers now hold will be given over to the public school teachers."[103]

Other critics portrayed the proposal as a threat to existing service providers. They argued that "the funding of programs by any single prime sponsor would prevent opportunities for growth of programs under other sponsors and might possibly extinguish them altogether" (Fishhaut and Pastor 1978, 123–24). Organizations representing private and community-based service providers, including Head Start, "saw Shanker's proposal as a threat to their existence" (E. Rose 2010, 66). Rather than bringing together a stronger coalition in favor of an expanded role for the national government in early childhood policy, the AFT proposal exacerbated tensions within the child development coalition. Some early childhood educators viewed it as no more than a power grab.

Summary: The Demise of the Child and Family Services Act

Supporters of the Child and Family Services Act of 1975 knew that they faced an uphill battle. The shifting political and economic environment made the enactment of expansive social policies unlikely, and opponents of a child development program were better organized than they had been just four years earlier. Whereas the Comprehensive Child Development Act cleared Congress only to be vetoed by President Nixon, the Child and Family Services Act made limited progress. The opposition campaign against the measure, represented by an anonymous flyer that sparked a flood of irate letters to Congress, was sometimes cited as the primary cause of the bill's demise. However, the rhetorical claims made by its opponents and supporters had not changed much from earlier congressional debates. What had changed in the intervening years was the universe of actors who viewed themselves as stakeholders. State governments were more active in this policy arena, and their representatives were more engaged in congressional policymaking than they had been in 1971. The role of organized labor also shifted as the American Federation of Teachers advanced a proposal that helped split the child development coalition into competing camps. These divisions contributed to the demise of the Child and Family Services Act and the further fragmentation of American early childhood programs.

Early Childhood Policy and the Carter Administration

In November 1976, Democrat Jimmy Carter defeated Gerald Ford to win the presidency. Walter Mondale, the primary Senate advocate of child development legislation, was elected vice president. Before taking office, Carter had lamented the incoherence of American family policy and argued that "the enactment of a comprehensive child development bill to provide quality, non-profit child care must be one of our major national priorities."[104] His campaign rhetoric and the presence of a familiar ally as vice president fostered cautious optimism among the supporters of increased public investment. Brademas, who had become majority whip in the House, noted that he and others were "anxiously awaiting the policies that the Carter Administration will propose."[105] Although the change in presidential administrations seemed to herald a more hospitable political climate for child development legislation, the late 1970s were a period of frustration and disillusionment for advocates. The Carter administration did not prioritize early childhood policy, and even the president's modest proposal to host a conference on the American family generated controversy.

The struggling economy was an important barrier to the consideration of comprehensive child development legislation. The economic environment limited the prospects for ambitious initiatives in domestic policy and reduced Carter's ability to collaborate with Congress on new entitle-ment programs (Berkowitz 2006, 113). In the words of the vice president, there were "high expectations for what was possible under a new Demo-cratic president, and a lot of backlogged expectations—only we didn't have the economy that would pay for it" (Mondale 2010, 192).

Even if economic circumstances had been more favorable, however, it is far from certain that the administration would have forcefully advo-cated major policy change. It "strengthened the federal role in education," but "it did not make education a central component of its domestic pol-icy" (Thomas 1983, 283). The most controversial action Carter took was the creation of the national Department of Education. This action repre-sented the fulfillment of a campaign pledge. The National Education As-sociation had long supported the creation of a freestanding education de-partment. In 1976, "in exchange for receiving the NEA's first presidential endorsement, Jimmy Carter pledged to back the idea" (Kahlenberg 2007, 213). The move was criticized by conservatives who invoked states' rights and opposed the growth of the federal bureaucracy. It also drew fire from liberals who worried that the NEA would exercise outsized interest over the department. Carter nevertheless used the power of the presidency to achieve departmental status for the education agency.

Other education issues, including early childhood policy, did not re-ceive a similar presidential commitment. In fact, the creation of the De-partment of Education caused Carter to be characterized as "the president who almost ended Head Start as we know it" (Zigler and Muenchow 1992, 171). At the behest of the Office of Management and Budget, which advo-cated a broad-based agency, Carter called for Head Start to be placed in the new department. Head Start parents, the National Head Start Associa-tion, and other advocates of the program objected vehemently to this pro-posal. They feared that a broad-based department would be dominated by teachers unions and administrators, and they argued that inclusion in the new department would undermine the basic rationale of Head Start. With its emphasis on comprehensive services and parent involvement, Head Start was more than an education program. Carter's proposal was viewed as a betrayal of Head Start and his African American supporters, and by the time the Department of Education bill was enacted, Head Start had been deleted. The episode resolved the relationship between Head Start and the Department of Education, but it was a harrowing experience for program advocates (Zigler and Muenchow 1992, 188).

As a presidential candidate, Carter proposed to convene a White House conference on the American family. Even this modest initiative, however, greatly frustrated several constituencies. Activists complained that the White House failed to take the conference seriously. Organizations representing African Americans, Catholics, and those with an interest in social welfare policy "complained in common about ignored requests for meetings, perfunctory replies to questions about the conference planning process, and promised deadlines for action that were not met" (Steiner 1981, 40). Furthermore, the original conference leadership team dissolved in a matter of months. Wilbur Cohen, a former HEW secretary who had helped draft the Social Security Act in 1935, agreed to serve as national chairman but then announced that a health problem would preclude his participation.[106] The potential appointment of Patricia Fleming as executive director also aroused controversy. Critics questioned whether Fleming, a divorced working mother of three, was an appropriate choice. After agreeing to accept the position, she resigned before her appointment was announced publicly (Steiner 1981, 42–43). Rather than being an "uplifting, feel-good event, the conference degenerated into arguments over whether one type of family was better than another" (Berkowitz 2006, 111). The promised conference finally took place in the summer of 1980, and its recommendations focused on such traditional issues as job-related pressures and the tax treatment of families (Steiner 1981, 45). Thus the Carter administration proved itself both unwilling to advance a major proposal on early childhood policy and incapable of exercising leadership on the broader issue of family policy.[107]

The Child Care Act of 1979

With the executive branch essentially sidelined, the initiative shifted back to Capitol Hill. Senator Alan Cranston (D-CA), a fierce critic of how the administration handled the conference on the American family, was joined by four Senate colleagues in introducing the Child Care Act of 1979.[108] The bill was the culmination of more than two years of work. The Senate Subcommittee on Child and Human Development, chaired by Cranston, held a series of hearings in California and Washington during which it heard from parents, child care providers, and others as it shaped the legislation.[109] The proposal differed in several important ways from the Comprehensive Child Development Act and the Child and Family Services Act.

At a basic level, the Child Care Act lacked the ambition and scope of its predecessors. It was characterized as a "very limited and incremental child care bill [that] attempted to reach a compromise among the important interest groups over the design of new programs" (McCathren 1981, 126). Its eligibility provisions were illustrative. Previous proposals targeted the children of poor and middle-class families and viewed universal access as a long-term goal. Cranston, in contrast, described the target constituency of his proposal as families "whose incomes are too low to get any substantial benefit from the tax credit and too high in many cases to be eligible for programs . . . which are targeted on welfare or poverty-level families."[110] The Child Care Act focused on poor and working women who were struggling to remain in the workforce and off of welfare. Its "very limited goal" was "to create a modest system of child care not limited to low-income parents" (McGill-Franzen 1993, 70).

The Child Care Act also moved away from its predecessors' emphasis on comprehensive services and the Head Start model. The title of the legislation reflected this shift. The bill acknowledged that some families might need health, nutrition, or social services, but it carefully avoided use of the term *comprehensive*. Instead, it emphasized child care services for working mothers. At a subcommittee hearing in February, Cranston described existing programs as "severely overtaxed" and argued that policy changes were necessary "as the rising cost of living and other social conditions bring more and more mothers of young children into the workforce in order to maintain decent standards of living for their families."[111] Cranston's rhetoric and the move away from comprehensive services implied a custodial model of early childhood programming whose goal was to enable mothers to work. This shift was also reflected in the legislation's limited provisions for parental involvement. Though it guaranteed that services would be voluntary, it "did not establish the parent- and consumer-dominated councils with specific policymaking powers as did the 1971 bill" (Beck 1982, 328).

The Child Care Act also advanced an alternative approach to the issue of prime sponsorship. It went even further in expanding state government prerogatives than had the Child and Family Services Act. Cranston's proposal "assumed that states would be prime sponsors (or would determine to which state and local agencies to delegate these responsibilities)" (Beck 1982, 328). The Child Care Act did not deliver funds from the national government to local projects run by community organizations or to local governments. Rather, its "clear meaning was to pass federal funds to states, which would make major policy and allocation decisions" (Beck 1982, 328). State governments would possess tremendous discretion in program implementation.

While it would be a mistake to attribute this provision exclusively to the lobbying efforts of state governments, it is important to recognize their visible presence in the late 1970s. For example, the ECS chairman sent President Carter a letter in February 1977 urging the new president "to publicly adopt the position that education improvement is directly tied to the improvement of state/federal relations and that the primary direction of federal activity should be to support and supplement the states."[112] State officials often complained that federal regulations duplicated state government efforts, a claim that resonated especially strongly in early childhood policy. With its assumption that states would serve as prime sponsors, the Child Care Act seemed responsive to this line of argument. The executive director of the ECS described the bill as "well suited to furthering ongoing efforts at the state level to improve child and family service delivery systems."[113]

The limited ambition of the Child Care Act reflected political and economic realities. Politically, Cranston hoped that the bill would be acceptable to the diverse constituencies with a stake in this policy arena. One objective of the subcommittee hearings in 1977 and 1978 was to "smoke out the supporters and detractors and read the present sentiments of those most directly involved in the child care debate" (McCathren 1981, 126). After the demise of the Child and Family Services Act of 1975, there was little doubt that support from those individuals and groups would be necessary to overcome the strong opposition of conservative policymakers, columnists, and interest groups. Such support failed to materialize, however, and the bill failed to generate much enthusiasm from the child development community.

The Child Care Act of 1979 was also modest financially. Reflecting the public mood of austerity and the promise of the Carter administration to cut government spending, Cranston attempted to portray the bill as efficient and cost-effective legislation whose "ultimate savings will far outweigh the short-term expenditures."[114] Revisiting a line of argument that had appeared in 1971 and 1975, Cranston argued that the bill would pay for itself through tax revenues from increased parental earnings and through reduced expenditures on other government programs. Recognizing the budgetary constraints under which lawmakers operated, Cranston argued that public spending on child care was money well spent.

Cranston hoped his modest proposal would be acceptable to the wide-ranging stakeholders with an interest in early childhood policy. But the coalition that had come together in 1971 had splintered in 1975 and was "hopelessly divided" by 1979 (McCathren 1981, 131). The divide over the role of public schools, growing enrollment in proprietary child care centers, and the political solidification of Head Start meant that his moderate proposal generated limited enthusiasm.

The unequivocal opposition of the Carter administration further disappointed Cranston. At a subcommittee hearing in February, one administration official described existing national government child care funding. Citing Head Start, services provided under Title XX of the Social Security Act, and the child care tax credit, she concluded, "Given the size and nature of this commitment, we do not believe that another categorical program for child care is warranted at this time."[115] In a testy response, Cranston argued that the administration position would be "more credible if your agency acknowledged the need for a systematic and coordinated approach such as provided in [the Child Care Act] but said that the federal government did not want to pay the price at this point."[116] He could not resist noting the irony of "a Carter-Mondale administration appearing before this subcommittee in opposition to child care legislation."[117] At a March 15 press conference, the senator announced that he was canceling further hearings on the bill, effectively killing it for the 1979 congressional session.

The Continued Growth of Head Start and the Tax Credit

Despite the demise of comprehensive congressional initiatives like the Child and Family Services Act and modest proposals like the Child Care Act of 1979, the national government's role in early childhood policy evolved throughout the decade. In terms of enrollment and spending, Head Start grew dramatically during the late 1970s. Program enrollment had declined from 374,000 during fiscal year 1972 to 279,340 during fiscal year 1977, but by fiscal year 1979, Head Start served 429,500 children, an increase of more than 50 percent over a two-year period. During the same period, expenditures rose from $376 million during fiscal year 1972 to $425 million during fiscal year 1977, before rising sharply to $680 million during fiscal year 1979.[118] These figures suggest that President Carter, despite proposing to locate Head Start within the new Department of Education, was an important ally. He publicized Head Start's effectiveness and began a trend of requesting substantial increases in its budget. In doing so, the president "put Head Start on a course that would be difficult for the next president to reverse" (Zigler and Muenchow 1992, 190). The political solidification of Head Start, however, contributed to further programmatic fragmentation in this policy arena.

Parental involvement was a central component of Head Start and a key source of policy feedback, especially after the formation of the National Head Start Association in 1973. A May 1978 Head Start assessment report is illustrative. The assessment team visited twenty-nine Head Start programs in twenty-three states and interviewed over a thousand people. Its report noted that parents "who actively participate in the program gain valuable personal and consumer skills, are often motivated to pursue higher life goals, and sometimes experience career development through employment in the program."[119] Many Head Start parents began as volunteers but eventually became aides, cooks, teachers, and even program directors. The transition from volunteer to teacher was especially common. Of the twenty-nine sites visited by the assessment team, "at least 17 [58.6 percent] had teachers who were, at one time, parents of Head Start children and had worked their way up the career ladder."[120] This common transition occurred at a time when the program was focused on improving the educational credentials of its staff. The report concluded, "From the teams' perspective as outsiders, the many personal success stories of parents who became actively involved suggest that it is in reality an area of significant program achievement."[121] Some officials argued that the employment of Head Start parents aided the broader community because the employees served as "role models helping to motivate their peers."[122]

The centrality of parent involvement had broader political implications that reflected Head Start's origins within the Community Action Program of the Office of Economic Opportunity. The report therefore included a stand-alone section devoted to the program's community role. Head Start served both as an information and referral service for low-income families and as "an advocate for all children and families. Programs have helped develop parent self-confidence and leadership, introduce concepts such as parent involvement and teacher aides into the school systems, and provide economic upward mobility for many parents."[123] In other words, community activism was a crucial component of Head Start's organizational mission. According to the report, Head Start advocacy had evolved "from confrontation to cooperation" as Head Start programs became "part of the system in their communities."[124] Although the report focused on local affairs, the program also developed a strong presence in congressional politics.

The heightened political status of Head Start altered the political landscape. The Child Care Act of 1979, with its restrictive eligibility provisions and its move away from comprehensive services, reflected this shift. The bill "did not envision a competitive or parallel program to Head Start" (McCathren 1981, 127). Instead, it tried to accommodate existing stakeholders in the hope that they would endorse the legislation. Such support did not materialize, however. Head Start supporters warily viewed the Child Care Act as a potential threat to their existing prerogatives. For example, a witness testifying on behalf of the Child Welfare League of America argued that Head Start should be expanded and "appropriately shielded regardless of what kind of new early childhood legislation is enacted."[125] Head Start backers had made similar claims after the president proposed to include Head Start in the Department of Education. Their defensive posture in both contexts illustrates how policy feedback contributed to divisions within the child development coalition. Head Start backers concentrated on preserving their gains. They nominally backed more-ambitious legislative proposals but expressed reservations about them.

Head Start was not the only national program to experience considerable growth during the 1970s. With relatively little fanfare, Congress modified the dependent care tax deduction on several occasions, embedding these changes within omnibus tax reform legislation. Established in 1954, the tax deduction originally was limited to six hundred dollars per year and was phased out for families with income between forty-five hundred and fifty-one hundred dollars. The Revenue Act of 1964 raised the income threshold from forty-five hundred to six thousand dollars and made husbands with incapacitated wives eligible for the deduction. In the 1970s, Congress made a series of more-substantial changes, transforming the deduction into a tax credit with considerably broader eligibility provisions.

The first major change occurred in 1971, when President Nixon signed the Revenue Act of 1971 a mere day after vetoing the Comprehensive Child Development Act. The Revenue Act made any individual maintaining a household eligible for the deduction, subject to a gainful employment requirement. It also modified the definition of a dependent, increased the deduction limit to forty-eight hundred dollars per year, and increased the income threshold at which the deduction began to be phased out from six thousand to eighteen thousand dollars. In terms of services covered, the Revenue Act allowed the deduction for household services in addition to direct dependent care and limited the deduction with respect to services outside the taxpayer's household. The law sought to encourage the hiring of domestic workers, encourage the care of incapacitated persons at home, and provide relief to middle- and low-income taxpayers.[126]

President Nixon praised the Revenue Act in the same veto message in which he lambasted the Comprehensive Child Development Act. Utilizing the tax code to achieve social policy goals, he wrote, "reflects my conviction that the federal government's role wherever possible should be one of assisting parents to purchase needed day care services in the private, open market, with federal involvement in direct provision of such services kept to an absolute minimum."[127] Nixon claimed that the revised tax deduction would potentially benefit 97 percent of all families in the country in which two parents were employed, offering them "free choice of the child care arrangements they deem best for their families."[128]

The treatment of dependent care in the tax code changed again in the mid-1970s. The Tax Reduction Act of 1975 raised the income tax threshold at which the deduction would be phased out from eighteen thousand to thirty-five thousand dollars, and the Tax Reform Act of 1976 replaced the tax deduction with a nonrefundable tax credit. Supporters of the latter change argued that a tax credit would be especially beneficial for taxpayers in the lower tax brackets. Table 1 illustrates the deduction's limited reach as of 1973, especially among low-income taxpayers. More than 90 percent of the individual returns in the lowest income category claimed the standard deduction, making them ineligible, and only 0.2 percent of the returns in that category claimed child and dependent care expenses.[129] Supporters of the shift to a tax credit also praised its administrative benefits. They argued that the rules governing married couples, divorced and separated persons, and payments to relatives were unduly restrictive and that computation of the deduction was too complex.[130] The shift to a tax credit

TABLE 1. Expenses for Child and Dependent Care on Individual Income Tax Returns, 1973

Income Level	Number of Returns	Standard Deduction Claims (%)	Itemized Deduction Claims (%)	Child and Dependent Care Expense Claims (%)	Total Amount of Child and Dependent Care Expense Claims ($)
Less than $5,000	27,038,000	25,283,000 (93.5%)	1,311,000 (4.8%)	52,300 (0.2%)	$35,981,000
Less than $10,000	20,582,000	14,811,000 (72.0%)	5,771,000 (28.0%)	453,231 (2.2%)	$333,562,000
Less than $15,000	15,804,000	8,098,000 (51.2%)	7,706,000 (48.8%)	715,050 (4.5%)	$486,738,000
Over $15,000	17,269,000	4,009,000 (23.2%)	13,260,000 (76.8%)	605,320 (3.5%)	$435,275,000

Source: Statistics of Income 1973: Individual Income Tax Returns, Internal Revenue Service Publication 79 (11-76) (Washington, DC: Department of the Treasury, 1976), tables 1B (p. 2), 2A (p. 40), and 2.9 (p. 60).

seemed to have an immediate impact. Between 1976 and 1980, the number of tax returns on which the dependent care credit was claimed increased from 2,660,000 to 4,231,000 (59.1 percent), and the amount of credit claimed rose from $548 million to $956 million (74.5 percent).[131]

Using the tax code to achieve social policy objectives is one of the distinctive features of the American welfare state (Hacker 2002; Howard 1997). Supporters of this approach often argue that tax expenditures are less intrusive and less bureaucratic than the direct provision of services by government agencies and that tax expenditures provide a wider range of potential options. Politically, tax expenditures represent a potentially easier road to policy change because "whereas direct spending programs require new legislation, which Congress is not obligated to act upon, tax expenditures can be tucked away in must-pass bills" (Howard 1997, 179). As an illustration of this distinction, the transformation of the dependent care tax deduction in 1970s did not receive much media or public attention. It occurred in a series of omnibus revenue bills that were enacted at the same time that direct spending programs repeatedly failed to gain enactment. Tax expenditures can have profound long-term implications. They "can continue indefinitely because they are not subject to periodic budget battles" (Kelly 2003, 608).

The transformation of the tax code generated two forms of policy feedback with crucial political implications. First, it altered middle-class parents' stake in the ongoing debate. The changes "may have removed a potentially powerful constituency for direct public spending on day care" by entrenching a system of tax subsidies that supported private day care for the middle class rather than embracing the goal of universally available, publicly provided services (Morgan 2001, 243). The creation of the child care tax credit, in combination with other factors, facilitated the proliferation of employer-sponsored, voluntary, for-profit, family-based, and other forms of early childhood care. As government assistance "became inextricably associated with poverty and its remediation, nonpoor parents chose or were compelled to turn to private alternatives" (Michel 1999, 237).

Changes in tax policy thus contributed to the divide between the public and private sectors that is one of the distinctive features of early childhood education in the contemporary United States. The clients and advocates of different kinds of care were a "divided constituency that was, in turn, perpetuated by congressional vacillation between targeted and universal forces" (Michel 1999, 278). Parents who were satisfied with the quality and availability of early childhood care options might fear that such options would no longer exist under a universal government program, making them suspicious of initiatives like the Child Care Act. The average dependent care credit per tax return was only $207 in 1979,[132] so material self-interest was probably less important to these parents than was their perceived autonomy.

The second form of policy feedback generated by the transformation of the tax code was the political mobilization of service providers. One of the distinctive features of the politics of tax expenditures is the political mobilization of third-party providers (Howard 1997, 9). This dynamic emerged as Congress considered the Child Care Act. During a subcommittee hearing on February 21, the chairperson of the Private Child Care Providers Allied Association listed private providers' concerns about the bill. She noted that they "represent the majority of center delivery in the United States through owner-directed for profit and director or board directed not for profit programs."[133] In a prepared statement, the National Association for Child Development praised the bill for its "promotion of availability and diversity of child care services by involving the entire range of providers, proprietary, public, and nonprofit" and for its "increased emphasis on participation by the states."[134] It expressed concern, however, about the "standards with which a provider would have to comply to participate in the program."[135] The prominence of third-party providers at congressional hearings was an important development because it illustrated how the contours of this policy arena had shifted during the 1970s. Fueled by the growth of governmental programs like Head Start and the transformation of the tax code, a more diverse set of stakeholders mobilized to defend their existing prerogatives.

Conclusion: The Shifting Terrain of the Late 1970s

In assessing the impact of a critical juncture in the policymaking process, one must distinguish between its short-term and long-term consequences. This chapter focused on the former, examining congressional developments immediately after Nixon's veto of the Comprehensive Child Development Act. On the surface, not much seems to have changed. The ambitious Child and Family Services Act of 1975 was justified and criticized in language that resonated with earlier debates and failed to gain enactment. The Child Care Act of 1979 was narrower in scope and bowed to economic and political realities. It also did not come close to being adopted by Congress. Many of the same actors were involved in all three episodes.

Focusing solely on the failure of Congress to adopt major legislation, however, overlooks important ways in which the early childhood policy sector changed during the 1970s. The absence of a comprehensive national policy did not imply stasis. The social and political forces that put the issue on the nation's political agenda, including the widespread entry of mothers into the labor force and changing perceptions of the value of early childhood education, contributed to heightened demand for child care and dramatic increases in preschool enrollment in both the public and the private sector. Public policy changes contributed to these trends, even though they garnered significantly less attention than did the episodes mentioned in the preceding paragraph. The transformation of the tax code entrenched a system of tax subsidies that supported private day care for the middle class and that facilitated the proliferation of various forms of early childhood care (Michel 1999; Morgan 2001, 2006). The political solidification of Head Start contributed to the tremendous growth of that public program in terms of enrollment and expenditures. The policy changes of the 1970s helped solidify the divide between the public and private sectors that is a distinctive feature of early childhood policy in the United States. Low-income and middle-class families tended to rely on the public and private sector, respectively.

Focusing solely on the repeated failure of the national government to enact major child development legislation also overlooks crucial political changes. Most important, the 1970s witnessed the gradual dissolution of the coalition that had come together to support the Comprehensive Child Development Act. Many of the same actors were involved in later debates, but their perspectives and preferences changed along with the shifting contours of this policy arena. The growth of the private sector removed a potentially powerful constituency for universal legislation—middle-class parents—and helped mobilize third-party providers. Defenders of Head Start became increasingly wary of how proposals to expand the role of the national government would affect their authority and funding. Representatives of state governments argued that any changes to national policy should recognize and build on what was occurring at the state level. Finally, the American Federation of Teachers exacerbated existing tensions within the child development coalition with its call for giving the public schools responsibility for administering a universal program. In sum, the 1970s witnessed increased fragmentation and decentralization in terms of both the shape and the politics of early childhood policy. This trend would continue into the following decade.

6 | Policy Stability and Political Change in the 1980s

The fragmentation of early childhood policy in the United States can be traced to developments in the late 1960s and early 1970s, especially Nixon's veto of the Comprehensive Child Development Act. The veto was a critical juncture not only because it dashed the hopes of those who wanted a larger role for the national government. It also caused those advocates to engage in venue shopping, an attempt to move the debate to more favorable institutional terrain. Their tactical shift produced numerous short-term victories, from the political solidification of Head Start to the creation of several state-level programs. These short-term victories, ironically, created additional long-term hurdles to their objectives, hurdles that advocates were unable to overcome. In fact, the heritage of this venue shopping was a more splintered and fragmented coalition supporting major policy change. Rising enrollment in early childhood programs of various types, the creation and expansion of state programs, and the growth of Head Start shifted the political terrain on which later congressional debates occurred.

The 1980s were not a period of major change in early childhood policy at either the national or the state level. The issue fell off the congressional agenda in the early part of the decade, and when Congress devoted more attention to it in the late 1980s, ambitious and incremental reform proposals did not make much legislative progress. Several policy changes occurred at the state level, but most state programs remained limited in scope. They served a targeted clientele and did not adopt the comprehensive approach to child development that had been popular during the late 1960s and early 1970s. Examining the limited changes of the 1980s is analytically useful, however, because it illustrates how the politics of early childhood policy had shifted in subtle ways.[1] Advocates of greater public investments made limited progress partly because they were unable to coalesce into a unified force for policy change.

Congressional Politics: Critics Coalesce
and Supporters Split

After the demise of the Child Care Act of 1979, congressional interest in early childhood education and care fell dramatically. The presence of Republican Ronald Reagan in the White House represented a seemingly insurmountable obstacle to major policy change, and retrenchment replaced expansion as the overarching objective of policy reform. Programs like Head Start were not immune from the administration's efforts to reduce spending on social programs. Head Start supporters thwarted a proposal to turn the program over to the states and a drive to undercut its national leadership. The program's budget survived virtually intact, but Head Start was forced to serve more children while cutting back on its hours, services, and technical assistance.

Head Start's ability to resist any more dramatic changes was attributed to a combination of "the dedicated federal agency staff who remained to administer the program; the increasingly sophisticated organization of Head Start directors, parents, and staff; the resulting bipartisan support in Congress; and the well-publicized research on the effectiveness of Head Start and "Head Start–like" programs" (Zigler and Muenchow 1992, 193). Working with program administrators and such organizations as the Children's Defense Fund, the National Head Start Association emerged as "a force with which all politicians must contend" (Zigler and Muenchow 1992, 210). Its mobilization and largely successful defense of Head Start illustrates the political significance of policy feedback.

In terms of early childhood policy more broadly, the 1980s were a period of minimal policy change. In 1990, one advocate of reform lamented, "The primary problem, in my opinion, is that in the 1980s early education was removed from . . . the nation's agenda."[2] Most of the nation's political and intellectual energy focused on the "excellence" movement, an effort to raise educational quality through various changes in elementary and secondary education.[3] Policy discussions regarding children who were too young for formal schooling focused on custodial child care rather than educational programming. The Reagan administration successfully advanced a combination of tax cuts and tax breaks that sought to "facilitate parent choice and spur child care initiatives in the private sector" (Michel 1999, 256). These policies were especially helpful to middle-class women who needed care upon entering the labor force and were capable of the financial planning the policies required.

Partisan politics undermined more-ambitious initiatives. Republicans called for state and local control, flexible solutions, and "reasonably firm" answers to questions about the impact of child care, in advance of further national government involvement (Hatch 1982, 258). Democrats generally envisioned a more expansive role for the national government and described child care as a "necessity for families of all types of conditions" (Kennedy 1982, 261). This stalemate was not broken until Republican presidential candidate George H. W. Bush proposed a national child care program during the 1988 campaign, and Congress endorsed the Child Care and Development Block Grant Act two years later. The legislation funded child care subsidies for low-income working families and other efforts to improve program quality (Cohen 2001). It required every state to develop a child care plan for working families and galvanized a series of public and private activities in the states, while distributing most of its funds to parents through vouchers (Lombardi 2003, 40).[4]

Short-term political forces helped prevent major change, yet several long-term forces were also influential. Congress, particularly the House of Representatives, had changed significantly in the decade since comprehensive child development legislation was first proposed. These reforms, such as the Subcommittee Bill of Rights, created a more diffuse power structure that increased the time and effort required to enact legislation. Brademas noted that the changes had made "all the more complicated the task not only of the president but of the leadership of the House in putting together majorities for both domestic and foreign-policy legislation" (Brademas 1987, 126). Critics argued that the reforms made Congress "dramatically less effective and accountable" (Frum 2000, 280). Those who desired a more expansive role for the national government in early childhood policy faced a challenging institutional environment.

Long-term shifts in the political terrain, especially in the interest group universe, were especially significant. The political heritage of Nixon's veto included a mobilized opposition movement and a fragmented supporting coalition. Blocking the comprehensive proposals of the 1970s was a key learning experience for opponents of national government involvement. By the early 1980s, the opposition was "tough and well organized" (Beck 1982, 309). It included such organizations as the National Coalition for Children, the American Conservative Union, the Moral Majority, the Heritage Foundation, the Eagle Forum, and the National Conservative Research and Educational Foundation. Observers were struck by the "promptness with which opposing groups organize when child care legislation is under consideration" (Grotberg 1981, 11). Their political engagement meant that a stealth campaign like the one conducted on behalf of the Comprehensive Child Development Act was no longer possible. Opponents were too well organized for that strategy to work.

Furthermore, divisions within the early childhood policy community hamstrung supporters of national government intervention. The developments of the 1970s meant that "active political support for child care [was] more splintered and more difficult to mobilize than it was a decade ago" (Beck 1982, 308). Political frustration was one source of this fragmentation. In addition, since the early 1970s, the private sector, religious organizations, and state and local agencies had sought to meet the increased demand for programs serving young children. Their efforts expanded the range of stakeholders with an interest in early childhood policy.

These stakeholders held competing views about whether and how the existing policy repertoire should change. In defending their prerogatives, they sometimes undercut the effectiveness of reformers whose objectives they claimed to share. The subsequent "rifts between public and private provision, and among the clients and advocates of different kinds of care, created a divided constituency" (Michel 1999, 278). The existence of new subnational early childhood programs exacerbated this fragmentation and created another set of actors with an interest in maintaining existing arrangements. When Congress returned to the issue in the late 1980s, divisions within the early childhood policy community dampened the prospects for either comprehensive or incremental change. The fate of two unsuccessful initiatives from the late 1980s illustrates how the politics of early childhood policy had shifted over time. The coalitions on both sides of the issue had changed so substantially that the obstacles faced by advocates of increased government intervention were higher.

Smart Start: The Community Collaborative for Early Childhood Development Act of 1988

In the late 1980s, members of Congress introduced several bills on early childhood policy. Smart Start: The Community Collaborative for Early Childhood Development Act, introduced by Senator Edward Kennedy (D-MA) in 1988, was especially noteworthy because its ambitious scope resonated with the comprehensive legislation of the 1970s. Congress did not endorse Smart Start, an outcome that did not surprise its sponsor.[5] Its provisions, its failure to gain enactment, and the arguments advanced by its supporters all resonated with earlier congressional debates. Those areas of overlap, however, mask crucial differences in the politics surrounding Kennedy's proposal. Growing enrollment in preschool programs, the creation and expansion of state programs, and the political solidification of Head Start helped change the terms of the congressional debate. The diverse witnesses who testified on Smart Start pledged fealty to its overarching goals, but they also worried that its adoption would negatively affect their prerogatives.

Smart Start was an ambitious piece of legislation whose emphasis on universal access to comprehensive preschool services resonated with the proposals of the early 1970s. Kennedy said that its main objective was to "make early childhood development programs universally available to the nation's four-year-old children."[6] Most witnesses focused on its educational component, but Smart Start sought to promote good nutrition and parental involvement and to provide prenatal and diagnostic services on a full-day, full-year basis. The bill reserved at least half of its slots for children in families with incomes below the poverty line. Children in families with incomes under 115 percent of the poverty line would receive services at no cost, while eligible children from families with incomes above this benchmark would be subject to a sliding fee scale. Smart Start called for up to $500 million in government funds in its first year of operation, with that figure rising to $750 million and $1 billion in subsequent years. Senator Robert T. Stafford (R-VT), a member of Congress since 1961, noted that Smart Start constituted a sharp shift from the congressional agenda of the early 1980s: "I recall that several years ago the options put forward for serving the young were primarily grounded in employer incentive programs. Much has changed. Now we in Congress are seeing major legislative initiatives designed to expand services to preschool children."[7] Senate hearings on Smart Start therefore provide a good analytical opportunity to examine whether and how preschool politics had changed since the early 1970s.

The witnesses who testified on behalf of Smart Start made claims that echoed those made by their predecessors in the 1970s. They highlighted trends in the American labor market and in preschool enrollment. Increased participation in the labor force by the mothers of young children, they argued, meant that "the demand for good day care far exceeds the availability of good day care."[8] One witness noted that from 1970 to 1985, rates of participation in the labor force by mothers with children under the age of five had risen from 30 percent to 54 percent, while preschool enrollment rates among children whose mothers were not in the labor force had increased from 37 percent to just over 50 percent.[9]

These figures suggested that preschool attendance was an increasingly standard part of American life, which caused some witnesses to focus on

equity concerns. One witness lamented the existence of a "two-tier system" in which children from lower-income families were less likely to enroll in high-quality preschool or child care programs.[10] This concern helps
explain why Smart Start reserved at least 50 percent of its program slots
for children in low-income families. Some supporters claimed that these
children were at risk for later school failure and were therefore especially
likely to benefit from preschool enrollment.[11]

Many witnesses portrayed early childhood programs as cost-effective
investments. This argument was not new, but during the 1980s, it was
ubiquitous. Supporters cited successful examples like the Perry Preschool
Program and compared them to "a vaccine to help ensure healthy development of many children and youth."[12] Senator Jeff Bingaman (D-NM)
claimed, "Several studies have documented that every dollar spent for
quality preschool education can return up to $6 in lower cost for later
education, for public assistance and for the criminal justice system. Even
with our current budget deficits, I do not see how we can afford *not* to invest in quality education and child care."[13] This high rate of return was
contingent on the existence of quality options, but few witnesses added
this important caveat.[14] Instead, they claimed that every dollar invested in
Smart Start would pay for itself over the long term.

The political terrain on which the debates of the late 1980s occurred
differed in several important ways from that of the 1970s. In an editorial
calling for increased public investment, the *New York Times* asserted that
attitudes about children had changed dramatically since Nixon's veto,
making it possible "to identify and energize a potential coalition on behalf
of early childhood intervention."[15] Indeed, the witnesses who testified on
behalf of Smart Start were strikingly diverse. Kennedy claimed that the
appearance of business leaders, government officials, educators, and advocates at one hearing reflected a "spirit of community and cooperation,
which is the basis of this legislation."[16]

The engagement of the business community was especially important.
The Committee for Economic Development issued a policy statement entitled *Children in Need: Investment Strategies for the Educationally Disadvantaged*. Several witnesses mentioned the report. Owen Butler, vice-
chairman of the organization, chaired two subcommittees on early
childhood education, visited twenty-three states to meet with individuals
and groups working on the issue, and appeared before Congress to discuss
Smart Start. He said, "The single most important investment that the nation can make for its future is to provide comprehensive preschool prepa-
ration for every educationally and economically disadvantaged child in

the country."[17] Smart Start supporters treated this strong endorsement from a business group as further evidence that early childhood programs should be viewed as cost-effective investments.

Several other constituencies appeared at the hearings, suggesting widespread interest in early childhood policy. One hearing featured a bipartisan panel of governors who had been involved in early childhood education. Several educational associations also appeared. For example, the National Association of State Boards of Education (NASBE) had convened its National Early Childhood Education Task Force in 1988, and an NASBE representative discussed what it had learned at hearings in Atlanta, Chicago, Boston, and San Francisco.[18] Other witnesses represented groups whose members worked with young children and their families, such as the National Alliance of Pupil Services Organizations.[19] Another witness appeared on behalf of the National Black Child Development Institute, which was leading the Ad Hoc Day Care Coalition, a group of more than seventy organizations seeking to expand access to quality child care programs.[20] This coalition resonated with the one that Marian Wright Edelman led in the late 1960s and early 1970s.

It is tempting to describe the expanding range of constituencies with an interest in early childhood policy as a resource for advocates of expanded public investment, as the *New York Times* did in the aforementioned editorial, but doing so overstates their cohesiveness. While state officials, Head Start supporters, and the educational community agreed on the merits of expanded access to high-quality early childhood programs, they advanced competing visions of how to achieve that goal. Their main areas of disagreement illustrate how the existing policy repertoire constrained the options available to national lawmakers during the late 1980s.

Several lawmakers and witnesses argued that any increased policy reform should, in the words of New Jersey governor Thomas H. Kean, "build on what we've got."[21] Testifying before Smart Start was formally introduced, Kean advised, "Don't create new mechanisms and new bureaucracies. . . . I would rather see you put your energies into nurturing these proven winners than proceed with a bill that departs from the basic principles which have already proved successful."[22] Several senators expressed similar views. Kennedy explained, "Basically, my vision of Smart Start is that it is really a funding stream to build on existing agencies that are providing services within the community."[23] When another witness expressed concern that Smart Start would have a negative impact on Head Start, Kennedy responded, "We build on those types of programs which have been effective for preschool children. We're not trying to reinvent the wheel."[24] Senator Claiborne Pell (D-RI) argued that Smart Start would enable existing programs like Head Start and the Chapter I Compensatory Education Program to reach a greater percentage of eligible young children: "We must be very sure as we go along that we build on the already-proven successes of the programs in being. What we need here is a tremendous infusion of funds for this very good objective."[25] Senator Christopher Dodd (D-CT) said, "Smart Start . . . is intended to build upon already existing programs to upgrade their services, extend their hours. Obviously, we don't want to duplicate programs if they already exist. That would be a waste of money."[26]

Many witnesses also argued that Smart Start should build on existing programs. The president of the National Education Association claimed, "The most prudent investments build on existing programs."[27] A representative of the National Association for the Education of Young Children used language echoing that of Senator Kennedy: "Given the tremendous need for services that exists, particular care must be given in both planning and implementation stages to avoid overlap and duplication of services. . . . Resources are too desperately needed within the field to spend money on reinventing the wheel."[28] The prominence of this theme suggested a consensus that Smart Start should not create a new program from scratch.

Witnesses disagreed, however, about the specific direction Smart Start should pursue. By 1988, the national government and many state governments allocated funds to early childhood programs, while community-based organizations and private-sector entities across the country provided preschool services. As a result, the witnesses representing these varied constituencies had different things in mind when they asked the senators to build on existing programs. The need for better coordination and program integration came up repeatedly. Even more revealing, however, is the fact that diverse witnesses who embraced the overall objectives of Smart Start nonetheless viewed it as a potential threat to existing programs.

The governors who appeared before Congress hoped Smart Start would provide additional funding for but refrain from onerous mandates on state programs. They claimed that state governments, unlike other jurisdictions, were capable of marshaling the resources necessary to ensure that child development efforts were well coordinated and cost effective. They argued that the national government should be relegated to a support role. Minnesota governor Rudolph G. Perpich, a Democrat appearing on behalf of the National Governors Association, focused "on how your early childhood legislative proposal can best assist and encourage our efforts on the state level."[29] Perpich seemed to find a receptive audience. During his opening statement, Senator Kennedy had explained that he had asked the bipartisan panel of governors "for their ideas about how we can best complement the early childhood education programs in their states."[30]

The fact that state officials lobbied for additional funds and authority is unremarkable, but it represented a sea change from the debates of the early 1970s. Recall that state officials felt excluded from the debate over the Comprehensive Child Development Act. Seventeen years later, the governors were consulted before similar legislation was introduced. Furthermore, Congress seemed to heed their requests. At a subsequent hearing, a witness praised Smart Start by saying, "[It] is dedicated to quality. It has the appropriate regulations. It is also building on state initiatives. . . . And that is a really valuable thing."[31]

What explains this remarkable shift in the role of the states? The states were seen as integral players in early childhood policy partly because of their history of activity. Some of this activity dated back to the early 1970s, while some of it was of more-recent vintage. During an exchange with Perpich, Senator Orrin Hatch (R-UT) noted that the states "haven't sat around waiting for the federal government to come up with solutions."[32] Other witnesses also highlighted recent developments at the state level. One explained, "You could make [an] argument that since states have already begun, why create another agency to deliver educational services? It seems to me, that would be a replication of effort."[33] Another noted, "The individual states have already begun to move aggressively in the direction you propose. Your proposals, if adopted, will encourage all states to move and will greatly expand the programs in states and cities where movement had already begun."[34] Another witness praised Smart Start for its deference to the states: "Rather than attempting to impose a new uniform federal program, Smart Start builds on the active efforts of 23 states which have already begun preschool initiatives in the 1980s."[35] Smart Start was often described as a partnership between local, state, and national governments, a portrayal that would not have applied to the Comprehensive Child Development Act.

Another key concern was the relationship between Smart Start and Head Start. Smart Start supporters often invoked Head Start in claiming that the wider availability of preschool access would benefit children. Some Head Start supporters worried, however, that Smart Start would divert resources from a program they regarded as successful. The president of the National Head Start Association said, "We are concerned about the possible establishment of two federal funding streams. . . . [The] solution of taking money from Head Start and giving it to Smart Start is exactly what we fear."[36] Responding that Smart Start sought to support and enhance Head Start, Dodd acknowledged, "I appreciate your concern, because it is one expressed by an awful lot of people. In fact, I had that initial concern. Because I think Head Start has been so successful that I did not in any way want to see it diminished at all, or eroded, through well intended legislative efforts that would distract dollars from a very worthwhile, proven, successful program."[37]

Indeed, the possibility that the existence of Smart Start would have negative consequences for Head Start arose repeatedly. Pell described himself as "very concerned that these efforts not diminish successful existing programs such as Head Start and Chapter I."[38] A witness representing business and professional firms in Colorado noted that Head Start reached "far too few children and parents who are clearly eligible. . . . [Head Start] must not be neglected by the Congress, even as you make additional forward movement with other proposals."[39] In addition to concerns about Smart Start's potential financial impact on Head Start, there was a possibility that the programs would compete for personnel. Staffers at Head Start centers and other community-based organizations generally received lower wages than public elementary school teachers, and some witnesses worried that these professionals would leave Head Start once they fulfilled Smart Start's training requirements. One witness explained, "As public-funded programs come in, if they act as a drain to teaching staff, it can be a very serious problem in terms of what local communities are sometimes facing."[40] The mobilization of Head Start supporters illustrates how existing arrangements constrained the options of those who favored policy change. Because Head Start was generally viewed as successful, senators emphasized how Smart Start would complement it and facilitate its expansion. They did not want to be perceived as promoting legislation that would potentially lead to its demise.

Finally, the educational community endorsed Smart Start and other early childhood initiatives but was an ambivalent ally. Governor James Blanchard of Michigan, a Democrat, described "elements in the education community that won't support a major, new initiative in preschool until they receive what they feel are an adequate sum of dollars for their programs."[41] Educators worried about possible competition for scarce public funds, and the issue of administrative responsibility also provoked tension. The tension surrounding prime sponsorship had helped derail the comprehensive legislation of the 1970s. Reprising that debate, several witnesses insisted that Smart Start should give school systems the primary responsibility for running early childhood programs. The president of the National Education Association, noting that the schools offered safety, trained personnel, and facilities, argued "that the programs should not duplicate what we are offering in the public schools."[42] Albert Shanker of the American Federation of Teachers described prime sponsorship as an area of concern and said that state and local education agencies should be given administrative priority. He argued that "the education community at all levels has the major role to play in a new program such as Smart Start."[43]

Other witnesses were skeptical of ceding too much control to the public schools. They questioned whether public schools provided an appropriate pedagogical environment for young children: "[S]chools have not been known for allowing children a lot of freedom. And young children need that opportunity. . . . [T]hey learn in an active way, not sitting passively behind the desk."[44] The arguments advanced on both sides of the debate reflected tensions within the early childhood policy community. These tensions made coalition formation and maintenance difficult.

In sum, Smart Start's ambitious scope and lack of success resonates with the comprehensive legislation of the 1970s. In the intervening years, however, shifts in the policy and political landscape had created fissures within the early childhood policy community. Representatives of state governments, Head Start, and the educational community appeared before Congress in an attempt to move the legislation in their desired direction, sometimes contradicting one another in the process. They endorsed the general idea of policy change but sought to prevent the creation of new programs that would impinge on their existing prerogatives. The existence of a diverse range of early childhood programs represented a political constraint for those who wanted to alter the status quo. This feedback dynamic made it more difficult to mobilize the support necessary to navigate the legislative process.

The Prekindergarten Early Dropout Intervention Act of 1988

Members of Congress considered several proposals that were less ambitious than Smart Start. Senator Lawton Chiles (D-FL) introduced the Prekindergarten Early Dropout Intervention Act of 1988, which would have authorized grants to local educational agencies, community-based organizations, and nonprofit private organizations that operated early intervention programs for dropout prevention. The main goal of the legislation, according to Chiles, was "to reduce the number of children who later drop out of school by providing high-quality early education which focuses on the development of language and cognitive skills."[45] It would have provided twenty-five million dollars to programs for three- and four-year-olds. The Senate Committee on Labor and Human Resources held a hearing on the bill in May, but the chamber took no further action. Despite its limited legislative progress, the Senate testimony illustrated four important features of the debate over early childhood policy in the late 1980s.

First, early childhood education was increasingly viewed through an economic lens and framed as an investment. Multiple witnesses cited its cost-effectiveness. A major theme of the hearing was that every dollar spent on preschool would pay for itself by reducing long-term spending on various government programs. One witness said of high school dropouts, "Many of these children will, of course, drop out of school, but they will not drop out of our lives. They will linger to haunt our pocketbooks, if not our individual or collective consciences. They will . . . fill our welfare rolls and our jails."[46] An academic researcher claimed that early childhood programs would reduce spending on the criminal justice system, welfare, and special education and would increase the taxable earnings of older youths.[47] Other witnesses cited the results of the Perry Preschool Project and the recent report by the Committee for Economic Development in their calls for massive investments in prekindergarten and child care. Committee chairman Edward Kennedy summarized this line of argument: "We have benefited in recent times from the very convincing evidence that this investment in early intervention—and it is an investment—has enormous potential."[48]

Second, the bill's supporters generally envisioned a circumscribed role for the national government. A representative of the American Federation of Teachers argued that "there is a federal role in providing leadership and support aimed at stimulating additional early childhood education services."[49] Another witness explained, "One of the things that excites me about this bill is that it suggests that state and local agencies really do need to take a very strong role in implementing appropriate programs."[50] Multiple witnesses described the national government as an agenda-setting force that could highlight the significance of early childhood programming or as a potential funding source. Program development was generally viewed as something that was better left to service providers or state and local officials. Kennedy noted that national officials had "a lot to learn from the local experiences," a sentiment that was not expressed during the hearings of the late 1960s and early 1970s.[51] The Prekindergarten Early Dropout Intervention Act envisioned a demonstration project in which the national government would fund local projects and assess them to determine which ones merited expansion. This objective was less ambitious than the goals espoused by Smart Start and the comprehensive legislation of the 1970s.

Third, several witnesses characterized program coordination as crucial in light of the shifting programmatic terrain of early childhood policy. Describing a prekindergarten program in Florida, one witness noted, "Interagency cooperation, with Head Start, Title XX, church and private day care facilities, has improved markedly [and] resulted in joint efforts to improve programs and share information and resources."[52] Other witnesses focused on the need for coordination between prekindergarten and Head Start. Chiles explained, "We see literally jealousies between people who are involved in Head Start and the educators on the other side, and many times there are overlapping bureaucracies and jurisdictions."[53] A representative of the American Federation of Teachers expressed concern "about the relationship between these programs, Head Start, and other existing early childhood programs."[54] A witness representing the American Association of School Administrators (AASA) was blunter: "AASA does not believe it is necessary to create a new early childhood educational structure. Existing programs should be supplemented, not supplanted."[55] This testimony suggests that existing stakeholders viewed the creation of new programs as potentially threatening. Program coordination was not only a bureaucratic problem to be addressed during implementation. It also represented a political hurdle to policy change. Existing providers wanted to expand access to preschool services but were wary of new programs that might encroach on what they perceived to be their turf.

Fourth, the question of service delivery continued to divide the early childhood policy community. Given the incremental nature of the measure being discussed, it is especially striking that witnesses zeroed in on the issue of administrative responsibility. The Prekindergarten Early Dropout Intervention Act would have enabled community-based organizations and other nonprofit organizations to receive grants for early childhood education, and the educational community reacted warily. Noting that the proposal called for local matches and additional resources, they argued that local educational agencies possessed financial resources that they could dedicate to early childhood programs. A representative of the

American Federation of Teachers argued, "We believe that at the local level the mechanism for choosing the administering agency should emphasize the local education agency exclusively."[56] The AASA representative said, "We maintain that governance should be in the hands of local school boards where early childhood programs are provided."[57] Head Start centers, community-based organizations, and other providers found such proclamations troubling. Even in the context of incremental reform, the question of service delivery generated open hostility among different constituencies in the early childhood policy community.

Summary: The Changing Congressional Politics of Early Childhood Policy

The 1980s were a difficult period for advocates of a more expansive role for the national government in early childhood policy. Both comprehensive and incremental proposals failed to make much legislative progress. It was a decade "when all social service programs in this country were cut and were at risk."[58] Retrenchment replaced expansion as the overarching goal of policy change, and defenders of programs like Head Start focused on consolidating their earlier gains.

By the late 1980s, the rhetoric and the politics of early childhood policy had changed significantly. Supporters increasingly portrayed program expansion as a cost-effective long-term investment as they lobbied for a relatively circumscribed role for the national government. Changes in the political terrain were even more important than these rhetorical shifts. In the years since Nixon's veto, constituencies including the public schools, Head Start centers, and private service providers had developed stakes in this policy arena. They mobilized to defend their prerogatives whenever Congress considered changes to the status quo. Intramural squabbles within the early childhood policy community emerged in the context of both ambitious legislation, such as Smart Start, and incremental proposals, such as the Prekindergarten Early Dropout Intervention Act of 1988. While they were not the only factor that caused these bills and others like them to make limited progress, they represented a significant hurdle to policy change.

While major legislative proposals languished, the tax code continued to evolve in significant ways.[59] By the end of the 1980s, the child and dependent care credit amounted to 30 percent of qualifying expenses for those with adjusted gross incomes of ten thousand dollars or less. The credit amount then fell by a percentage point for each two thousand dollars of adjusted gross income over ten thousand dollars, until it bottomed out at 20 percent for taxpayers with adjusted gross incomes greater than twenty-eight thousand dollars. The maximum amount of qualifying expenses to which the credit could be applied was twenty-four hundred dollars if one child was involved and forty-eight hundred dollars if two or more children were eligible. The maximum credit ranged from $480 to $720 annually for taxpayers with one eligible child and from $960 to $1,440 for taxpayers with two or more eligible children.[60] In the eyes of its supporters, the tax credit facilitated parental choice and enabled various nongovernmental providers to deliver the desired services. It facilitated "a healthy pluralism of child care providers [and did] not create a monopolistic bureaucratic system."[61]

The political dynamics surrounding early childhood policy in the late 1980s illustrate the constraining effect of the existing policy repertoire.[62] Such stakeholders as state government officials, Head Start supporters, and the operators of public- and private-sector programs repeatedly told national lawmakers that they should build on the existing system. Testifying in 1990, the president of the California Child Care Resource and Referral Network asked Congress to "use our experience and our knowledge [and] learn from our mistakes and successes. We implore you to build on what we've got in California, and now elsewhere in the country; that you will build on a model that works."[63] This type of lobbying effort was not unique to the early childhood policy community. In the early 1980s, one study of American education policy noted that a "major effect of federal [education] policy has been, for better or worse, to establish certain dependencies, interest group structures, and action channels across local, state, and federal levels" (Elmore and McLaughlin 1983, 320). In the context of early childhood education, these developments contributed to the fragmentation of a potential coalition supporting major policy change. Constituencies that agreed on the desirability of program expansion failed to coalesce around a specific proposal, in part because they viewed the creation of new programs as a political threat. Moving the issue onto the congressional agenda proved significantly easier than did altering the status quo.

The Education Reform Movement and Early Childhood Policy in the States

The contours of education policy shifted dramatically during the 1980s, especially in terms of intergovernmental relations. Organizations of local administrators, teachers, and school board members had traditionally dominated education policymaking, with state governments concentrating on such tasks as enforcing minimum standards for teachers and facilities. The 1980s, however, were a period of centralization during which state governments exercised considerable authority. This shift "was led by a 'new breed' of governors who became far more involved in shaping local education policy than in years past" (Fusarelli 2002, 140; see also Wong 2008). Inspired by several critical studies of American public education, including *A Nation at Risk,* many of them made education their top legislative priority.

The need for reform was often portrayed as an economic necessity during an era of rapid globalization. Governors and other state officials argued that stronger schools would attract businesses and jobs, because they believed that businesses valued educational systems that produced well-trained workers and provided quality schools for employees' families. An economic recession and fear of increased economic competition from such countries as Japan contributed to the appeal of education reform, especially, but not only, in southern states (McDermott 2011). For example, the Education Commission of the States proclaimed, "Increasing economic competitiveness from foreign countries has stirred interest in greater *productivity* and in *talent development.* . . . International competition requires higher achievement for all students."[64] More-demanding school curriculums, stricter requirements for teachers, minimum competency tests for high school graduation, and a variety of other reforms were portrayed as ways to compete in the global economy. This "new politics of education productivity" affected how people discussed education reform and their perceptions of what was at stake (Cibulka 2001).

Two important political shifts accompanied the emergence of education reform as an electoral issue. The first shift was the heightened involvement of the business community. Many business leaders felt a strong stake in education reform and made a concerted effort to set the political agenda and influence policy decisions. The second shift was the more prominent role of national organizations and networks. The Education Commission of the States, the National Conference of State Legislatures, the Council of Chief State School Officers, and the National Governors Association all accelerated their education policy activities during the 1980s (Mazzoni 1995). Their involvement meant that even though many important policy changes occurred at the state level, "a national discussion shaped the way the problem was framed and the specific solutions were advocated" (Cibulka 2001, 25). Beginning in the early 1980s, the influence of national and international forces grew considerably (Mazzoni 1993).

The primary impact of the education reform movement was felt at the elementary and secondary levels, but it also aroused interest in early childhood education. The imposition of more-stringent standards generated a need for more remedial programs and a rationale for compensatory pre-kindergarten programs. The results of the Perry Preschool Program reinforced this rationale by suggesting that low-income and disadvantaged children would benefit from early childhood education (Grubb 1987, 19).[65] In combination with the growing prevalence of working mothers and an emerging emphasis on moving welfare recipients into the workforce, the education reform movement placed early childhood policy on the political agenda.

At least eleven states enacted some form of early childhood education between 1979 and 1987, and others used existing school-aid mechanisms to fund such programs in the schools. Several states formed commissions to study the options available to them (Grubb 1987, 1). It is important not to overstate the importance of these early childhood initiatives, however. They were generally limited in scope. Beginning in 1984, for example, school districts in Minnesota offered its Early Childhood Family Education program to all families with children under age five. The program included parent discussion groups, home visits, parent-child activities, health and developmental screenings for children, and information about community services. In 1984, all school districts in Missouri were required to offer similar services through the state's Parents as Teachers program. Arkansas created the Home Instruction Program for Preschool Youngsters in 1986. It offered home visits from paraprofessionals and group activities for the parents of at-risk four- and five-year-olds.[66] Supporters of greater public investment praised these initiatives but noted that they fell far short of a comprehensive approach.

Several factors prevented the adoption of more-expansive programs, including their potential cost. Such exemplary initiatives as the Perry Preschool Program had high operating costs because they exhibited high adult-child ratios and employed staff with strong educational credentials. Policymakers therefore faced a trade-off between cost and quality: the most beneficial early childhood programs were likely to be very expensive. With finite resources, officials knew that high-quality programs would not be able to reach all of the young children who would potentially benefit. Universal, high-quality programs were not financially feasible. State programs varied their services, operating hours, staff salaries, and other features in order to accommodate these fiscal realities (Grubb 1987).

Divisions within the early childhood community represented a second obstacle to a more expansive approach. Diverse groups lobbied for expanded access and funding, but they remained wary of one another. For example, virtually every major professional organization affiliated with the public schools endorsed universal schooling for four-year-olds, but their endorsements generated limited enthusiasm from groups representing child care providers and minority children. The National Association for the Education of Young Children and the National Black Child Development Institute believed that traditional child care was incompatible with traditional kindergarten or first-grade education and felt that programs serving preschoolers should not fall under the aegis of the public school bureaucracy (McGill-Franzen 1993, 8). Educators downplayed the developmental content of early childhood programs, and early childhood professionals argued that the schools were too rigid and didactic to serve a younger constituency. This split led one observer to claim that "the real question for future policy is not whether these differences exist, but whether they can be contained and narrowed—whether educators and early childhood advocates can reach some compromise" (Grubb 1987, 29). Differences in teaching philosophies contributed to turf battles that prevented the supporters of expanded preschool services from organizing themselves into a unified and effective political force.

In September 1989, the early childhood community received a boost when President George H. W. Bush called a meeting with the nation's governors to develop a plan to improve public education. The president, members of his cabinet, and the governors addressed several topics as they met for two days at the University of Virginia. Before the summit, the president of the Education Commission of the States described early childhood education as a potential discussion topic. He hoped that the summit would reset and refocus federal spending on early childhood and clarify the roles of the states and the national government. He argued that the "federal government must get its act together since multiple departments presently have differing approaches."[67] The executive director of the National Association of State Boards of Education said, "We are especially excited about the focus on goals for the nation and the states, and the attention given to early childhood education."[68]

As the summit concluded, President Bush and the governors issued a joint statement in which they committed themselves to developing a defined set of national education goals, to building a federal-state partnership based on flexibility and accountability, and to restructuring education in all states. The statement highlighted early childhood education at several points. The "readiness of children to start school" was the first item listed in its section on performance goals. The financial role of the national government was "to promote national education equity by helping our poor children get off to a good start in school." The statement urged that "priority for any further funding increases be given to prepare young children to succeed in school."[69] The education summit, which drew significant publicity as only the third time in American history that the president called a meeting with the governors to discuss a single major issue, devoted considerable attention to school readiness and, by extension, to early childhood policy.[70]

In sum, many states attempted to increase the number of children enrolled in early childhood programs during the 1980s and early 1990s. They funded prekindergarten programs, supplemented Head Start, or did both. The number of states providing education-related services to prekindergarten-aged children nearly tripled from 1979 to the early 1990s.[71] Policy initiatives for three- and/or four-year-olds were endorsed by education commissioners and gubernatorial panels in such geographically and politically diverse states as California, Connecticut, Kentucky, Massachusetts, Michigan, New York, North Carolina, and South Carolina (McGill-Franzen 1993, 4–5).

Even after this period of activity, however, the reach of state early childhood education programs remained limited. By the mid-1990s, twenty-five states funded their own programs, five supplemented Head Start, and nine did both. Most state-funded prekindergarten programs reached a limited clientele. The Arkansas Better Chance program, for example, served at-risk or poor three- to five-year-olds. Michigan spent $42.6 million to support school districts operating comprehensive compensatory education programs for educationally disadvantaged four-year-olds in 1994–95. In 1993–94, Oregon spent $24.5 million to support the needs of low-income three- and four-year-olds, early childhood special education services, and preschool children with disabilities. In most states where such services were offered, spending on prekindergarten programs represented 2 percent or less of total state school aid.[72] Nationwide, publicly sponsored programs served only 8 percent of the approximately eleven million American children who attended preschools or some form of child care facility.[73]

Conclusion: Policy Stability and Political Change

For the most part, the 1980s were a period of limited policy change. Many congressional initiatives were considered but ultimately rejected, and the state programs that gained enactment were mostly targeted programs that were narrow in scope. The most significant shifts in early childhood policy had to do with the political dynamics surrounding the issue. More constituencies viewed themselves as stakeholders, and they mobilized both to voice their support for increased public investment and to protect their existing prerogatives. As the episodes profiled in this chapter make clear, it became increasingly difficult to construct a coherent coalition supporting major policy change. The political landscape began to shift in the late 1980s and early 1990s, however. The education summit drew heightened attention to the issue of school readiness, and a handful of developments at the state level suggested that more-profound changes might be in the offing.

7 | The Congressional Heritage of a Critical Juncture

During the past fifteen years, national and state officials have devoted substantial attention to early childhood policy. After chronicling the demographic, intellectual, and political forces that returned the issue to the political agenda, this chapter focuses on the congressional developments of the late 1990s and early 2000s. During the last two decades, Congress has held many hearings on early childhood policy and considered numerous legislative proposals. Its activity resulted in limited policy change, however, and evinced little interest in an expanded role for the national government.

The primary focus of contemporary congressional discussions illustrates how the legacy of previous policy decisions constrains the options available to reformers. Instead of recapitulating the debate over comprehensive programs, Congress paid more attention to program coordination. The creation and expansion of early childhood programs at the state and national levels led to concerns about duplication and inefficiency. Program coordination not only invoked administrative concerns. It also reflected the political challenges involved in altering existing arrangements. Governors and state officials, Head Start supporters, and various educational and professional associations viewed themselves as having a stake in the education and care of young children.

These constituencies agreed on the merits of investing additional public resources, portraying additional spending as a cost-effective investment in the country's future. They also agreed that national lawmakers should build on existing programs rather than implementing new initiatives. Each of them had programmatic turf to defend, however, and they reacted warily to proposals they perceived as encroaching on their prerogatives. As a result, translating increased interest in early childhood into concrete policy change proved difficult. Even when the different groups agreed that changes were desirable, they could not agree on the form those changes should take.

Increased Interest in Early Childhood Education

Early childhood policy gained heightened prominence in the late 1990s. Scholars attributed this "surge of interest" to such forces as female employment patterns, neuroscience research, and a political emphasis on school readiness (Clifford et al. 2005, 127). In some ways, these forces were analogous to the demographic, intellectual, and political factors that placed early childhood policy on the national political agenda in the 1960s. Indeed, the rhetoric used to justify attention to this policy arena resonated with the claims of an earlier era.

Changes in the American workforce contributed to the renewed interest in early childhood policy. The percentage of mothers working outside the home rose sharply between the Second World War and 1970, and this trend continued for the next quarter century. By 2000, 53 percent of married mothers with infants, 59 percent of unmarried mothers with infants, and more than 60 percent of mothers with children under age three were in the labor force.[1] Supporters of government intervention argued that officials should accommodate this trend rather than debating its desirability. One report explained, "These changes are unlikely to be temporary shifts in social and economic patterns. . . . Employed parents, and young children needing high-quality early care and education options, are a fact of life in today's world."[2] Labor force participation patterns were described as one of the "contemporary realities" that justified doing more for young children than American society had done in the past.[3] They did not necessitate a specific course of action but "generate[d] pressure for schools to deal with day care, early childhood education, after-school care and proposals for new school calendars."[4]

Intellectual trends also contributed to the renewed interest in early childhood policy. In the late 1990s, supporters of program expansion invoked neuroscience research to make the case for additional public investment. They argued, "A steadily growing body of scientific evidence [suggests] that the quality of young children's environment and social experience lays the groundwork for success in school and has a decisive impact on children's lives."[5] It was discovered that the fetal brain begins early in pregnancy to form the trillions of brain cell connections it will use during its lifetime. This rapid development continues through a child's early years and does not begin to taper off until around age eleven. The plasticity of the brain meant that early positive experiences could help facilitate future learning and cognition. Negative environments would have the opposite effect, but their impact could be mitigated if such conditions were reversed.[6] Scientists found that "countless potential connections may wither away or never form at all" without a healthy prenatal environment and appropriate sensory input starting at birth.[7] One supporter concluded, "The brain, that great plastic vessel of expanding knowledge, is a wondrous device that undergoes exponential growth in the earliest years at a rate unequalled at any later age. Opportunities not exploited during the preschool years may be lost forever" (Maeroff 2006, 36–37). This melodramatic language was fairly common.

By emphasizing the significance of a nurturing and stimulating environment during the early years and suggesting that the absence of such an environment would produce "long-term costs to children and society,"[8] neuroscience research provided preschool supporters with another item for their rhetorical tool kit. To them, the research findings "looked like nuggets of pure gold" (Kirp 2007, 100). They argued that custodial programs were insufficient to facilitate brain development and that only educational programs would have a positive impact. Thus intellectual forces played a crucial role in raising the public profile of early childhood policy. One scholar describes a "near-consensus that the academic research on brain development in infants has been enormously influential at focusing attention on the importance of a child's experiences in the early years on subsequent development" (L. White 2004, 670).

The education reform movement and the related emphasis on "school readiness" increased the prominence of the economic rationale for investing in early childhood initiatives. Proponents argued that the long-term benefits individuals gained by attending a high-quality preschool program redounded to society as a whole in terms of reduced spending on welfare and criminal justice programs and the existence of a well-trained workforce that was better able to compete in the global economy. Some economists portrayed high-quality early childhood education as a smart public investment that would produce a strong return. Their findings enabled preschool supporters to "appeal directly to pocketbook interests" (Kirp 2007, 92). For example, New York lieutenant governor Betsy McCaughey Ross argued that an expansion of prekindergarten would lead to reduced state spending on special education.[9] Arguments about the cost-effectiveness of preschool were common by the late 1990s.

Indeed, advocates focused intensely on the economic benefits of early childhood spending.[10] They argued that preschool attendance would help ameliorate disparities in school readiness among children of different ethnicities and socioeconomic statuses and that children who entered kindergarten "ready to learn" would be less likely to need remedial services. Supporters cited the North Carolina Abecedarian Project, the Perry Preschool Project, and the Chicago Child-Parent Centers as examples of cost-effective preschool programs. Colorado governor Roy Romer, a Democrat, explained that he had "become increasingly convinced that the early childhood years represent a significant opportunity to implement public policy actions that can help us address some of our most pressing social problems—school dropouts, welfare dependence, crime and youth violence."[11] Many preschool supporters shared his views.

Early Childhood Policy in the 1990s: Heightened Salience but Limited Change

The demographic, intellectual, and political forces described in the preceding section helped place early childhood policy on the national political agenda in the 1990s. Despite heightened interest in the topic and the inauguration of President Bill Clinton, the nation's first Democratic chief executive in more than a decade, no major shifts in national policy occurred. The Clinton administration "strongly support[ed] early childhood intervention strategies" (Wong 1995, 30). It "placed a high priority on steady increases in early childhood funding."[12] Its most important programmatic innovation was Early Head Start, a federally funded community-based program for low-income pregnant women and families with infants and toddlers. Secretary of Health and Human Services Donna Shalala formed an advisory committee in 1994 to design Early Head Start, which "evolved out of Head Start's long history of providing services to infants and toddlers."[13] The program served children under the age of three and represented an extension of what already existed, rather than a new policy direction. The creation of Early Head Start epitomized the trajectory of early childhood policy during an era of heightened political salience but incremental policy change.

The absence of innovation was not due to a lack of interest. Goals 2000, the 1994 reauthorization of the Elementary and Secondary Education Act, declared that by the year 2000, all children in the United States would enter school ready to learn. Legislators and executive branch officials at the national level concentrated on the relationship between student achievement and what happened before children entered school, leading to a heightened focus on early childhood education. For example, the U.S. commissioner of education statistics described early childhood education as a "critical area of focus."[14] Several corporations expressed an interest in the education of young children. For example, DuPont offered financial incentives to encourage child care programs in Delaware to pursue accreditation through the National Association for the Education of Young Children, because it believed that the existing state licensing requirements were minimal. The corporation hoped that the incentives would "communicate the message that [it] believed in the importance of good-quality care."[15]

In 1997, the White House hosted two conferences on early childhood policy. The first, entitled "What New Research on the Brain Tells Us about Our Youngest Children," focused on recent advances in developmental neuroscience. It sought to bring heightened attention to the educational content of programs serving young children. The second conference was a multidisciplinary, multiday affair that was intended to galvanize nationwide interest in the education and care of young children. It seemed successful initially. According to David Kirp (2007, 150), the conference caused attendees to consider "expanding Early Head Start and Head Start to include working- and middle-class families, or helping parents to become better consumers of child care, or adopting nationwide quality standards, or maybe even enacting a version of the fabled 1971 [Comprehensive] Child Development Act."

It did not take long, however, for this enthusiasm to evaporate. Advocates grew frustrated with the pace of change, arguing that lawmakers had not done nearly enough to pursue their school readiness goals. One activist complained, "It would be as if we had declared our national intent to go to the moon and back in a decade but had not created NASA or a new space center to make sure that it happened."[16] The absence of major new funding or major new programs frustrated those who had expected the 1990s to be a more auspicious era.

Program coordination was a major stumbling block, due to the existing maze of competing programs administered by different agencies at different levels of government. According to the Government Accountability Office, the national government administered approximately ninety early childhood programs through eleven agencies and twenty offices by the late 1990s.[17] In 1997, slightly over half of the federal funds devoted to early childhood were administered by the Department of Health and Human Services, the Treasury Department was responsible for approximately one-fourth of the funds, and the Department of Agriculture and Department of Education were each responsible for about one-tenth of the funds.[18] This extraordinary range did not include the rising number of programs administered by subnational governments. Major programmatic change would therefore require the administrators and constituencies who benefited from existing arrangements to set aside their jurisdictional turf battles and work together. Although many of them acknowledged the desirability of better coordination, they could not agree on how best to achieve this objective.

In 1999, a Senate committee held two days of hearings on program coordination in early childhood education. Senators and witnesses described jurisdictional conflicts among existing programs and lamented their effects. According to Senator Richard Durbin (D-IL), "Some of the agencies involved here and some of the people involved here, despite their best intentions, get caught up in a mind set, a turf battle, jurisdictional problems. . . . That is a recipe for duplication and inefficiency."[19] Senator George Voinovich (R-OH) pointed out that a key hurdle to program coordination was the fact that the disparate government agencies involved in early childhood did not share the same goals. For example, the Department of Education prioritized school readiness to a greater extent than did the Department of Health and Human Services.[20] Like his Democratic colleague, Voinovich worried that the multiplicity of existing programs was inefficient. He said, "I cannot believe that out of all of these education programs that we have got up here, there are not some of them that ought to be closed down or, in the alternative, the money that is being spent could be better allocated into something that is going to provide a better return in terms of investment."[21] It was easier to draw rhetorical attention to the shortcomings of the status quo, however, than it was to address them.

The relationship between Head Start and other early childhood programs drew special scrutiny. A representative of the Department of Education described the challenges involved in coordinating Head Start and the Child Care and Development Block Grant. She explained, "A lot of our work . . . is about how to work with both communities and states in building partnerships across those two pieces."[22] Successful collaborations had occurred in some states. Voinovich described how the expansion of Head Start in Ohio was made possible by locating Head Start centers and child care programs "at the same place so you do not duplicate the physical facilities."[23] The sharing of facilities represented a basic form of coordination, however, and most observers hoped for more-extensive collaboration.

The relationship between Head Start and the public school system also received substantial attention. Tensions between these two constituencies dated at least to the mid-1970s, when the American Federation of Teachers proposed a universal system of preschool run under the auspices of the public schools. Head Start supporters were wary of this administrative prescription and worried that the schools would not offer developmentally appropriate programming. This disagreement represented a crucial hurdle to program coordination and arose repeatedly in the late 1990s. Durbin asked witnesses to discuss "this whole question of whether or not integrating [Head Start] into the school system is really putting a clash between two cultures that have been created over the last three decades."[24] Many witnesses provided anecdotal examples of collaboration and suggested that the two constituencies were taking steps to confront the issue. They nevertheless acknowledged that significant gaps remained and that more work needed to be done. One witness pointed out that Head Start leaders tended to view themselves as offering a comprehensive child development program that included educational services, whereas school leaders tended to view themselves as part of the educational system.[25]

The hearings focused on program coordination at the national level, but several witnesses claimed that the issue was also relevant in the states. Senator John Edwards (D-NC) explained, "I have been in a bunch of Head Start centers, and I have been in a lot of Smart Start centers, and I had this visceral reaction that there is very little coordination."[26] He was troubled by program overlap and service gaps, and his observations are especially striking because the state-level Smart Start program to which he referred was often portrayed as exemplary. Coordination across government levels was a related issue. One Department of Education official explained that her agency wanted to help states and local communities provide high-quality early childhood education. When she convened meetings with various stakeholders, however, she often found that they were suspicious of one another: "There was a lot of discomfort initially. People [felt] they were going to lose their identity and might even lose their funding."[27] Taking the time to overcome these initial suspicions was essential because "the personal relationships really matter in order to get past the turf battles and the other obstacles. People need to know each other and be able to pick up the phone to talk to each other."[28] Systematically addressing the shortcomings of the status quo proved difficult despite this heightened emphasis on program coordination.

In sum, a supportive presidential administration and multiple conferences on early childhood education produced minimal policy change at the national level. A crucial obstacle to more-encompassing changes was the difficulty of bringing together a unified supporting coalition. The programmatic fragmentation that characterized early childhood policy meant that multiple stakeholders had turf to protect. They reacted warily to proposals to change the status quo (even if these proposals sought only to coordinate existing programs), because they feared that change would negatively affect their administrative prerogatives or their budgets. Fragmentation among the early childhood policy community was not, of course, the only obstacle to major policy change. The Republicans who took over both houses of Congress after the 1994 midterm elections viewed the retrenchment of government programs as a top objective. It is therefore revealing that similar issues emerged as stumbling blocks once Republicans controlled Congress and the presidency in the early 2000s.

Early Childhood Programs and the Presidency of George W. Bush

By the early 2000s, there was bipartisan agreement that early childhood programs merited increased public investment. Democrats and Republicans pointed to neuroscience research suggesting the long-term significance of children's experiences before the age of five and agreed, in broad terms, about its policy implications. At a February 2002 hearing on early childhood education, Senator Christopher Dodd (D-CT) asserted, "We are no longer arguing about the science of this. . . . As far as I am concerned, that debate is over with."[29] An exchange between conservative Republican Christopher Bond (R-MO) and liberal director Rob Reiner encapsulated the emerging consensus about the need for greater government involvement. As the hearing concluded, Bond acknowledged its consensual tone, "I mentioned to Rob Reiner that it is unfortunate that we agree on everything, because this place thrives on controversy. . . . If there is not a fight, it does not get covered, and I do not see anybody picking any fights today."[30]

This emerging consensus did not lead to major policy changes, however. Republicans and Democrats focused on different dimensions of reform, and activists and other stakeholders offered their own policy prescriptions that rarely matched those of the officeholders they lobbied. During the presidency of George W. Bush, Congress held numerous hearings on early childhood policy. The hearings focused on school readiness, cognitive development, public-private partnerships, preschool access, program quality, and other issues. Most participants agreed that policy change was desirable, but they disagreed on the proper course of action.

Two issues proved especially controversial. First, the proposals of the early 2000s reignited the long-standing debate over the appropriate educational content of programs for children under five. Several initiatives emphasized early literacy and were criticized for neglecting other dimensions of child development. A second divisive issue concerned the appropriate way to address program fragmentation. There was nearly unanimous agreement that the existing system was fragmented and that such fragmentation was counterproductive, but proposals to integrate services aroused the suspicions of existing stakeholders.

Cognitive Development and Early Childhood Education

The signature education initiative of the early 2000s was the No Child Left Behind Act (NCLB). The central pillar of NCLB was accountability, which it sought to achieve through an extensive system of testing and a requirement that all schools, districts, and states make annual progress toward the goal of bringing all their students at least to "academic proficiency" by the end of the 2013–14 school year.[31] Although NCLB focused on elementary and secondary education, it had ramifications for early childhood policy because some members of Congress viewed its application to preschool education as a logical extension.

Two other features of NCLB were relevant to early childhood policy. The first, the Early Childhood Educator Professional Development Program, provided competitive grants to partnerships providing high-quality professional development to early childhood educators working with children from birth through kindergarten entry who came from low-income families in high-need communities. The second, Early Reading First, sought to enable children to start school with the skills they needed to become proficient readers. Early Reading First targeted children from low-income families and awarded grants directly to a variety of early learning programs, including Head Start and private child care providers.[32]

Shortly after signing NCLB into law in early 2002, President Bush launched his initiative Good Start, Grow Smart. This proposal sought to strengthen the academic focus of Head Start programs, encourage states to develop quality criteria for early childhood programs that were aligned with their K–12 standards, and expand research into effective prereading and language curricula and teaching strategies. One administration official explained, "The goal is to use the findings of scientifically-based research, particularly in the area of reading, to strengthen the education component of federal early childhood programs so that such programs effectively help prepare children for success in school."[33] With its focus on early literacy, the goals of Good Start, Grow Smart resonated with those of NCLB.

Even before the launch of Good Start, Grow Smart, the Bush administration had evinced a preference for programs that prioritized cognitive development. In February 2001, First Lady Laura Bush unveiled an initiative called Ready to Read, Ready to Learn, which "helped put early learning into the national spotlight."[34] Its two main goals were "first, to ensure that all young children are ready to read and learn when they enter their first classroom; and second, to help our Nation recruit the best and the brightest to become teachers, especially in classrooms in our most impoverished neighborhoods."[35] Reading skills and teacher recruitment would play prominent roles during subsequent congressional discussions. During the summer of 2001, the White House brought together hundreds of educators, researchers, librarians, business leaders, and federal officials for the Summit on Early Childhood Cognitive Development. At the summit, the administration announced the formation of an interagency task force "that will work to determine the best ways to ensure young children enter school ready to learn," and the secretary of education announced a plan to overhaul Head Start by placing a heightened emphasis on the development of literacy and prereading skills.[36] These diverse initiatives shared a focus on early literacy.

Critics of the administration's initiatives asserted that early childhood programs should pursue broader objectives. They favored a "whole child" approach that incorporated social and emotional development in addition to prereading skills. Edward Zigler explained, "If we want a nation of readers, we have to look beyond teaching phonics. We have to look at the whole child, the parents, and at all of the people and experiences that make up the child's early learning environment."[37] Another congressional witness made a similar appeal. He noted that behavioral problems compromised the learning of many young children and argued, "If we really want to enhance children's readiness for school, then we must pay as much attention to the development of their social and emotional competence as we do to their cognitive and linguistic abilities. . . . Knowing the alphabet on your first day of school is not enough if you can't sit still or control your temper in the classroom."[38]

Critics did not dispute the significance of cognitive development but argued that focusing exclusively on literacy would be myopic if programs did not address children's physical, social, and emotional development. Others worried that the accountability provisions of NCLB would trickle down to preschool-aged children and claimed that such testing would be counterproductive. One critic claimed, "People worry for good reason about subjecting children to experiences that really could be harmful and certainly would not enhance their cognitive development."[39]

The disagreement about the appropriate educational content of early childhood programs recapitulated a long-standing controversy about what such programs should accomplish. Some viewed them as custodial programs designed to assist working parents, while others viewed them as a means of facilitating child development. Even popular programs like Head Start were affected by this ongoing debate. In 2003, the Bush administration introduced a standardized assessment that was to be given to all Head Start students twice a year. Early childhood experts contended that the test was an inappropriate tool and would produce data of questionable usefulness due to its focus on letter, number, and word recognition. Congress ultimately halted the test in 2007 (E. Rose 2010, 206).

Head Start supporters frequently reminded other interested parties that the program pursued nutritional, social, and other goals in addition to its educational objectives. During a hearing on the appropriate role of the national government in early childhood education and care, Christopher Dodd noted that the balance between developmental and other goals varied across existing programs. He lamented that developmental standards had not been included in the Child Care and Development Block Grant program, explaining that "any effort we made to set additional developmental standards or qualities that teachers ought to have and so forth . . . was vehemently opposed at the time and has been over the years."[40] His observations highlighted how long-standing divides within this policy arena had hardened over time, making policy change even more difficult. Those with a stake in the status quo viewed potential changes with suspicion, a feedback dynamic that affected the reauthorization of Head Start.

Program Coordination, Block Grants, and Head Start

By the early 2000s, Democrats and Republicans agreed that program fragmentation represented one of the most glaring deficiencies of the status quo. The gradual evolution of early childhood policy had created a plethora of funding streams and programs, many of which served narrow constituencies. Senator James Jeffords (I-VT) explained, "Currently, parents must work through a maze of programs and an array of funding streams to learn about or gain access to quality early care and education programs. And, what we don't need is another narrowly tailored program which only addresses the needs of a few and provides few dollars."[41] Many congressional witnesses used similar language as they lamented this fragmentation. Rob Reiner described the existing system as a "haphazard, underfunded, incoherent approach that does not meet the needs of this vast majority of our nation's youngest children."[42] Edward Zigler said that the "variable quality and persistent fragmentation [of existing programs] result in a confusing array of services for families, marked inefficiencies in the use of public and private resources, a difficult environment for assuring accountability and assessing impacts, and significant inequalities in access to programs that are most effective."[43] Program fragmentation, in sum, contributed to an inefficient use of societal resources and an uneven playing field for young children. The issue elicited sufficient concern that a House subcommittee held a hearing in April 2005 on "improvement through integration." Witnesses from Georgia, Oklahoma, New Jersey, North Carolina, and elsewhere talked about collaborative efforts in their respective states, focusing primarily on the relationship between Head Start and other programs.

Program coordination was thought to be particularly problematic in the context of Head Start. When it was created in 1965, Head Start represented the only opportunity for many disadvantaged children and families to receive developmental services. By the turn of the twenty-first century, however, several national and state programs were pursuing similar goals. The programs evolved along separate tracks, with only "minimal formal coordination of efforts across child care, early intervention of services of children with disabilities, and preschool programs with Head Start."[44] Many observers, worried that the proliferation of early childhood programs was leading to inefficiencies, argued that coordinating or possibly integrating these programs was desirable. Such integration was difficult to achieve, because the programs operated by different, sometimes incompatible, rules. For example, the eligibility cutoff for Head Start was lower than that of every federal and state-funded child care program and many state prekindergarten programs. This variation made it "challenging to bring together children in the same classroom."[45]

In many states, Head Start and public prekindergarten programs had different governance structures. In Georgia, Head Start was "governed by a local entity, policy councils, and board of directors whereby parents take a very active role in the governance of the program. [The] Georgia Pre-K Program is governed on the state level, through contractual agreements with [its] providers."[46] Governance structures affected jurisdiction over programs, implicitly invoking the prime sponsorship debate that remained controversial. Local Head Start leaders were wary of ceding to state governments the authority they had traditionally exercised. One practitioner explained, "One of the strengths of Head Start . . . is its local autonomy, and in some instances that very strength becomes an impediment to collaboration and coordination, because local programs do not have to do that if they choose not to."[47] Many Head Start supporters viewed collaboration as undesirable.

In addition, Head Start and other early childhood programs sometimes viewed one another as competitors for scarce resources and staff. In the early 2000s, there was a concerted effort to increase the number of college graduates in Head Start classrooms. Supporters of more-stringent degree and certification requirements, including the Children's Defense Fund, the National Association for the Education of Young Children, and the National Institute for Early Education Research,[48] said that such requirements would "dramatically improve cognitive development, language, prereading, and premathematical skills in our young children as well as their social skills and emotional well-being."[49] Skeptics worried that individuals with bachelor's degrees and specialized training in early childhood would move to public school kindergartens where they could earn approximately twice as much[50] and receive benefits that private Head Start providers typically could not afford.[51] One member of Congress asked, "How is Head Start going to compete? . . . As you get to those economically competitive requirements, it is going to be more difficult for Head Start groups who are running the programs."[52] Without more-effective coordination, additional funding for Head Start, or another solution, critics worried that raising the educational credentials of Head Start staffers would have negative consequences.

The debate over program integration came to a head with the introduction of the School Readiness Act of 2003, which would have reauthorized Head Start for five years. Bill supporters argued that the legislation built on the "astounding success" of the program,[53] but Head Start supporters were troubled by its attempt at program integration. The main target of their ire was Title II, which allowed states "that have exhibited a substantial dedication to early childhood education and care" to participate in a statewide demonstration program.[54] Advocates of this provision claimed that it would better integrate preschool programs with Head Start and address the problematic patchwork nature of early childhood policy. Representative Michael Castle (R-DE), chair of the House Subcommittee on Education Reform, noted, "By coordinating efforts to recruit children, developing state guidelines for care, aligning school readiness standards with K–12 goals, and other activities, a state can leverage resources to spend funding more efficiently and also serve additional children better."[55] Similarly, the deputy executive director of the Council of Chief State School Officers wrote that a unified statewide effort would assure "greater consistency among programs and the cost benefit of a statewide system."[56] In sum, supporters claimed that the statewide demonstration project would increase the coherence of the existing system and improve program quality.

The Head Start community and its congressional allies, in contrast, viewed Title II as a block grant proposal that would water down or possibly dismantle Head Start. Representative Lynn Woolsey (D-CA) argued that the standards for state participation in the demonstration program were too weak, characterizing Title II as "one huge super waiver of current Head Start law that will weaken and eventually . . . kill Head Start."[57] Critics worried that the legislative language did too little to guarantee that participating states would preserve the quality standards and comprehensive services that made Head Start successful. One witness explained, "There are no guarantees, no requirements for performance standards, no enforcement mechanisms, and no specific minimum standards about classroom size, teacher-student ratio or teacher education."[58] Critics found the absence of such language very troubling.

One potential solution was to require that states meet existing performance requirements in order to receive block grant money. Critics responded that such a requirement would render Title II unnecessary. If the goal of the measure was to build on the successes of Head Start, they argued, why include the block grant proposal? Opponents of the School Readiness Act also worried about how states would use their newfound authority. Their primary concern was financial. Sending unrestricted block grants to the states during an economic crisis made it possible that cash-strapped states would use the funds to address their broader fiscal problems. Critics feared that the quality and comprehensive services of Head Start would be diluted simply because the states could not afford to maintain them.

Supporters of the School Readiness Act denied that it would weaken Head Start. Castle explained, "[T]his should not be taken as a threat or . . . as something which is going to be necessarily detrimental to Head Start. It is an effort to improve Head Start, and I would hope we would all look at it from that point of view."[59] The accusation that the bill would lead to the dismantling of Head Start, defenders claimed, was not consistent with its substance or congressional intent. They pointed out that many states administered early learning standards exceeding those of Head Start, suggesting that Title II "would entrust states to raise the bar for early childhood programs and develop cohesive, rational systems serving their youngest learners."[60] Supporters and opponents of the School Readiness Act viewed it through divergent lenses, and the measure became embroiled in partisan politics. The House eventually passed the bill by a 217–216 vote. All 203 Democrats voted against it and were joined by twelve Republicans and one Independent. The proposal died in the Senate, which took no action on it.

The debate over Title II illustrates the difficulty of reforming the fragmented and decentralized system of early childhood policy. Most observers agreed that better coordination among existing programs was desirable, yet the defenders of individual programs were suspicious of change and jealously guarded their prerogatives. Proponents of the School Readiness Act recognized the need to engage Congress, the executive branch, the states, and "the many other stakeholders in the Head Start program."[61] Their effort to do so was unsuccessful.

In fact, the dispute over the bill generated a minicontroversy about the political activities of the National Head Start Association (NHSA), which opposed Title II. On May 8, 2003, the associate commissioner of the Head Start Bureau sent a letter to all Head Start programs warning them that their "political activities are governed and, in many ways, restricted or limited by Federal law." The letter claimed that an advocacy group, presumably the NHSA, was encouraging programs "to use Head Start program funds and/or staff in a manner that is in direct violation of the laws that govern your political activities."[62] The executive director of the NHSA responded that the letter's legal references and "vague accusation of impropriety have had the effect of chilling the exercise of free speech expression by Head Start programs and their representatives."[63] This heated exchange suggests that both sides recognized the political significance of policy feedback. The mobilization of Head Start supporters like the NHSA represented a hurdle to policy change and helped preserve the status quo.

After the demise of the School Readiness Act, Congress worked on the reauthorization of Head Start for another four years. Program coordination and the removal of barriers to such coordination remained a central issue. In 2005, Castle said, "Head Start should be working toward integrating services with other school readiness programs and not competing against them."[64] His revised proposal, which would have given the states more authority over Head Start, did not gain enactment.[65] President Bush finally signed a Head Start reauthorization measure into law on December 12, 2007. It increased spending for Head Start, expanded eligibility for enrollment, eliminated the controversial standardized test that had been given twice a year to all four- and five-year-old enrollees, and set more-stringent educational credential requirements for Head Start teachers.[66] These changes, while important, left the basic structure of Head Start intact. They did not fundamentally alter the relationship between the program and other early childhood initiatives.

The Obama Administration and Early Childhood Programs

In 2007, Representative Mazie Hirono (D-HI) introduced the Providing Resources Early for Kids (PRE-K) Act. She called it a "federal/state partnership to provide better preschool opportunities for our country's children."[67] Such language would have been unthinkable in the early 1970s, when members of the early childhood policy community wanted to bypass the states completely and often succeeded in doing so. The PRE-K Act directed the secretary of education to award matching grants to states to enhance state-funded preschool programs. The grants would be awarded through a competitive process and could be used to increase the qualifications of and benefits provided to program staff, decrease class sizes and improve teacher-student ratios, provide comprehensive services, and extend program hours per day and weeks per year.

On June 25, 2008, the House Committee on Education and Labor approved the PRE-K Act by a resounding 31–11 margin. Like so many other congressional initiatives, however, it did not become law. Even though 120 members of the House had signed on as cosponsors, the committee vote proved to be the final action taken by that chamber on the proposal.[68] Supporters of a more expansive role for the national government in early childhood policy were unable, once again, to achieve their primary objective.

The presidential election of 2008, however, led many advocates to believe they were on the verge of a major policy breakthrough. After Barack Obama's victory, they were "atremble with anticipation over [his] espousal of early childhood education."[69] The new president had campaigned on a comprehensive platform for early childhood. During the campaign, he pledged to establish a Presidential Early Learning Council to coordinate federal, state, and local policies; to quadruple financing for Early Head Start; to provide challenge grants for states to use for early childhood programs; and to expand home visiting programs for low-income mothers. These initiatives remained a high priority for the administration despite the recession, and opposition to them seemed to be less intense than it had been in the past.[70] Three years later, however, some advocates expressed disappointment. Acknowledging that the Obama administration had launched several relevant initiatives, they wanted it to make early childhood an even higher priority.[71]

The American Recovery and Reinvestment Act (ARRA), popularly known as the "stimulus," included several provisions with implications for early childhood programs. It provided a total of $13 billion in supplemental funding for Title I of the Elementary and Secondary Education Act. Both Congress, in its conference report on the legislation, and the Obama administration, in departmental guidance issued after its passage, encouraged local education agencies to consider using these funds for early childhood programs.[72] The ARRA also included $39.5 billion in state fiscal stabilization funds to support educational programs. The funds supported early childhood, elementary, secondary, and postsecondary education, with the goals of providing fiscal relief and boosting student performance. Departmental guidance mentioned the expansion of early childhood programs and the modernization of early childhood facilities as potential uses for these funds.[73] Head Start and Early Head Start received an additional $1 billion and $1.1 billion respectively for program expansion or enhancement, and the ARRA also included preschool-related supplemental funding to the Individuals with Disabilities Education Act.

These provisions of the ARRA did not launch any groundbreaking initiatives. They simply worked through state governments and local education agencies to provide a boost for existing early childhood programs. Some observers nevertheless viewed this infusion of funds as an opportunity to promote program coordination. A report by the National Conference of State Legislatures explained that the legislation enabled states "to work with additional providers and explore new partnerships to expand services, support providers in meeting Early Head Start standards, or improve quality."[74] It encouraged state officials to leverage ARRA funds to build partnerships with school districts and other service providers. This recommendation implicitly acknowledged the diverse array of stakeholders in early childhood policy and suggested that program coordination remained a central concern.

As part of the ARRA, the Obama administration also launched a competitive grant program entitled Race to the Top. The program featured two grant phases that awarded a total of $4.35 billion in education funding to "reward states that are creating conditions for education innovation and reform; achieving significant improvement in student outcomes, . . . ; and implementing ambitious plans in four core education reform areas."[75] The core reform areas included standards and assessments, data systems, great teachers and leaders, and turning around the lowest performing schools. Race to the Top drew a great deal of interest from state officials. Forty states and the District of Columbia submitted applications for the first phase of the program, and Delaware and Tennessee were each awarded a grant. In August 2010, an additional ten winners were announced in the second phase of the program.

One section of the Race to the Top application was entitled "Innovations for Improving Early Learning Outcomes." States were encouraged to include practices, strategies, or programs that would promote school readiness among at-risk children by improving the quality of their early childhood experiences. This section was an invitational priority, meaning states were encouraged to complete it, but it had no effect on how the applications were scored. Even though it was not a part of the grading structure, most state applications incorporated early childhood education policies and practices.[76] The applications included initiatives to develop early learning standards, align the standards with those for the later grades, and incorporate early education information into longitudinal data systems. Many states mentioned increasing enrollment in or funding for early childhood programs as a way to improve their education systems.[77] Some states also included plans to strengthen professional development.

Program coordination was not a common topic. The District of Columbia proposed "blending Head Start funds and local resources to provide comprehensive programming for all children and their families [as part of an effort to] build a more seamless early childhood program."[78] Although few applications included that sort of structural reform, advocates recognized that several constituencies would be affected by the changes the states proposed. One report urged early childhood advocates to consider how their initiatives would affect the prerogatives of existing stakeholders. It noted that a memorandum of understanding in California provided that prekindergarten quality and expansion efforts would be an allowable district-level expense if the state won a grant award. Other advocates should follow that example, it concluded, and "consider meeting with local education leaders including teachers unions and school district superintendents to solicit their buy-in."[79] The fragmented terrain of early childhood policy made such calculations a practical necessity.

The peripheral role of early childhood education in the Race to the Top program troubled some advocates. In 2011, it was granted a central place in a $500 million round of the contest entitled the Race to the Top–Early Learning Challenge (RTT-ELC). The goal of RTT-ELC, which was described as "the administration's signature early learning reform initiative"[80] and a "historical opportunity to support early learning,"[81] was to support quality enhancements for programs serving high-need children. The competition focused on "improving development standards and assessment, program standards, tiered rating and improvement systems, and early childhood educators."[82] Reprising earlier debates about the role of cognitive development in early childhood programs, critics noted that the initiative did not say "anything about giving children time to creatively explore and learn through play."[83] RTT-ELC nonetheless generated a great deal of interest, as thirty-seven states and territories submitted proposals.

State leaders reacted favorably to the administration's early learning initiative. They believed that it represented an opportunity to build on many of the initiatives profiled in chapter 8 of this book. A letter from several leaders of the National Conference of State Legislatures asked the administration to "use federal funding to expand and supplement existing programs" and to "leave eligibility decisions regarding who is served in early education programs to the states."[84] Increased funding and autonomy are common themes when state officials lobby the national government, yet the letter's tone and content illustrates an important long-term shift in the politics of early childhood policy. Significant state-level activity is a defining feature of the contemporary debate, whereas the states were less powerful stakeholders in the late 1960s and early 1970s.

In December 2011, the White House announced that nine states would receive awards through the grant competition. The RTT-ELC provided financial support for state efforts to "increase access to high-quality programs for children from low-income families, providing more children from birth to age five with a strong foundation they need for success in school and beyond."[85] The grants were important to state officials grappling with a challenging fiscal environment. Like the other early childhood initiatives adopted during the first three years of the Obama administration, however, they left the basic structure of early childhood policy intact. Advocates welcomed increased funding for early childhood initiatives but continued to lament a lack of coordination among existing programs.

Conclusion: The Limited Impact of Increased Congressional Activity

Over the past two decades, members of Congress have held hearings on school readiness, public-private partnerships, program quality and effectiveness, preschool access, and cognitive development. In short, there has been no shortage of congressional activity. This assortment of hearings, however, has produced minimal policy change. Most congressional initiatives have failed to gain enactment, and new programs like Early Head Start essentially built on what already existed. More-innovative programmatic shifts have been stymied repeatedly. The initiatives of the Obama administration made more money available for early childhood programs but did not alter the fragmentation and coordination issues that many observers view as the main weakness of the status quo.

The political terrain on which these recent congressional battles have been fought, however, differs from that of the late 1960s and early 1970s. Earlier generations of reformers operated on something approaching a tabula rasa. When they debated the appropriate role of the national government in early childhood policy, there were few entrenched programs and constituencies whose concerns needed to be addressed. By the 1990s, several constituencies viewed themselves as having a stake in this policy arena and jurisdictional turf to defend. Major policy change required the accommodation of state and local officials, Head Start supporters, and various educational associations who viewed new programs as threats to their authority and their budgets. Nixon's veto and the venue shopping and other reactions it spurred had created a dense thicket of interests and actors through which any reform proposal would have to pass. Even when there was broad agreement about the desirability of change, this fragmentation limited reformers' political prospects. The administrative and political hurdles to major policy shifts were simply too great.

8 | The Contemporary Preschool Movement in the States

During the last two decades, many states have expanded access to and increased public spending on preschool education. Some recent initiatives built on the publicly funded programs that were established during the 1970s, while other states created new programs. One source of heightened state-level activity in the late 1990s and early 2000s was the absence of policy action at the national level and reformers' effort to find a more favorable institutional venue (Bushouse 2009, 8), but the venue shopping of the contemporary period was not a recapitulation of what occurred in the 1970s. Increased enrollment in such government programs as Head Start and in private-sector programs meant that many service providers had a strong stake in the status quo. Policy change required accommodating or at least addressing the concerns of these stakeholders. Some states provided favorable terrain for reformers, while others did not due to the relative political strength of these invested constituencies. This chapter combines secondary evidence, case studies of developments in individual states, and an original quantitative analysis of preschool funding decisions in all fifty states to illustrate how the existing slate of service providers affected early childhood policymaking.

In keeping with a primary theme of this book, the existing policy repertoire constrained reformers' options. Most of the state-level policy shifts of the late 1990s and early 2000s built on or combined existing public and private programs. Accommodating multiple providers was necessary both politically and logistically. It was a political necessity because the early childhood policy community consisted of constituencies who disagreed with one another about the purpose of preschool, teacher certification requirements, program eligibility, and other fundamental issues. Teachers unions, Head Start supporters, private service providers, and other groups advanced competing visions of the future. Some of them viewed expanded public programs as a threat to their survival and lobbied against any proposed changes. As a result, major policy shifts often necessitated granting these groups a continued role in providing early childhood services. Accommodating multiple providers was a logistical necessity because program growth required additional facilities and personnel and a supporting infrastructure. The policy changes of recent years have consequently furthered, not mitigated, the fragmentation of early childhood policy in the United States.

The New Politics of Early Childhood Education

In 1999, the Education Commission of the States asked over three hundred attendees at its annual meeting to identify the most important education issues facing their state. Early childhood ranked tenth, mentioned by only 37 of the 388 respondents to the survey.[1] Things changed very rapidly, however. Governor Jeanne Shaheen (D-NH) made early care and education the focus of her term as chair of the ECS in 2000–2001, and the organization launched a two-year initiative entitled Early Learning: Improving Results for Young Children. The initiative emphasized two aspects of early childhood policy that the ECS believed had received insufficient attention. It sought to engage the business community as a full partner, portraying early learning as an investment in the development of the future workforce, and to establish systematic connections between early learning and elementary education.[2] Each of these goals testified to the increasingly dense array of stakeholders in this policy arena.

The political tactics of the Early Learning initiative resonated with those the ECS pursued in the early 1970s. The organization hoped to have a national impact, but it initially planned "to bring the national dialogue home to 20 or so states . . . by sponsoring workshops designed to jumpstart or accelerate state-level strategy development on early learning."[3] This venue shopping would become more targeted over time, as the ECS hoped to "establish and maintain a longer-term collaborative relationship with three to five states committed to carrying out an ambitious early care and learning agenda."[4] Within a year, the initiative had engaged twenty states through regional workshops and state-specific technical assistance, and it had plans to offer workshops to representatives from all fifty states within months.[5] Thus the Early Learning initiative illustrates both the increased salience of early childhood policy and the significance of venue shopping in facilitating policy change.

The profile of early childhood policy continued to rise in the early 2000s. One sign of its increased prominence was the frequency with which governors mentioned it in their State of the State addresses. For example, sixteen of the forty-four governors who had given their addresses by March 17, 2003, talked about early learning issues. Democrat Janet Napolitano of Arizona said, "The more we learn about the importance of early childhood learning, the more obvious it is that voluntary all-day kindergarten and universal pre-K should be standard offerings in our schools." Democrat Jennifer Granholm of Michigan cited brain development research as she advanced a program called Great Start to increase learning in the years from birth to age five. Democratic governors were especially enthusiastic, but the issue's appeal crossed party lines. For example, Republican Mark Sanford of South Carolina described teacher quality and early childhood education as high-priority areas and promised to ensure that they received an infusion of public funds.[6] Various initiatives launched by officeholders and national organizations produced state-level activity, leading some scholars to identify the emergence of a preschool "movement" by the middle of the decade (Fuller 2007, 5; Kirp 2007, 100).

In terms of its membership and leadership, the contemporary preschool movement bears a superficial resemblance to the child development movement of the late 1960s and early 1970s. Bruce Fuller (2007, 5) describes it as "led by earnest elites who work from within foundation offices, state governments, and universities." There is an element of truth in this portrayal. The David and Lucile Packard Foundation, the Pew Charitable Trusts, and the Schott Foundation for Public Education have actively promoted universal preschool,[7] and policy entrepreneurs in state government have been indispensable to the policy changes of the past decade. Many academic research centers are active in early childhood policy. For example, the National Institute for Early Education Research at Rutgers University publishes research and an annual report card on state preschool programs.

Preschool supporters consciously sought to expand the breadth of their coalition, however. As a result, the contemporary preschool movement includes several constituencies who previously had not been very involved in early childhood policy. Multiple analysts credit the Pew Charitable Trusts with developing this strategy. The foundation recognized that its campaign would achieve minimal results unless it was supported by children's advocacy groups and "unanticipated sources" (Kirp 2007, 161). It therefore cultivated support in the business and law enforcement communities as well as the media, engaging such organizations as the Committee for Economic Development, Fight Crime: Invest in Kids, and the Education Writers Association. Pew "successfully expanded the range of actors advocating for universal preschool" (Bushouse 2009, 116). The inclusion of Fight Crime: Invest in Kids was especially savvy. The organization "predicated its support on statistics showing that children of low economic circumstances who attend pre-K are less likely than peers to become delinquents and engage in antisocial behavior" (Maeroff 2006, 214). As a result, the universal preschool movement has been called "a big-tent coalition [that] includes politicians and pedagogues, philanthropists, pediatricians, and police chiefs" (Kirp 2007, 3).

The main rhetorical claims of the contemporary preschool movement match those of earlier periods. In the early 2000s, supporters of increased public investment cited recent trends in the labor market and the resultant need for early childhood services. They profiled scientific research that seemed to imply that environmental influences in the early years affected long-term cognitive development. They advanced arguments about "school readiness" and educational equity, justifying their position on both moral and cost-effectiveness grounds. Their arguments resonated with those of their predecessors. Despite this rhetorical overlap, however, the tone of the debate shifted in a subtle yet crucial way. The debate of the late 1960s and early 1970s had been about "child development," an umbrella term incorporating educational, nutritional, and other family services. In the late 1980s and early 1990s, the focus had been on child care and its availability. The debate of the early 2000s, in contrast, emphasized the provision of educational services for young children.[8]

Supporters hoped that an educational frame would lead to greater public support. Policymakers and advocacy groups used such terms as *early childhood education and care, early learning and care,* or *educare* to emphasize cognitive development.[9] This rhetorical shift was crucial in the United States, where child care is often viewed as a social welfare issue or a parental responsibility, while education usually connotes a public role and public responsibility (L. White 2004). Surveys suggested that the public viewed early childhood education more positively than child care, leading one scholar to conclude that "promoting early childhood care and education as part of comprehensive education reform efforts is a promising approach" (Beatty 2001, 181). Preschool supporters therefore separated policy for preschool-aged children from policy for infants and toddlers. This split enabled reformers to align preschool with education and to frame it as a program worthy of public investment (Bushouse 2009, 155–56).

Reframing early childhood education was not only important in shifting public attitudes. It also affected policymakers' views. Like the public, policymakers perceived a "big difference between prekindergarten and child care" (Kirp 2007, 137). The former was regarded as preparing young children to succeed in school, and the latter was regarded as not really preparing infants and toddlers for anything. This distinction was not novel. It resonated with the early twentieth-century divide between day nurseries and nursery schools. What differed about the rhetorical shift of the early 2000s was that proponents of increased public investment in early childhood programs generally coalesced around a single issue frame.

Changes in national education policy reinforced the appeal of an education frame. Passage of the No Child Left Behind Act was especially significant even though those involved in the education and care of young children disagreed about its implications. Some early learning professionals viewed NCLB's emphasis on annual assessments with concern. They questioned whether it was possible or desirable to assess preschoolers' progress and worried about "the trickle down of inappropriate testing of young children."[10] In their opinion, assessments promoted an emphasis on academic achievement at the expense of other developmental goals. Standards should therefore "include all of the dimensions of children's development that contribute to their well-being as well as their academic success" (Stipek 2006, 463). They argued that school readiness was best viewed as a multidimensional concept incorporating "language and cognition, social and emotional development, general knowledge, and skill development. [It should] be considered as a process that occurs over time and is not complete by the first day of kindergarten."[11]

Other practitioners, in contrast, viewed NCLB as an opportunity for expanded public support. By tying federal funding to school performance and focusing on educational quality, the legislation "put pressure on state legislatures to ensure that children entering primary school are 'ready to learn' so . . . their test scores do not drag down the school and affect school funding" (L. White 2004, 672). They argued that NCLB reinforced the focus on school readiness that had been part of the debate over early childhood policy since the late 1980s. In addition, some of them claimed that assessments would be useful for "identifying atypical patterns of development that warrant closer scrutiny by educators and parents, determining whether children are learning the content and skills that their district and school have set as goals, and ensuring that the education institution is responsible for its responsibilities."[12] While the early childhood policy community coalesced around an educational frame in its push for program expansion, early childhood specialists and elementary school educators disagreed about the implications of NCLB.

Program cost continued to affect the possibility of major reform. Universal, high-quality programs were costly, and state governments faced significant budget constraints. Many preschool supporters argued that all children needed opportunities to learn, but most state programs were narrowly targeted because universal programs were out of reach financially. For example, California's State Preschool Program enrolled three- and four-year-olds living in families at or below 60–65 percent of the state median income. Four-year-olds who met the Head Start income eligibility standards could participate in Delaware's Early Childhood Assistance Program. The Kentucky Preschool Program was available to four-year-olds who were eligible for free lunch and to all disabled three- and four-year-olds. Seventy percent of the funds for Early Childhood Projects in Nebraska were targeted to serve children eligible for Head Start, those in families with incomes less than 150 percent of the federal poverty line, those born premature or with a low birth weight, and those whose primary language was something other than English.[13] Funding concerns affected eligibility and quality provisions and represented one of policymakers' "key challenges" at both the national and state level (Clifford et al. 2005, 141).

Despite the aforementioned similarities between the universal preschool movement and its predecessors, the debates of the early 2000s occurred on distinct political terrain. The universe of actors who perceived themselves as having a stake in early childhood policy had changed considerably over the years. The debate over universal preschool was not simply a reprise of what had occurred previously. New interest groups and organizations became involved, as has already been discussed, and the positions advanced by some long-term participants shifted in important ways. These political changes represent the state-level heritage of Nixon's veto and the by-product of the reactions and counterreactions it produced. This policy feedback facilitated the development of programs that accommodated multiple providers, adjusting to, rather than addressing, the fragmentation that characterized this policy sector.

Fragmentation, Coordination, and the Politics of Early Childhood Education

By the early 2000s, early childhood policy in the United States had taken on its two most distinctive characteristics. The private sector was a crucial provider of services, and public-sector activity was highly decentralized. Commentators, practitioners, and advocates often described these attributes of the existing system as shortcomings. Preschool education consisted of "a hodgepodge of providers offering uneven services for young children and having no connection to the public education system that children enter at age 5 or 6."[14] One analysis concluded that the "elements of a system are in place, but the pieces are not designed to fit together in a cohesive way."[15] Another described the status quo as a "patchwork of diverse programs, each with its own infrastructure and no overarching policy framework encompassing a whole system of care and education."[16] A complex conglomeration of providers and funding streams existed.

Many reformers argued that the status quo was unacceptable because many American children lacked access to high-quality early childhood programs. They recognized, however, that policy change would require the mobilization of a wide range of constituencies. One report concluded, "Filling the gaps and building a high-quality system of early care and education require the attention, investment, and action of many people—parents and families, business leaders and philanthropists, teachers and preachers, senior citizens and students, media and policymakers."[17] Those who hoped to establish a cohesive system rather than "sprinkling more unconnected programs on the landscape" realized that they needed substantial commitments from the business, political, philanthropic, and faith communities.[18] The inherent difficulty of merging these constituencies into a cohesive coalition was exacerbated by the fact that they lacked a formal, common language to describe their objectives.[19] Diverse terms like *preschool, prekindergarten, nursery school,* and *early care and education* suggested agreement that early childhood programs should feature educational content, but they hinted at more politically significant divisions among potential supporters.

The unsystematic creation and growth of early childhood programs since the 1970s meant that even though reformers agreed on the need for policy change, many of them had a stake in a particular element of the status quo. As a result, it was difficult for them to work together, because they had distinct bureaucratic and programmatic turf to defend. In other words, policy feedback represented a critical obstacle to policy change, because it produced constituencies who mobilized to defend specific programs. When state officials sought to merge existing initiatives into a single program, they often found that "turf battles and different funding sources impede[d] those efforts" (Cohen 2001, 275). Those who agreed that change was desirable advanced different goals and sometimes found themselves in opposition to one another.

The status of Head Start is illustrative. One report on early childhood policy described a "striking disconnect between Head Start, the more general world of early care and learning, and the K–12 education system."[20] Another report noted that such states as Mississippi, Wyoming, and North Dakota lacked state-funded preschool programs but had high enrollments in Head Start and programs for children with disabilities. It seemed to imply the existence of a "crowding out" effect, at least in certain states. For example, it juxtaposed Mississippi and New York. In the former, 35.9 percent of the state's three- and four-year-olds attended a preschool program funded by Head Start or the Individuals with Disabilities Education Act. In New York, a state with a large state preschool program, 35.2 percent of the state's three- and four-year-olds attended a state or federal prekindergarten program.[21] This comparison seemed to suggest that a large Head Start program substituted for a large state preschool program.

The relationship between Head Start and the "more general world of early care and learning" was one of many tensions within the early childhood community. Proponents continued to debate the appropriate role of the public school system. Some warned that "early care and education cannot be constructed as a simple extension of K–12 learning."[22] They claimed that children under the age of five had developmental needs that would not be well served by the public schools and charged that teachers unions were more interested in generating jobs for their members than in providing preschool services. In 2004, for example, the California Teachers Association helped draft a ballot initiative that would have generated $1.5 billion for preschool. It did not consult other preschool operators in the state, so the measure was "widely perceived as a full-employment act for the teachers' union" (Kirp 2007, 211). Eventually the union withdrew its proposal.

The diverse and cross-cutting cleavages involved in early childhood policy led one analysis to conclude, "While nearly every level of government and sector of society has a stake in improving early care and learning, the responsibilities are so fragmented that no single actor holds enough of the levers for change to get it done."[23] The range of interests with a stake in the existing "nonsystem" was an obstacle to governance reform. Constituencies that nominally shared the same objectives regarded reform warily when it seemed likely to move the status quo in a direction that did not suit their interests. Reform advocates recognized that they faced significant hurdles and called for the "transcendence of selfish interests in the higher pursuit of a more integrated system."[24] Policy change required the mobilization of diverse constituencies. Their identities and the prospects for reform "var[ied] from state to state according to the history and political will of each."[25] Despite these formidable obstacles, the early 2000s were a period of significant reform. The most dramatic changes took place in states where officials developed programs that accommodated multiple providers and came to terms with this legacy of fragmentation.

Overcoming the Obstacles to Reform

Historically, statewide early childhood programs targeted children who were of low socioeconomic status or who were otherwise considered to be "at risk." Beginning in the 1990s, however, states like Georgia and Oklahoma developed programs that allowed children from middle- and upper-income families to receive a free preschool education. Given the historical trajectory of early childhood policy in the United States, the adoption of universal preschool represented a noteworthy shift (Barnett and Hustedt 2003, 54). Many scholars closely examined these state-level episodes of policy change, attempting to understand how the political barriers that had frustrated past reform efforts had been surmounted (Bushouse 2009; Fuller 2007; Kirp 2007; Maeroff 2006; E. Rose 2010). Their case studies suggest that divisions within the early education policy community were a hurdle that could be cleared by designing programs that accommodated multiple providers. Most state-level initiatives built on or combined existing public and private programs.

Incorporating multiple service providers into the expanded state preschool programs was a logistical necessity, because rapid expansion necessitated additional classroom space and teachers and the existence of a supporting infrastructure. Space and personnel constraints in public facilities meant that partnerships with the private sector were the only way that many states could meet their enrollment objectives. Every state subsidizing preschool therefore included such providers as day care centers, licensed family child care homes, faith-based agencies, and private schools. The exact mix varied from state to state, but according to the National Center for Education Statistics, nearly 30 percent of the institutions operating state preschool programs were not affiliated with the public school system as of 2002.[26] Relying on this spectrum of providers led to concerns about uneven program quality and sparked controversy about the importance of teachers' educational credentials.

The rapid expansion of Georgia's ambitious preschool program illustrates the internal tensions among the early childhood community. The program's origins dated to the gubernatorial campaign of Democrat Zell Miller. Miller pledged to create a lottery for education and proposed earmarking some of the funds it generated to preschool. After his election, the idea was endorsed by the state legislature and a citizen referendum. The referendum campaign focused on the lottery itself, with preschool receiving "virtually no attention" (Bushouse 2009, 29).

The Georgia program served nine thousand at-risk children when it opened its doors in September 1993. The number of enrollees doubled in its second year, and forty-five thousand children were signed up in its third year. A key change occurred during its fourth year of operation. All four-year-olds in the state were eligible for enrollment, and sixty thousand of them were signed up to enroll. The rapid expansion of the program spurred the state to incorporate both public and private providers in order to find adequate facilities and qualified teachers. Logistical challenges meant that "the state needed [private providers] to make the experiment of universal prekindergarten work" (E. Rose 2010, 107). In 1996–97, over half of its enrollees attended publicly funded private programs, even some based in churches.[27]

Incorporating multiple service providers was also a political necessity. After the referendum passed, various groups expressed concerns about how the preschool program would be implemented. The program sparked numerous battles "among a narrow set of actors, mainly within the child care industry" (Bushouse 2009, 67). For-profit preschool providers wanted to ensure their place in the expanded program, and Head Start providers worried that the state planned to take over Head Start. The fears of the latter group existed because many of the local coordinating councils for the state program, which initially focused on at-risk children, did not involve Head Start in program planning. The program guidelines were subsequently modified so that coordinating councils were advised to include Head Start representatives.[28] The implementation of universal preschool in Georgia required both strong gubernatorial support and a willingness to accommodate existing stakeholders.

The development of Oklahoma's universal preschool program provides similar lessons about the political necessity of accommodating multiple providers. In contrast to Georgia, where universal preschool was linked to a high-profile gubernatorial campaign and a lottery referendum, universal preschool "quietly emerged" in Oklahoma through a complex series of incremental changes (Bushouse 2009, 47). In 1980, the state legislature funded a small pilot program. A decade later, a technical change in the school finance formula enabled local school districts to be reimbursed for educating four-year-olds (Kirp 2007, 181). In 1998, legislation creating a universal preschool program was signed into law without significant controversy or media coverage. The program accommodated established preschool service providers, including Head Start operators and faith-based programs (Finn 2009).

Head Start supporters in Oklahoma viewed the expansion of public preschool as a threat. Two factors contributed to winning their support in 1998. First, the architect of the proposal convinced Head Start leaders that expanding the preschool program would increase revenues to Head Start, because its centers would be eligible for public funding if they established "collaborative" relations with their local school districts. This legislative language allowed Head Start to "create partnerships with the public schools, either to run preschool classrooms or to offer wrap-around programs for children attending a half-day class within an elementary school" (Fuller 2007, 111). Second, the revised school finance formula had led many districts to place four-year-olds in kindergarten, a trend that the Head Start community viewed with alarm. It was hoped that expanding the public preschool program would end or at least limit this practice (Bushouse 2009, 43). Once these concerns were addressed, the expansion of the state preschool program did not face any significant opposition. Framed as an incremental shift and buttressed by national praise and favorable evaluations (Gormley and Phillips 2005; Gormley, Phillips, and Gayer 2008), the Oklahoma program boasts "a stable institutional structure and a cohesive policy image. It has attained a policy monopoly with no challengers on the horizon" (Bushouse 2009, 86).

The uneasy relationship between Head Start and public preschool programs was also evident in West Virginia. When universal preschool legislation gained enactment in 2002, it constituted only four pages of a fifty-one-page bill and was the handiwork of a small inner circle of legislators and political appointees. Its main opposition came from the state's House Education Committee chairman, who feared that state funding would displace federal Head Start funding for preschool services. That competitive dynamic had emerged when one of the poorest counties in the state began to offer preschool but failed to coordinate with Head Start. The West Virginia bill required public schools to collaborate with county Head Start agencies in order to address this concern (Bushouse 2009, 48).

In Tennessee, legislation with the potential to establish universal preschool was adopted in 2005, only after the concerns of the Head Start community were addressed. The original bill required all preschool programs to comply with the standards of the State Board of Education, including a requirement that each classroom have a certified teacher. Head Start operators feared that their programs would not be able to participate in the state program, because Head Start does not require a certified teacher. Their concerns were addressed in a meeting between Head Start representatives and the State Board of Education. The final legislation placed a strong emphasis on collaboration, even though it did not mandate it (Bushouse 2009, 127–33). The tension between Head Start and public programs is often due to concerns about enrollment and funding, but developments in Tennessee highlight that integrating Head Start into state programs is generally difficult due to the extensive federal standards that regulate program governance, performance, and accountability. In some cases, these regulations must be modified or waived to enable Head Start centers to enter contracts with state programs (Barnett and Hustedt 2003, 56–57).

The relationship between Head Start and state preschool programs is only one manifestation of the policy feedback that characterizes early childhood policy. Head Start supporters are one of many stakeholders interested in maintaining the status quo or directing policy change in a particular direction. Such service providers as nonprofits, churches, for-profit firms, and local schools are also inclined to view proposed changes and one another suspiciously. In Texas, for example, "the public schools, Head Start centers, and child care centers viewed one another with disdain" (Kirp 2007, 198). Head Start leaders and for-profit child care providers feared the expansionist tendencies of the public schools and "were antagonistic to an expansion of state prekindergarten because it threatened their survival" (Kirp 2007, 206). In Texas, policy reform was possible only after state policymakers offered something of value to each of these constituencies.

Developments in California illustrate a similar dynamic. Tensions between teachers unions and other preschool providers are another obstacle to developing a cohesive coalition. Bruce Fuller (2007, 10) describes a June 2002 conference call during which participants discussed the wide-ranging groups that already served three- and four-year-olds in Los Angeles. They agreed that coalescing around a single model of service provision would be challenging because "this patchwork quilt of child care organizations would be difficult to move in any one direction."

The organizational pluralism that characterizes early childhood programs represents an obstacle to policy change. Tensions exist even in states where advocacy groups have a better working relationship. In Illinois, organizations including Voices for Illinois Children, the Ounce of Prevention Fund, and Illinois Action for Children, which typically join forces to lobby, fight in private over the appropriate policy approaches and political strategies to pursue (Kirp 2007, 21).

Tensions among service providers also affected initiative campaigns. In 2002, Florida voters amended the state constitution to guarantee high-quality prekindergarten for every four-year-old in the state. The operators of for-profit preschools and faith-based schools feared that the initiative would drive them out of business but were reassured by promises that any prekindergarten, public or private, that satisfied state standards would be able to participate. Critics viewed the reassurances as obstacles to genuine reform and a more cohesive system, but they demonstrate the political necessity of accommodating existing stakeholders. They also suggest that "this powerful lobby will seek to protect private providers and incorporate them into any system of universal prekindergarten" (Maeroff 2006, 40). This resistance continued during implementation, leading one analyst to describe the program as "a classic example of how a diffuse majority, those who voted for the constitutional amendment, lost out to a concentrated and determined minority, the operators of private and faith-based preschools" (Kirp 2007, 188). Private and faith-based service providers enroll most four-year-olds, and the regulations governing the Florida program largely reflect their preferences.

In summary, program expansion typically reflected the logistical and political necessity of accommodating multiple service providers. Most of the changes described in this section of this chapter sought "to build on and combine existing private and public programs into a more coordinated system with consistent standards" (Barnett and Hustedt 2003, 56). A May 2006 report described state officials as "grappling with the challenges of accommodating existing programs and services while at the same time maintaining some uniformity of quality, outcomes, and coordination across programs."[29] This effort also reflected a growing consensus that such coordination would lead to more-effective programs. Dozens of states established governance bodies designed to give greater priority to children and family issues and to improve program operations.[30]

These programmatic benefits were exceeded, however, by the political benefits of incorporating multiple service providers. In many states, reformers faced opposition from stakeholders who believed their survival was at risk. They responded by emphasizing public access to programs (rather than the direct provision of services) and by encouraging participation by public and private preschools, because the "existence of a large lobby group for private preschools [left] little space for a unilateral approach" (Beatty 2001, 182). In many states, policy change became possible only when the concerns of Head Start centers, faith-based preschools, and other providers were addressed. Incorporating multiple providers also offered rhetorical benefits. Supporters could then plausibly claim that they were not offering a "big government" solution that usurped parental rights and responsibilities.[31]

Policy Feedback and Preschool Funding at the State Level

The developments profiled in the previous section of this chapter suggest that accommodating the preferences of existing providers, including Head Start, is often a prerequisite for major policy change. It is insufficient, however, to examine only states in which the creation of a universal program or the expansion of an existing program occurred. Only by examining both successful and unsuccessful attempts to change the status quo is it possible to isolate the political sources of early childhood policy. This section describes a quantitative analysis of contemporary preschool education across all fifty states. Its goal is to extend and reassess existing case study research. By examining all fifty states, including many where major policy change did not occur, its systematic analysis acts as a tentative validity check on the conclusions drawn in the preceding section.[32]

Turning to the state level offers the added benefit of providing a largely untapped venue in which to assess the impact of policy feedback. Most studies of policy development examine national politics. This focus is understandable given the scope of national programs like Social Security, yet it means that scholars must be cautious about developing broad generalizations about the policymaking process. The underlying similarity and manageable variation of the American states makes them a propitious venue in which to evaluate hypotheses about policymaking (Gray 2008; Mooney 2001). State-level analysis can assess the conditions under which the conclusions drawn from national studies "travel" to other venues, thereby producing more-robust generalizations. The quantitative analysis presented in this section therefore represents a robustness check accompanying the historical evidence presented elsewhere in this book. It simultaneously evaluates the impact of policy feedback and several other political and economic factors on early childhood policy.[33]

The outcomes of interest are whether and how states fund preschool education. During the 2006–7 school year, forty-one states dedicated public funds to preschool (Rigby 2007). These state-funded programs come in three basic forms. States may fund freestanding preschool programs, supplement Head Start, or combine the two approaches. In 2006–7, thirty states funded freestanding programs, Oregon dedicated all of its preschool spending to a Head Start supplement, and ten states used a combined approach.[34] Nine states did not dedicate public funds to preschool.

The long-standing tension between Head Start supporters and other members of the early childhood policy community suggests that interest group politics might affect the category into which a state falls. If Head Start supporters feel threatened by a freestanding preschool program, they may press state officials not to create one. As a result, states with a strong Head Start community may be especially likely not to fund preschool education. The first outcome on which the analysis focuses is therefore a dichotomous variable indicating whether a state does not dedicate any public funds to preschool. A positive relationship between the strength of the Head Start community and this outcome is expected. The second outcome examined is a dichotomous variable indicating whether a state dedicates all of its public preschool spending to a freestanding program. A negative relationship between the strength of the Head Start community and this outcome is expected.[35]

The strength of the Head Start community is the key factor in the analysis that follows. The proxy used to assess its strength is the percentage of preschool attendees in the state who are enrolled in Head Start.[36] This proxy captures the potential strength of the Head Start community because it emphasizes its size. State Head Start organizations possess divergent views on many issues, and the political effectiveness of their leaders also varies. The chief limitation of the proxy employed here is that it does not account for these important differences. Its main advantage, however, is that it offers an objective measure of Head Start's reach relative to other early childhood programs. The Head Start percentage ranges from a low of 9.2 percent in New Hampshire and New Jersey to a high of 65.3 percent in Mississippi. Based on the historical episodes and case study evidence profiled in this book, states in which a relatively high percentage of preschool enrollees are enrolled in Head Start are likely not to fund preschool education and unlikely to dedicate all preschool spending to a freestanding state program. Head Start supporters are often reluctant to support the creation or expansion of state-funded preschool programs, and state officials will presumably be more attentive to their preferences when they represent a larger proportion of existing stakeholders.

Many state characteristics might affect decisions about preschool funding. One potential demographic influence is the age profile of the population. The issue might resonate more strongly in states with a relatively high proportion of young children, where policymakers might perceive a greater need for publicly funded programs. The logic of this relationship is analogous to the idea that policy adoption is driven by underlying societal conditions or needs (Nice 1994). The analysis that follows therefore includes the proportion of the state population that is under five years old.[37] States with a younger population base might face stronger demand for preschool services and therefore be especially likely to fund them.[38]

State wealth also has the potential to affect preschool funding decisions. Its potential impact is related to both the population served by Head Start and the general impact of state wealth on policymaking. Most Head Start enrollees live in low-income families, though the correlation between income and enrollment is imperfect, because Head Start does not reach the entire eligible population. Including a proxy for state wealth therefore ensures that a significant relationship between the strength of the Head Start community and preschool funding decisions is not due to states' socioeconomic profiles. In addition, wealthy states may have more resources to devote to preschool, while less wealthy states may be reluctant to use their scarcer resources for that purpose. Political scientists have long noted a general relationship between wealth and policy outcomes (Dye 1966; Tweedie 1994; Walker 1969).[39]

Other demographic factors might affect preschool spending decisions. Formal education levels might affect societal attitudes toward preschool and the willingness to fund it. Individuals with higher levels of formal education might be more sympathetic to public spending on education in general and on preschool education in particular, leading to a positive relationship between state education levels and preschool spending. The analysis that follows uses the percentage of the state population with a high school diploma or higher as its proxy for state education levels.[40] Another potential influence is racial diversity. Scholars have linked racial heterogeneity to policy choices (Fellowes and Rowe 2004; Soss et al. 2001) and educational outcomes at the state level (Hero and Tolbert 1996). They have found that states with larger minority populations tend to implement less generous policies. The analysis that follows uses the percentage of the state population identified as non-Hispanic white as a proxy for homogeneity and, based on prior research, expects a positive relationship between population homogeneity and preschool funding.[41]

Preschool funding decisions might also be influenced by the state political environment. Party control of government institutions (Roh and Haider-Markel 2003; Spill, Licari, and Ray 2001) and the ideological environment (Berry et al. 1998; Erikson, Wright, and McIver 1993) have been linked to various public policies. Democrats tend to be more enthusiastic than Republicans about publicly funded preschool. Democratic control of the governorship or state legislature might therefore make it more likely that a state will devote public funds to preschool, while Republican control might make such funding less likely. The analysis that follows therefore includes a dichotomous variable that indicates whether Democrats exercise unified party control of state government.[42] The potential relationship between preschool funding and ideology is based on similar logic. Conservatives generally prefer to reduce the scope of government activity, while liberals typically support its expansion. Many conservatives characterize publicly funded preschool as an undesirable intrusion on parental autonomy. States in which residents hold relatively liberal political views might be more likely to dedicate public funds to preschool. The analysis therefore includes an annual estimate of citizen liberalism (Berry et al. 1998). Both Democratic control and citizen liberalism are expected to have a positive effect on preschool funding.

To evaluate the aforementioned relationships, the following analysis examines five years of cross-sectional data on state preschool spending from 2001 to 2005 (Rigby 2007). The unit of analysis is a state-year. The outcomes of interest, whether a state chose not to dedicate funds to preschool and whether a state funded only a freestanding state program, are examined in two separate models. Each model includes the variables described in this section and indicator variables for each year of the analysis. Both dependent variables are dichotomous, so standard logistic regression methods are used to evaluate the determinants of preschool funding.

Why do some states not dedicate public funds to preschool? Table 2 displays the results of a logistic regression model examining this decision.[43] As expected, the division within the early childhood policy community seems influential. The size of the Head Start community has a significant positive effect on the likelihood that a state will not allocate public funds to preschool. When other independent variables are fixed at their central values, moving from a state with a small Head Start community (12.95 percent of total preschool enrollment) to a state with a large one (35.30 percent) increases the likelihood that it will not fund preschool, by 12.72 percentage points. In combination with the evidence presented throughout this book, this result suggests that some Head Start supporters perceive other publicly funded preschool programs as a potential threat.

State officials appear to respond to their preferences when they represent a large proportion of those with a stake in preschool.

The decision not to fund preschool also seems to be influenced by other factors. As predicted, there is a significant negative relationship between state wealth and this decision. Wealthy states are more likely to allocate public funds to preschool.[44] When other independent variables are fixed at their central values, moving from a wealthy state to a poor one decreases the likelihood that it will fund preschool, by 12.57 percentage points. Resource availability appears to facilitate preschool funding. Citizen ideology has the expected effect. Liberal states are more likely to dedicate public funds to preschool. When other independent variables are fixed at their central values, moving from a liberal state to a conservative one decreases the likelihood that it will offer publicly funded preschool, by 6.53 percentage points. The presence of unified Democratic government also appears to increase the likelihood that it will fund preschool education, but this relationship does not achieve conventional levels of statistical significance.[45]

Table 3 displays the results of a model examining the decision to devote all public preschool funds to a freestanding state program. The division within the early childhood policy community has the expected impact.

TABLE 2. Determinants of the Decision Not to Fund Preschool Education

Variable	First Difference	Confidence Interval
Head Start Enrollment (+)	12.72**	[3.12, 30.31]
Population under Five (−)	0.71	[−5.26, 7.88]
Per Capita Income (−)	−12.57*	[−31.53, −2.02]
Education Level (−)	15.20**	[4.54, 33.01]
Population Homogeneity (−)	2.71	[−4.82, 14.40]
Democratic Government (−)	−3.15	[−9.05, −0.14]
Citizen Ideology (−)	−6.53**	[−17.21, −1.17]
2002	−0.49	[−6.42, 6.15]
2003	0.88	[−6.13, 8.33]
2004	5.61	[−3.13, 18.47]
2005	4.82	[−3.26, 16.13]
Number of observations	250	
Log likelihood	−65.368	
Chi-square	98.79	
Prob. chi-square	0.000	
Pseudo R^2	0.430	

Note: Expected directions in parentheses. All tests of statistical significance are two-tailed.
*Significant at the .05 level; **significant at the .01 level.

The size of the Head Start community has a significant negative effect. When other independent variables are fixed at their central values, moving from a state with a small Head Start community to a state with a large one reduces the likelihood that a state will fund only a freestanding preschool program, by 43.25 percentage points. Like the analogous result in table 2, this finding seems to imply that some Head Start supporters feel threatened by freestanding preschool programs and that their political strength affects whether state officials respond to their preferences. As anticipated, interest group politics seems to influence state decisions about whether and how to fund preschool.

The performance of the other variables examined in the model is disappointing. As expected, unified Democratic government makes it more likely that a state will fund only a freestanding program. When other independent variables are fixed at their central values, moving from a state without unified Democratic control to a state with it increases the probability that the state will fund only a freestanding preschool program, by 24.50 percentage points. Citizen ideology also has the anticipated effect. Liberal states are more likely to fund only a freestanding program, but this relationship does not attain conventional levels of statistical significance.[46]

TABLE 3. Determinants of the Decision to Fund Only a Freestanding Preschool Program

Variable	First Difference	Confidence Interval
Head Start Enrollment (−)	−43.25**	[−61.90, −23.32]
Population under Five (+)	−5.48	[−25.95, 15.49]
Per Capita Income (+)	−15.47	[−39.27, 7.32]
Education Level (+)	−50.21**	[−65.52, −32.60]
Population Homogeneity (+)	−3.97	[−21.87, 15.08]
Democratic Government (+)	24.50*	[2.18, 43.45]
Citizen Ideology (+)	3.23	[−17.16, 21.65]
2002	4.57	[−17.20, 27.60]
2003	−0.34	[−22.67, 22.61]
2004	21.82	[−0.68, 43.31]
2005	24.48*	[2.87, 46.09]
Number of observations	250	
Log likelihood	−132.611	
Chi-square	75.55	
Prob. chi-square	0.000	
Pseudo R^2	0.222	

Note: Expected directions in parentheses. All tests of statistical significance are two-tailed.
*Significant at the .05 level; **significant at the .01 level.

The results presented in this section suggest that the size of the Head Start community may influence whether and how states fund preschool education.[47] A large Head Start presence seems to make it more likely that a state will not fund preschool education and seems to decrease the likelihood that it will only fund a freestanding public program. The chief limitation of the preceding analysis is that it cannot identify the precise mechanisms through which the Head Start community affects preschool funding. Its impact may be due to supporters' political activity, worries about the financial implications of policy change for Head Start, or a feeling among state political leaders that large Head Start enrollments obviate the need for state activity. Additional case study research comparing successful and unsuccessful attempts at major policy change would add greater depth to the results presented here, and they might illuminate the impact of factors like inertia and individual leadership that are not addressed in the preceding analysis. Furthermore, Head Start is a national funding stream and a disparate, intensely local collection of programs. It is important to recognize that Head Start supporters may have blocked the growth of other preschool programs in some states but not others.[48]

Despite its limitations, the preceding analysis supports one of this book's key assertions. The impact of the Head Start community is consistent with the concept of policy feedback. Supporters of policy change often must overcome the opposition of constituencies who benefit from the status quo, and the clout of program beneficiaries can constrain the options that policymakers possess. Existing policies affect the possibilities for future policymaking by shaping the identities, interests, and incentives of key actors (Skocpol 1992). The mobilization of existing stakeholders has been an obstacle to comprehensive change in such areas as retirement security and health care (Campbell 2003; Hacker 2002; Mayes 2004; Walker 1991), and a similar dynamic seems to have affected the state-level impact of the contemporary preschool movement.

State Programs and the "Great Recession"

The preceding analysis examined a period of extensive state government activity in early childhood policy. In 2005 and 2006, thirty-one states increased preschool funding by a total of more than one billion dollars, Illinois and West Virginia endorsed programs to make preschool available to all children whose parents want it, and several states established task forces to examine the issue. A strong economy in South Carolina, for example, made possible a project that distributed \$23.7 million in new funding to schools, child care centers, Head Start, and faith-based providers.[49] Shortly thereafter, however, the economic context changed dramatically and effectively removed major programmatic expansions from the political agenda. Beginning in 2007, the United States entered a recession that "caused the largest collapse in state revenues on record."[50] Increased demand for public programs accompanied these revenue declines, as residents lost jobs, income, and health insurance. States had experienced recessions in the early 1980s, early 1990s, and early 2000s, but the recession of the late 2000s was unusually severe. Sluggish economic growth and high unemployment persisted well after its official conclusion in June 2009, and state officials continued to face major fiscal challenges into 2012.[51]

Unlike the national government, virtually all states are required to balance their operating budgets every year or biennium. Plunging revenues and the increased need for government services opened sizable budget gaps that state officials were forced to close. The combined shortfalls for 2009 through 2012 totaled more than \$530 billion.[52] States met this challenge by drawing down the record reserves they had accumulated heading into the recession,[53] using the roughly \$140 billion in funds provided by the American Recovery and Reinvestment Act, and adopting a combination of tax increases and spending cuts. The spending cuts affected nearly every domain of state government activity, including early childhood education. Arizona eliminated preschool services for 4,328 children and funding for schools to provide additional support for disadvantaged children from preschool to third grade. Massachusetts reduced spending on early intervention services for children with special needs by 16 percent. Rhode Island reduced the number of children served by Head Start and similar services.[54]

Ongoing fiscal challenges slowed but did not stop state-level activity in early childhood policy. During the 2008–9 school year, the percentage of three- and four-year-olds enrolled in state prekindergarten programs rose in twenty-nine states and fell in nine states. Total funding rose, albeit at a slower pace than in previous years, and state funding per child declined in twenty-four of thirty-eight states, after adjusting for inflation (Barnett et al. 2009, 4). According to the National Conference of State Legislatures, the number of bills on early care and education fell from 2008 to 2009, but "a number of states protected investments in young children and avoided cuts to early childhood programs; some states even increased their commitment."[55] Alaska and Rhode Island, two states that previously did not have publicly funded prekindergarten programs, provided new appropriations to pilot programs.[56] Even so, some observers worried that the reduced pace of change foretold more-dramatic shifts as state budgets more fully bore the brunt of the recession. Acknowledging that it would be inappropriate to read too much into a one-year dip in real spending, they nevertheless speculated that "given states' budgetary problems this could be the start of a new downward trend that will erode the value of these programs and turn them into ineffective, cheap substitutes for real education" (Barnett et al. 2009, 13).

States continued to cope with difficult economic conditions in 2010 and 2011. Their actions drew mixed reviews. One sanguine report concluded that fiscal challenges had not kept state governments from finding "innovative ways to increase availability and even create new programs aimed at improving the accessibility and quality of early childhood services."[57] A handful of states enacted legislation to address student readiness and assessment standards and to expand access to existing facilities, while Minnesota and Washington expanded state-funded programs for educationally at-risk children.[58] Other observers highlighted what they viewed as more-troubling trends. One study concluded, "The grim fiscal climate makes dramatic program expansions unlikely and impractical in the near term."[59] Due to the recession, total enrollment in state prekindergarten programs barely increased, total spending by the states decreased, and spending per child declined in inflation-adjusted dollars during the 2009–10 school year. The slow economic recovery and the exhaustion of federal stimulus funds caused some observers to speculate that these trends would have a significant negative impact on the quality of state programs over the longer term. They concluded, "Funding levels in some of the states have fallen so low as to bring into question the effectiveness of their programs by any reasonable standard" (Barnett et al. 2010, 10).

As state officials grappled with a challenging fiscal environment, they also sought to coordinate existing programs more effectively through the creation of early childhood advisory councils. The goal of this administrative reform was "to guide investments and ensure that resources are used efficiently and toward the greatest effect."[60] National legislation spurred and facilitated state activity. The 2007 Head Start reauthorization mandated the creation of the councils and required them to identify opportunities for and barriers to coordination among extant national and state programs. The American Recovery and Reinvestment Act provided one hundred million dollars in grants to states to establish the councils. The need for better coordination "across early childhood programs" was "an underlying thread in all state early childhood advisory councils' applications for federal funding."[61] The councils built on existing state initiatives and drew their membership from public agencies and private stakeholders in the business, philanthropic, and other communities.

Responding to contemporary fiscal challenges requires striking a balance among several competing priorities. In addition to allocating public funds, state policymakers must also determine the eligibility requirements, curricular standards, personnel credentials, and classroom regulations that govern state-funded programs. Such decisions are substantively significant because they determine who gains access to the programs and what type of services they will receive. In an era of resource scarcity, preschool advocates must carefully consider how changes will affect the effectiveness or quality of public programs. Despite general agreement about the deficient quality of existing programs (Barnett and Hustedt 2003; Henry, Gordon, and Rickman 2006), different constituencies within the early childhood community offer competing prescriptions for improvement.

The conflict over teacher certification requirements is illustrative. In recent years, many organizations and politicians have recommended that all preschool teachers hold a bachelor's degree with specialization in early childhood education. They argue that highly credentialed caregivers produce stronger academic performance and "yield significant improvements in program effectiveness for all children, especially those from low-income families."[62] Representatives of Head Start and other community-based programs tend to be less enthusiastic. The Improving Head Start for School Readiness Act, signed into law by President George W. Bush in December 2007, established new educational goals for Head Start teachers. Many program administrators expressed misgivings about this change, arguing that additional funds would be necessary to provide "tuition and book scholarships, provide release time and substitute teachers while teaching staff were in school, and increase compensation once credentials were earned."[63] The National Head Start Association characterized it as an "unfunded mandate" that failed to recognize the fiscal realities involved in hiring, training, and retraining teachers with advanced degrees.[64]

The fiscal impact of higher certification requirements does not end once a degree has been earned. Many Head Start centers find it "impossible to keep highly qualified teachers because there are better opportunities in the public schools."[65] One study found that Head Start directors and private program providers feared that teachers took positions in their programs "only as stepping stones to more lucrative jobs in the public schools" (Barnett and Hustedt 2003, 56). Many Head Start leaders and private-sector providers fear that more-stringent certification requirements will exacerbate this competition for personnel. The acquisition of more formal education may even lead staffers to seek employment outside the early childhood field, which has historically offered very low wages.[66] Although these concerns are not new, they resonate especially strongly in an era of resource scarcity. Whereas some members of the early childhood policy community favor higher credentials as a way to promote program quality, others worry about their considerable financial implications.

Fiscal challenges also threaten to exacerbate the ongoing controversy surrounding program eligibility. The contemporary debate invokes both the long-standing question of the age at which children should begin their formal education and the question of whether public programs should be targeted or universal. The universal preschool movement has gained momentum since the 1990s and has received considerable popular and scholarly attention (Bushouse 2009; Fuller 2007; Kirp 2007; E. Rose 2010). Universal programs are expensive, however, and program cost is a serious concern in an era of limited resources. In addition, some critics have questioned whether universal programs are responsive to the needs of all parents, especially if they are run by the public schools. Such programs may not appeal to parents who prefer less institutional forms of care, and they may be inappropriate for parents with unusual work schedules (Fuller 2007, 16). The claim that early childhood initiatives must accommodate parental preferences is also not new, but the contemporary policy landscape, with more American children enrolled in a diverse array of public- and private-sector programs, highlights one of reformers' central challenges: programmatic diversity represents a political obstacle for those who hope to construct a more collaborative and less fragmented system.[67]

Conclusion: Early Childhood Policy at a Crossroads

In the late 1960s and early 1970s, supporters of increased public investment in child development believed that they were living through a critical moment. Contemporary supporters view themselves as being in a similar situation, and their rhetoric bears a striking resemblance to the proclamations of Harold Howe II and Albert Quie with which this book began. In 2002, Georgia governor Roy Barnes echoed Howe's optimism by predicting "that within ten years early childhood will be as accepted (and be state funded) as kindergarten is today."[68] In contrast, David Kirp (2007, 266) channeled Quie's wariness with his assessment that the preschool movement "has arrived at a crossroads. Even as more states are offering preschool, more children are enrolling, and more public dollars are being spent, the quality of instruction remains mixed and the amount of money being spent on each child has declined." Their contrasting perspectives hint at a potential tension between improved preschool access and better program quality.

Other observers approach the future with a combination of optimism and wariness. One survey of the contemporary landscape concludes, "Eventually, public school will begin for most children at age three or four. [Prekindergarten], in many ways, is at a crossroads, caught between early child care programs, Head Start, and schools" (Clifford et al. 2005, 141). Its abrupt shift from confidence to wariness is noteworthy, and its observation about competing constituencies resonates with the evidence presented in this chapter. Existing policy arrangements, rather than being the foundation on which reforms can build, sometimes represent an obstacle to policy change. Stakeholders like teachers unions, Head Start supporters, private-sector providers, and others endorse expanded access to early childhood programs but offer distinct visions of how best to accomplish that goal. Moving the fragmented system of early childhood policy in a single direction is both a political and a logistical challenge. Regardless of whether reformers focus their attention on the national level or the fifty states, they confront a policy landscape that is significantly more complicated than the one their predecessors faced four decades ago. The accumulated policy choices of the intervening years privileged a diverse array of stakeholders, and accommodating their preferences is often a prerequisite for major policy change.

Conclusion: The Future of Preschool Politics

In a November 2011 interview, House minority leader Nancy Pelosi (D-CA) was asked what her legislative goals would be if the Democrats were to retake control of the House of Representatives. The former Speaker of the House answered that her top priority would be to push for comprehensive change in early childhood policy. Describing how she struggled to find reliable care for her children, she spoke approvingly of the Comprehensive Child Development Act that President Richard Nixon vetoed in 1971. She observed, "One of the great pieces of unfinished business is high-quality child care; I wonder why we just can't do it."[1]

Many preschool advocates shared Pelosi's goals but not her optimism. At the end of 2011, the Pew Charitable Trusts ended its ten-year commitment to a campaign for high-quality, voluntary prekindergarten for all three- and four-year-olds. In a final report outlining its "Pre-K–12 vision" for the future of public education, the foundation noted that major reform would require collaboration among diverse stakeholders. Effective collaboration, it argued, "will demand more than merely cooperating better. At every stage of implementation, these stakeholders must be willing to change how they think, talk and operate, especially with respect to entrenched systems and long-held maxims about early childhood, pre-k and public education."[2] A December 2011 column by the executive director of the Minnesota Early Learning Foundation touched on similar themes. Describing the barriers to major policy change, it noted that "change is popular in the abstract, controversial when it hits home. . . . We saw change quickly become controversial when reform requires adults with a stake in the failed status quo to do things differently."[3]

The developments profiled in this book illustrate the many challenges involved in early childhood policymaking. Beginning in the late 1960s, both comprehensive bills to create a permanent national framework for the universal provision of preschool services and incremental proposals to shift the status quo in a more modest direction have foundered on the shoals of the legislative process. The most famous proposal, the Comprehensive Child Development Act cited by Pelosi, cleared both congressional chambers only to be vetoed and denounced in extraordinarily harsh terms by the president. It is tempting to read this congressional history as a story of repeated rejection and policy stasis.

Interpreting the evolution of early childhood policy in this manner, however, underestimates the dramatic political and policy shifts that have occurred even in the absence of landmark national legislation. Some of these changes are rhetorical. Legislation in the late 1960s and early 1970s focused on child development and sought to provide a wide range of services to young children and their families. In recent years, the focus at both the national level and in the states has turned to educational programs and cognitive development, with terms like *school readiness* and *prekindergarten* moving to the fore. Similarly, supporters of increased public investment have responded to concerns about the cost of high-quality preschool services by describing it as an investment that will pay for itself over the long term.

More important for the purposes of this book, the politics of early childhood policy in the early twenty-first century differ profoundly from those of the late 1960s and early 1970s. For example, significant state-level activity is a defining feature of the current debate. The emergence of state governments as powerful stakeholders is illustrative of broader changes in the interest group universe. Other stakeholders, including Head Start supporters, educational associations, and private-sector service providers, are more active and influential than they used to be. Their involvement, ironically, has splintered the coalition supporting major policy change. Diverse stakeholders have endorsed additional government intervention, but they often disagree on its form. This political complexity is a by-product of the programmatic fragmentation that is a central feature of American early childhood policy, and it has contributed to the maintenance of a status quo that many observers find problematic.

Policy Development and Preschool Politics

Early childhood education in the United States differs from that of other countries along two key dimensions. First, the private sector plays an unusually large role in service provision. This pattern resonates with other policy arenas and is a defining feature of the American welfare state (Gottschalk 2000; Hacker 2002; Howard 1997). It is important because public- and private-sector programs tend to serve different constituencies. Economically secure families tend to rely on the private sector for preschool services, while most government-administered programs are targeted on such specific subgroups as children from low-income families. The second distinctive attribute of early childhood education in the United States is its public-sector decentralization. Government programs are administered by numerous executive agencies at the national, state, and local levels. In recent years, the uneasy relationship between these diverse programs and funding streams has received substantial attention. Many observers cite insufficient coordination as one of the primary deficiencies of the contemporary system. This book has sought not to assess the merits or demerits of what presently exists but, rather, to explain how and why preschool education in the United States came to take on its distinctive form.

Isolating the political origins of the contemporary American system requires a developmental approach that treats policymaking as a long-term causal chain. The present system developed gradually. Its origins can be traced to the temporally distant events of the early 1970s, when several efforts to establish a national framework fell short. Nixon's veto of the Comprehensive Child Development Act was a critical juncture, because it set in motion a series of reactions and counterreactions that produced the present fragmentation of the contemporary system. The absence of a comprehensive national policy facilitated the growth of nonprofit and for-profit programs in the private sector. In addition, supporters of expansive governmental initiatives, largely stymied at the national level, sought a more favorable institutional venue for their campaign. Their successful venue shopping led to substantial policy activity in the states as well as to the expansion of Head Start and the Child and Dependent Care Tax Credit. The long-term political consequences of their successes were profound. Various constituencies mobilized to defend their stake in existing arrangements, and their successful lobbying made it more difficult for the national government to adopt a more coherent approach to preschool service delivery. As existing programs and the constituencies defending them grew more entrenched, preschool education evolved into a fragmented and decentralized system.

This evolution offers broader lessons for the study of public policy. It illustrates how the existing policy repertoire can affect the positions that interest groups take and the strategies they employ. Preschool advocates adjusted to changes in their social, institutional, and political environment. Constituencies who agreed that additional government involvement was desirable differed on the specific form that it should take, and this disagreement led them to work at cross-purposes. The broad coalition that came together in the early 1970s to support child development legislation eventually disintegrated, torn apart by a combination of political frustration and disagreements over the details of various legislative proposals. State and local officials and Head Start supporters viewed many recent initiatives as threats to their existing prerogatives and budgets. Their shifting positions are instructive in terms of both explaining the contemporary fragmentation of American preschool education and illustrating the complex interplay between public policy and interest group activity.

Consider, for example, the evolving role of state governments. A key controversy during the congressional debates of the early 1970s concerned prime sponsorship and administrative responsibility. Many state officials expressed frustration with the Comprehensive Child Development Act, believing that the vetoed bill bypassed the states and privileged local governments and community organizations. Motivated by an interest in early childhood and a desire to protect state prerogatives against national encroachment, they devoted more attention to the issue. At the same time, preschool advocates viewed the states as an increasingly viable venue for policymaking on child development. As a result, the early to mid-1970s were a period of significant activity at the state level. The number and the size of state early childhood programs grew, and the states became more involved in the education and care of young children. For example, officials in many states created offices of child development, a bureaucratic reform designed to improve the administration of early childhood programs.

The state-level reforms of the early to mid-1970s were not broad in reach, but they nonetheless had significant short- and long-term political consequences. In the short term, they contributed to the increased assertiveness of state officials during congressional debates about early childhood policy. As Congress considered the Child and Family Services Act of 1975 and the Child Care Act of 1979, state officials were more assertive about protecting their prerogatives. They urged their congressional counterparts to support the efforts that were already underway at the state level. The Child Care Act granted the states significant administrative discretion, assuming that they would serve as prime sponsors. While it would be a mistake to attribute this shift solely to state officials' lobbying efforts, it is important to acknowledge their mobilization and increasing assertiveness. By the time Congress returned to early childhood policy in the late 1980s, state officials were viewed as crucial stakeholders. Prior to introducing Smart Start in 1988, for example, Senator Edward Kennedy (D-MA) convened a bipartisan panel of governors who provided suggestions about how best to achieve the goal of universal preschool access. This consultative process represented a sea change from the debates of the early 1970s.

The states have played a central role in early childhood policy over the past two decades. State lawmakers consistently appear before Congress to protect their policymaking prerogatives and to lobby for increased financial support, and the states represent an institutional venue in which crucial policy decisions are made. Many congressional initiatives, including the PRE-K Act and the Race to the Top–Early Learning Challenge contest profiled in chapter 7, limit the national government's role to agenda setting and financial support. In contrast, they tend to view program development as a task best left to state officials and service providers. The early 2000s have been a period of widespread state-level activity, during which state lawmakers have enacted new programs and expanded access to and increased spending on existing programs.[4] The universal preschool movement is perhaps the most visible manifestation of this heightened state prominence.

Thus the evolution of early childhood policy in the United States highlights a dimension of federalism that is often overlooked. The fragmentation of political authority among national and subnational governments is often described as a constitutional hurdle to the adoption of expansive social policies (Huber, Ragin, and Stephens 1993; Robertson 1989). This one-dimensional portrayal of federalism and its impact overlooks how the institutional fragmentation of the American political system provides reformers with several avenues through which they can achieve their goals. Thwarted in one institutional arena, they can pursue their objectives in another setting. Such venue shopping is a common element of American politics (Baumgartner and Jones 1991, 1993), and it helped shape the contemporary preschool system. When the states emerged as an important locus of policymaking activity, the scale of their efforts was less important than the fact that their very existence created a new set of stakeholders. The dynamics described in this book suggest that scholars should devote more attention to the role of subnational units as autonomous actors in federal systems (Pierson 1995). Successful venue shopping at the state level can have significant long-term political consequences (Orloff 1988). Scholars of American social policy must be more attentive to the complex and ongoing interplay between the national government and the fifty states.

The long-term impact of federalism may vary across policy areas due to the structure of existing programs and their political appeal. Programs that offer the states considerable discretion might facilitate the mobilization of state officials, while those constraining subnational authority might limit it. The varying administrative role of state governments across programs like Medicaid, unemployment insurance, and Temporary Assistance to Needy Families therefore represents an analytical opportunity to examine and refine the argument advanced in this book. Furthermore, the popularity of existing programs might influence whether state officials will mobilize to defend their prerogatives. If a program is viewed as a political liability because of the financial burden it imposes or the social construction of its target populations (Schneider and Ingram 1993), state officials might be willing to cede administrative control to Congress. Future research on the long-term impact of federalism and venue shopping should seek to identify the conditions that are most likely to generate feedback effects.

The political evolution of Head Start, a targeted national program that serves disadvantaged young children and their families, also illustrates how policy feedback contributed to the fragmentation of American preschool education. Established as part of the War on Poverty in 1965, Head Start maintained a tenuous existence during its early years but was placed on surer footing during the 1970s (Vinovskis 2005; Zigler and Muenchow 1992). It is a comprehensive program that provides educational and other services. Head Start parents value the decision-making authority the program allows them to exercise and the job opportunities it provides. Recent survey evidence suggests that recipients view Head Start as effective (Mettler and Stonecash 2008). Experience with the program also seems to increase political participation (Schneider and Sidney 2009; Soss 1999). The existence of Head Start spurred the creation of the National Head Start Association in 1973, which has been an outspoken and active defender of the program for the past four decades.

Ironically, the mobilization of Head Start supporters contributed to the fragmentation of the early education policy community. They generally favored the expansion of publicly funded programs but viewed major changes as potential threats to their prerogatives and their budgets. Tensions between Head Start supporters and other advocates were evident in the 1970s, when a California official described Head Start teachers as an obstacle to an early childhood bill and when the Child Care Act of 1979 sought to accommodate the Head Start community by avoiding any direct conflict with the program. By the late 1980s, Head Start supporters often viewed new early childhood programs as substitutes for, rather than complements to, their favored program. At a congressional hearing in 1988, for example, the president of the National Head Start Association openly expressed her fear that a new national program would compete with Head Start for funding. The case study evidence and quantitative analysis presented in chapter 8 of this book suggest that Head Start also generated policy feedback at the state level. Accommodating the concerns of the Head Start community was often a prerequisite for major reforms.

The shifting positions of state governments and Head Start supporters illustrate how the mobilization of those who benefit from existing policy arrangements can constrain policymakers' options. This feedback dynamic helps explain why contemporary discussions of early childhood policy tend to emphasize the potential costs of programmatic fragmentation and the potential benefits of coordination. Promoting collaboration among different stakeholders is a challenge, but there have been some noteworthy successes (Gormley, Phillips, and Gayer 2008). Accommodating existing stakeholders seems to be a logistical and political necessity for major policy change. It is a logistical necessity because program expansion requires additional facilities, personnel, and supporting infrastructure. It is a political necessity because the early childhood policy community includes diverse constituencies who disagree about many basic questions, and some of these groups view the expansion of public programs as a threat to their survival. Reform often requires concessions that grant these groups an ongoing role in service provision. As a result, most of the major policy changes of recent years accommodate existing providers. This approach, however, furthers, rather than mitigates, the fragmentation of the contemporary preschool system.

In summary, the present structure of American early childhood education can be traced to the late 1960s and early 1970s. At that time, several efforts to establish a permanent national framework were defeated, and reform advocates engaged in venue shopping. Their successes resulted in a mélange of public-sector programs at the national and state levels. Those who benefited from these programs mobilized to defend their prerogatives. Their mobilization, in combination with the growth of the private sector that was fostered in part by expansions of the Child and Dependent Care Tax Credit, reshaped the political terrain on which subsequent discussions of early childhood policy took place. Although many observers expressed reservations about the status quo, major policy change was usually controversial, because it offended the mobilized groups who benefited from existing arrangements.

With its emphasis on critical junctures, venue shopping, and policy feedback, the present analysis applies concepts that have been developed in other contexts to a largely unexamined but substantively important domain. This endeavor represents the sort of "test case" without which scholarly literatures are inadequately integrated and fail to advance. It is an especially valuable enterprise because recent research on American social policy has been criticized for a lack of integration (Hacker 2005). The evidence presented in this book suggests that the central concepts of the policy development approach may be applicable to a wide range of policy arenas.

Indeed, future research on social policymaking should incorporate education programs more systematically. Scholars of American and comparative politics have devoted relatively limited attention to this topic.[5] As a result, most existing research on education policy consists of program analyses that offer valuable insights about how policies function but that produce static portraits of phenomena that are constantly in motion (Sroufe 1995, 79). Furthermore, program variation across different education levels provides an analytical opportunity to assess hypotheses about the policymaking process. The enactment and implementation of No Child Left Behind, for example, has shed light on the impact of federalism and various institutional and ideological changes (Manna 2006; McGuinn 2006). Efforts to impose NCLB-like accountability mechanisms on higher education were decisively rebuffed, however (Lowry 2009). In addition, the role of the private sector is more pronounced in early childhood education than it is in elementary and secondary education. For a variety of reasons, education policy represents fertile terrain for scholars who wish to develop generalizations about the politics of American social policy. Additional research is likely to prove both substantively and theoretically illuminating.

Finally, subnational policymaking merits a more prominent place in the study of policy development. In addition to illuminating the impact of federalism, turning to the state level provides a virtually untapped venue in which to assess the applicability of key concepts of the developmental approach. Most existing studies concentrate on the national level,[6] an understandable focus, but one that presents several challenges in terms of developing generalizations. One can overcome these challenges using the underlying similarity and manageable variation offered by the fifty states to evaluate hypotheses about policymaking. During an era in which state governments are a central locus of policymaking activity, there are both substantive and analytical reasons why scholars of social policy should be more attentive to state politics.[7] Analyses of state-level developments will allow scholars to make more-confident generalizations about social policymaking.

In sum, the argument and analytical approach advanced in this book suggest three avenues for future research. First, scholars must acknowledge the multiple dimensions of federalism, devoting particular attention to the role of subnational units as autonomous actors in a federal system. Federalism provides opportunities for venue shopping that can have significant short- and long-term political implications. State governments are not only the source of crucial policy decisions. They also lobby the national government, acting to protect their policymaking authority. Second, scholars must expand their frame of reference to include a wider range of program areas. Retirement security and health care policy undoubtedly merit the attention they have received, but the concepts developed and generalizations made in studies of those two program areas might not be applicable to other domains. Additional "test cases" of the sort offered by this book would be valuable. Third, scholars would be well served to turn their attention to the American states. The subnational level represents a favorable venue for assessing the validity and limitations of concepts like policy feedback, and it offers an opportunity to conduct historical and quantitative analyses of policy choices. Examining temporal and spatial variation at the state level will enable scholars to refine their knowledge about the dynamics of the policymaking process.

The Future of Preschool Politics

Almost four decades after Nixon's landmark veto, former vice president Walter Mondale (D-MN) reflected on its implications and on whether supporters could have done anything to produce a different outcome. He explained, "I have often wondered if we had put in place the same controls but operated it through the public school system if it would have had more support."[8] Such a tactical shift may have been beneficial, but it also may have dampened the enthusiasm of advocates who preferred the Head Start model and were wary of giving too much authority to state governments or the public school system. When Albert Shanker of the American Federation of Teachers described early childhood education as a job for the public schools in September 1974, those constituencies viewed his proposal as a power grab. Even if Mondale and his congressional allies had overcome these intramural disagreements within the early childhood policy community, the presence of Richard Nixon in the White House made the enactment of comprehensive child development legislation unlikely.

Over time, the obstacles confronting potential reformers grew more difficult to surmount. The evolving positions and political activities of state governments and Head Start representatives in the public sector, in combination with a growing number and range of service providers in the private sector, meant that more actors perceived themselves as stakeholders. Anyone wishing to alter the status quo had to grapple with this growing organizational density. The difficulty of this task was apparent by the late 1970s: "If you put your hand on Head Start, for example, you'd find a lot of people who knew exactly what it meant to them and what sort of budget they expected from Washington" (Mondale 2010, 270). The Head Start community was one of many constituencies whose mobilization affected subsequent political debates over early childhood policy. Many of these constituencies opposed proposals to alter existing arrangements. Though they expressed fealty to the general objective of increased public-sector investment, they worried that policy changes would affect their administrative prerogatives and their financial support.

What do the dynamics described in this book portend for the future of preschool education in the United States? Major policy change is always a difficult undertaking in the institutionally fragmented American political system, and it becomes even more challenging when the interests and political influence of existing stakeholders are taken into account. Even so, one should not interpret the preceding analysis to mean that the present system is frozen in place. One of the striking developments of the last two decades is the extent of policy change in states like Georgia and Oklahoma. These episodes suggest that substantial shifts are most likely to occur when reformers accommodate existing stakeholders in the public and private sectors. Contemporary reformers seem to be cognizant of this dynamic, and they often assert that new programs will not cause anyone who is satisfied with the preschool services their children receive to lose access to them.

In conclusion, the fragmented and decentralized preschool system that exists in the contemporary United States is the legacy of Nixon's veto of the Comprehensive Child Development Act and the reactions it sparked across several institutional venues. This historical legacy limits reformers' alternatives, because "policy options are always constrained by the legacies of existing policy, politics, and administration, and our choices today are burdened by our past" (Orloff 1988, 80). Some of the possibilities that existed in the late 1960s and early 1970s are unlikely today, a point that can be illustrated by returning to the prediction made by Harold Howe II, as commissioner of education, in 1968. Howe predicted that publicly provided preschool education would eventually be universal for four-year-olds in the United States. Since that time, the number and proportion of children enrolled in preschool has grown significantly. However, the private sector has long played and continues to play a crucial role in providing preschool services. A universal public system is unlikely to develop in the United States, where the complementary roles played by the public and private sectors are likely to be defining features of preschool politics for the foreseeable future.

A Note on Archival Sources

One of the archival sources on which the preceding analysis relies is a collection of interviews housed at the National Library of Medicine in Bethesda, Maryland. The relevant notes incorporate only the names of the interviewer and the interviewee, the date of the interview, and the page number from which the relevant quotation is drawn. The full citation for this source follows:

Leona Baumgartner and Milton J. E. Senn. Transcripts and Tapes of Interviews on the Child Development Movement. NLM ID: 2935107R. National Library of Medicine, Bethesda, MD.

The analysis also relies on archival material housed at several other institutions:

the Association for Childhood Education International (ACEI), Special Collections, University of Maryland Libraries, in College Park, Maryland (shortened to "ACEI Archives" in the notes);

the Carl Albert Congressional Research and Studies Center in Norman, Oklahoma (shortened to "Carl Albert Center" in the notes);

the Education Commission of the States in Denver, Colorado (shortened to "ECS Archives" in the notes);

the Minnesota Historical Society in Saint Paul, Minnesota;

the National Archives and Records Administration in College Park, Maryland (shortened to "National Archives" in the notes); and

the New York University Archives in New York, New York.

Notes

INTRODUCTION

1. "Picking up the Options," address by Harold Howe II, U.S. commissioner of education, Department of Health, Education, and Welfare, before the Annual Meeting of the Department of Elementary School Principals of the National Education Association, Houston, Texas, April 1, 1968, 5, National Archives, RG 12: Records of the Office of Education, Office of the Commissioner, Office Files of the Commissioner of Education, 1939–80, A1, entry 122, box 382.

2. Current Population Survey, "Table A-2: Percentage of the Population 3 Years and Older Enrolled in School, by Age, Sex, Race, and Hispanic Origin: October 1947 to 2010," http://www.census.gov/hhes/school/data/cps/historical/index.html (accessed September 14, 2012).

3. Current Population Survey, "Table A-1: School Enrollment of the Population 3 Years Old and Over, by Level and Control of School, Race, and Hispanic Origin: October 1955 to 2010," http://www.census.gov/hhes/school/data/cps/historical/index.html (accessed March 13, 2012).

4. Undated memorandum from Albert H. Quie, chairman, to House Republican Task Force on Education, Minnesota Historical Society, Manuscripts Collection, Albert H. Quie Papers, "1965–1968 Files," box 148, 146.I.19.5B. The memorandum is undated but accompanied a document entitled *Report of the Republican Task Force on Education: A New Look at Pre-School Education, Present and Future*. The report was written in 1966, suggesting that the memorandum was authored around that time.

5. Current Population Survey, "Table A-1." Bainbridge et al. (2005) note that question changes in the October CPS in 1985 and 1994 may have increased reporting rates.

6. *Transforming Public Education: Pathway to a Pre-K–12 Future* (Washington, DC: Pew Center on the States, 2011), 14.

7. Education Commission of the States, *Early Learning: Improving Results for Young Children* (Denver: Education Commission of the States, 2000), 4, ECS Archives.

8. Due to its focus on preschool programs, the present analysis devotes limited attention to the history of kindergartens in the United States. Kindergartens are an important chapter in the story of early learning, but they currently fall outside the domain of "preschool" due to their integration into the public school system. Several superb studies examine the emergence of kindergarten as an educational innovation in the late nineteenth century and/or its relationship with the public school system (Beatty 1995,

2001; Cuban 1992; Dombkowski 2001; Kaestle and Vinovskis 1978; Ross 1976; Russell 2011).

9. This book uses several terms interchangeably. It refers to preschool education, child development programs, early childhood policy, and prekindergarten. These terms reflect the changing rhetoric of those who favor greater public investment in educational programs serving young children (Russell 2011; L. White 2004). They also reflect preschool service providers' contemporary diversity.

10. Programs serving infants and toddlers also fall outside the scope of the present analysis. Beatty (1995, xi) asserts that it is "historically correct" to distinguish between preschool education and child care. Several scholars focus on child care in the United States and examine some of the policies and programs that appear in this book (Beatty 1995; Cohen 2001; Michel 1999).

11. These cost estimates include both preschool and child care programs. Focusing solely on child care centers highlights the role of the private sector. In 1990, according to one analysis, about 90 percent of American child care centers were private. Two-thirds of the private centers were nonprofit, and one-third was for-profit. The nonprofit centers included 25 percent that were independent, 15 percent that were sponsored by religious organizations, 8 percent that were run by large nonprofit organizations, and 9 percent that were run by Head Start providers (A. D. White 2005, 17).

12. Kavan Peterson, "Preschool Gets Record Boost in '05," *Stateline.org*, November 16, 2005.

13. *NEA on Prekindergarten and Kindergarten* (Washington, DC: National Education Association, 2004), 5.

14. *Ensuring America's Future: Policy Statements and Recommendations from National Education Organizations* (Alexandria, VA: Pre-K Coalition, 2011), 5.

15. In addition to complaints about the general shortcomings of the contemporary preschool system, many observers lament the poor quality of individual preschool and child care programs (Barnett and Hustedt 2003; Henry, Gordon, and Rickman 2006).

16. The historical and contemporary political conflict surrounding preschool education is multidimensional. This book focuses on the interplay between the public and the private sector and between the national government and the states, but questions of program effectiveness, appropriate curricula, and teacher certification requirements have also proven controversial. Those debates lie beyond the scope of this analysis but have been examined elsewhere (Beatty 1995; Vinovskis 1999a).

17. A "political analysis" seems especially constructive because, in the words of one scholar, "far too many 'historians' of particular childhood policies are insiders with axes to grind" (Sealander 2004, 181).

18. A recent comparative analysis of "family policy" concludes that fewer significant policy changes since the mid-1990s have occurred in the United States than in such countries as the United Kingdom, Germany, France, and Australia (Daly 2010).

19. Many other public preschool programs are modeled on Head Start, especially in terms of their clientele and their comprehensive programming.

20. House Committee on Ways and Means, *1990 Green Book: Background Material and Data on Programs within the Jurisdiction of the Committee on Ways and Means*, 101st Cong., 2d sess. (Committee Print, 1990), 840.

21. This growth is impressive, but not all claims are based on preschool-related expenses. Claimants become eligible for the tax credit based on the expenses they incur for

children who are thirteen years of age or less. The substantial growth in claims is based on data from 1988, when the Family Support Act significantly tightened eligibility for the tax credit. It required that taxpayers provide the correct name, address, and taxpayer identification number of the dependent care provider. It also lowered the age at which a taxpayer identification number had to be submitted for children for whom the credit was claimed, from age five to age two. These more-onerous reporting requirements lowered the number of claimants from nine million in 1988 to six million in 1989. See House Committee on Ways and Means, *2004 Green Book: Background Material and Data on Programs within the Jurisdiction of the Committee on Ways and Means*, 108th Cong., 2d sess. (Committee Print, 2004), 13–43.

22. Tax Policy Center, "Dependent Care Tax Credit: Number of Families and Amount of Credit, 1976–2009," http://www.taxpolicycenter.org/taxfacts/displayafact.cfm? Docid= 180 (accessed March 27, 2012). The Tax Policy Center is a joint initiative of the Urban Institute and the Brookings Institution. Its estimate was last updated in July 2011.

23. This dynamic is not unusual. Third-party providers in the private sector are often the "core societal advocates" of tax expenditures because there are no interest groups that represent their nominal beneficiaries (Howard 1997, 7).

24. Head Start remains in existence nearly five decades after its creation, and its long-term political impact has exceeded that of either the emergency nursery schools or the wartime child care centers. It was created, however, as part of the broader War on Poverty, which, if successful, would not be permanent.

CHAPTER 1

1. Encouraging the involvement of the market and private sector in social provision is a distinguishing feature of liberal welfare states, of which the United States is an "archetypal example" (Esping-Andersen 1990, 27). Some comparative analyses of early childhood policy compare American programs to those in other liberal welfare states (Michel 1999; L. White 2002, 2004).

2. Current Population Survey, "Table A-1: School Enrollment of the Population 3 Years Old and Over, by Level and Control of School, Race, and Hispanic Origin: October 1955 to 2010," http://www.census.gov/hhes/school/data/cps/historical/index.html (accessed March 13, 2012).

3. See Skocpol 1992 for a broader critique of cultural accounts of welfare state development.

4. One might posit that public opinion represents such a mechanism. However, most studies of the relationship between public opinion and public policy suggest that public opinion sets the general ideological direction of policy but does not spur elected officials to comply with specific demands (Erikson, Wright, and McIver 1993; Stimson, MacKuen, and Erikson 1995).

5. Comparative scholarship on social policy often examines interest group politics through the lens of power resources theory, which emphasizes the significance of organized labor and social democratic political parties. Power resources theory offers valuable insights into the politics of the welfare state, but several scholars have questioned its applicability to early childhood education and care (Bonoli and Reber 2010; Morgan 2006).

6. Milton J. E. Senn, interview with Senator Walter Mondale, April 23, 1975, 6.

7. Milton J. E. Senn, interview with Jule Sugarman, November 2, 1972, 31.

8. Milton J. E. Senn, interview with Marian Wright Edelman, October 4, 1973, 29.

9. Morgan 2006 describes the conservative resurgence and its policy implications in more detail.

10. *Transforming Public Education: Pathway to a Pre-K–12 Future* (Washington, DC: Pew Center on the States, 2011), 5.

11. The decentralization of political authority set forth in the Constitution has been exacerbated by Progressive Era reforms and changes in congressional operations (Steinmo and Watts 1995).

12. Federalism has been characterized as a "necessary condition for the development of American exceptionalism" (Robertson 1989, 261).

13. Federalism scholars describe an increased willingness among national officials to preempt policy decisions that were made at the state level (Zimmerman 1991).

14. Political historian Julian Zelizer (2004) argues that the complex world of political actors described by political science scholarship might help political historians develop fresh approaches and frameworks for the study of the policymaking process.

CHAPTER 2

1. Several authors examine the early history of early childhood programs in greater detail than will be pursued in this chapter. See Beatty 1995; Cahan 1989; Michel 1999; E. Rose 1999.

2. School attendance data suggest that approximately 40 percent of all three-year-olds in Massachusetts were enrolled in school as late as 1840. Attendance then steadily declined until 1860. See Kaestle and Vinovskis (1978) and May and Vinovskis (1977) for more on Massachusetts, the state for which the best data on infant school attendance are available.

3. Abigail Adams Eliot, "Nursery Schools Fifty Years Ago," *Young Children*, April 1972, 212, Association for Childhood Education International (ACEI) Archives, Special Collections, University of Maryland Libraries, RG V, series I, box 11.

4. Eliot, "Nursery Schools Fifty Years Ago," 211.

5. "NAEYC's First Half Century, 1926–1976," *Young Children*, September 1976, 463, ACEI Archives, RG V, series I, box 11.

6. Eliot, "Nursery Schools Fifty Years Ago," 213.

7. Cravens (1993) examines the emergence of child development as an established science and profession in the American scientific and academic system, focusing on the history and impact of the Iowa Child Welfare Research Station. Some of the Iowa scientists, most prominently George D. Stoddard, were actively involved in political debates over the appropriate role of nursery schools.

8. Local control led the schools to take on a variety of forms. Some were connected to colleges or universities, others were part of high school home economics departments, and others were administered by local community agencies. See Sue C. Wortham, *Childhood, 1892–1992* (Wheaton, MD: ACEI, 1992), 36, ACEI Archives, acc. 99–116, box 8.

9. Mary Dabney Davis, "Nursery Schools in 1936," *School Life*, December 1936, 117–120, ACEI Archives, RG V, series 1, box 10.

10. Bureau of Child Development, University of the State of New York, *Essentials of Nursery Education* (Albany: University of the State of New York, 1938), 1, ACEI Archives, RG V, series 1, box 10.

11. This particular estimate may overstate peak enrollment in the emergency nursery school program. In a 1972 interview, someone who was on the faculty of the Child Development Institute at Teachers College at Columbia University when the program began claimed that the peak enrollment was in 1934–35, when seventy-five thousand children attended nineteen hundred nursery schools (Hymes 1979, 20).

12. *Federal Aid for the Day Care Program*, no. 8 (Washington, DC: Child Welfare Information Service, 1945), Carl Albert Congressional Research and Studies Center, Helen Gahagan Douglas Collection, box 141, folder 1.

13. Elizabeth Rose (1999, 145) uses language that is more flexible, explaining that the nursery schools provided services to children whose families were "on relief or near relief." Her description confirms the targeted nature of the program.

14. Children attending WPA nursery schools represented only 5 percent of children aged two to five years who were attending school. Most of the others enrolled in kindergartens in public schools, and school attendance was higher in urban areas than in rural areas. See Mary Dabney Davis, *Schools for Children under Six: A Report on the Status and Need for Nursery Schools and Kindergartens*, bulletin 1947, no. 5 (Washington, DC: Federal Security Agency, Office of Education, 1947), 23, ACEI Archives, RG V, series 1, box 10.

15. *Federal Aid for the Day Care Program.*

16. *Federal Aid for the Day Care Program*, 44.

17. Milton J. E. Senn, interview with James L. Hymes Jr., November 16, 1972, 16.

18. Some observers portrayed female employment as an economic necessity for individual families who had been affected by the war, arguing that the stipends received by the wives of men in the armed forces were "utterly inadequate" (*Wartime Care and the Protection of Children of Employed Mothers: Hearing on S. 876 and S. 1130 before the Senate Committee on Education and Labor*, 78th Cong., 1st sess. [1943], 91).

19. Senate Committee on Education and Labor, *Wartime Care*, 81.

20. Senate Committee on Education and Labor, *Wartime Care*, 5.

21. Senate Committee on Education and Labor, *Wartime Care*, 50.

22. *Day Care of Children in Post-war United States* (New York: Child Welfare League of America, 1945), Carl Albert Center, Helen Gahagan Douglas Collection, box 141, folder 1.

23. Senate Committee on Education and Labor, *Wartime Care*, 8.

24. *Federal Aid for the Day Care Program*, 46.

25. *Federal Aid for the Day Care Program*, 46–47.

26. *Federal Aid for the Day Care Program*, 47.

27. Many WPA nursery schools were converted into wartime child care centers by lengthening their hours and limiting their enrollment to children of working women. By May 1943, "1,150 of the 1,700 WPA nursery schools were operating in war-disrupted areas serving children and families regardless of income" (Cahan 1989, 42).

28. Senate Committee on Education and Labor, *Wartime Care*, 12.

29. *Federal Aid for the Day Care Program*, 46.

30. Davis, *Schools for Children under Six*, 30.

31. *Nursery Schools Vital to America's War Effort*, School Children and the War Se-

ries, leaflet no. 3 (Washington, DC: Federal Security Agency, Office of Education, 1943), 12, ACEI Archives, RG V, series 1, box 10.

32. David H. Russell, "With Books and Magazines," *Understanding the Child* 25, no. 2 (April 1946): 55–60, 55, ACEI Archives, RG V, series 1, box 15.

33. *Children in a Democracy,* general report adopted by the White House Conference on Children in a Democracy, January 19, 1940, 36, ACEI Archives, RG V, series 1, box 14.

34. *Who Will Need a Post-war Nursery School,* Kaiser Child Service Centers, Pamphlets for Teachers, no. 3, 12, ACEI Archives, RG V, series 1, box 10.

35. Letter from Henry L. Zucker, chairman, Ohio State War-Time Child Care Committee, Ohio State Council of Defense, to Congresswoman Helen Gahagan Douglas, June 5, 1945, Carl Albert Center, Helen Gahagan Douglas Collection, box 17, folder 4a.

36. Association for Nursery Education of Southern California, Mail Survey of the Families of the Children Enrolled in the Ninety Los Angeles Child Care Center Nursery Schools, Carl Albert Center, Helen Gahagan Douglas Collection, box 17, folder 4b. The memorandum describing the survey is undated but reveals that it was mailed on July 15, 1945.

37. "Letters about Day Care," *Day Care News* (Committee on Day Care of Children, Wayne County Council of Defense) 20 (April 1945), Carl Albert Center, Helen Gahagan Douglas Collection, box 141, folder 1.

38. Letter from Alice T. Dashiell, field secretary, Child Welfare League of America, to Congresswoman Helen Gahagan Douglas, June 4, 1945, Carl Albert Center, Helen Gahagan Douglas Collection, box 141, folder 1.

39. *Day Care of Children in Post-war United States,* 2.

40. James L. Hymes Jr., "The Road Ahead for Nursery Schools," *Understanding the Child* 25, no. 2 (April 1946): 36–39, at 39, ACEI Archives, RG V, series 1, box 15.

41. "Child Care," resolution adopted at the Convention of the International Union, United Automobile, Aircraft and Agricultural Implement Workers of America, CIO, Atlantic City, New Jersey, March 23–30, 1946, Carl Albert Center, Helen Gahagan Douglas Collection, box 17, folder 4b.

42. A similar campaign occurred in the United Kingdom, where the National Society of Children's Nurseries pressed for nurseries to become a permanent feature of the British social service system. Legislation passed in England in 1944 and in Scotland in 1945 made "the provision of fully equipped educational centers obligatory upon all local Education Authorities for children *from two years of age and up.*" According to that legislation, "Parents are not required to send their children but the school authorities are required to provide suitable facilities" (Russell, "With Books and Magazines," 59; emphasis in original).

43. Congress continued to support centers for poor children in Washington, DC, until 1953 (Beatty 1995, 192).

44. Hymes, "Road Ahead for Nursery Schools," 36.

45. H.R. 2362, 80th Cong., 1st sess. (March 4, 1947); H.R. 793, 81st Cong., 1st sess. (January 5, 1949). In 1949, Senator Claude Pepper (D-FL) introduced companion legislation in the Senate: S. 1216, 81st Cong., 1st sess. (March 9, 1949).

46. Davis, *Schools for Children under Six,* 17–19.

47. Dorothy W. Baruch, Evangeline B. Burgess, and Dorothy Blumenstock Jones, *How to Start Publicity for Nursery Education in Your Community* (Iowa City, IA: National Association for Nursery Education, 1940), 13, ACEI Archives, RG V, series 1, box 10.

48. Four states (California, Massachusetts, New York, and Washington) allocated state funds for child care immediately after the Second World War. California was the only one whose allocation preserved a large proportion of its centers (Reese 1996, 568).

49. *For Every Child a Healthy Personality: A Digest of the Fact Finding Report to the Midcentury White House Conference on Children and Youth* ([Washington, DC]: Midcentury White House Conference on Children and Youth, 1950), ACEI Archives, RG V, series 1, box 14.

50. *Platform Recommendations and Pledge to Children* ([Washington, DC]: Midcentury White House Conference on Children and Youth, 1950), ACEI Archives, RG V, series 1, box 14.

51. Michel (1999, 150) argues that the largely unsuccessful attempts to extend public funding for early childhood programs provoked a "broad-ranging debate about motherhood, paid employment, and child care that eventually led to the formation of a national child care movement." For example, postwar protests in Philadelphia illustrated mothers' "new sense of entitlement" to publicly funded care and eventually led the city to fund centers through the 1950s (E. Rose 1999, 6). While important, these debates and developments had a limited effect on national enrollment patterns.

52. Lillian L. Gore and Rose E. Koury, *A Survey of Early Elementary Education in Public Schools, 1960–61* (Washington, DC: U.S. Department of Health, Education, and Welfare, 1965), 46, ACEI Archives, RG V, series 1, box 15.

53. Gore and Koury, *Survey of Early Elementary Education*, 52.

54. Dorothea Andrews, "Highlights of the Recommendations," *Children* 7, no. 3 (May–June 1960): 92–95, at 94, ACEI Archives, RG V, series 1, box 14.

55. Proponents also linked the tax deduction to the Korean War and other policy initiatives. They contended that "women's labor was necessary to the nation's economic and security interests, claimed that the deduction would help promote rapid mobilization in a wartime emergency, and insisted that child care was as legitimate a business expense as entertainment, travel, and country club membership" (E. Rose 1999, 196).

56. "The White House Message on Poverty," March 16, 1964, 2, National Archives, RG 12: Records of the Office of Education, Office of the Commissioner, Office Files of the Commissioner of Education, 1939–80, A1, entry 122, box 125.

57. This discussion of Head Start draws heavily on three excellent accounts of its emergence and early years: Vinovskis 2005, Zigler and Muenchow 1992, and Zigler and Styfco 2010.

58. "Preschool Programs for Disadvantaged Children," memorandum from Harry Levin to Frances Keppel, U.S. commissioner of education, August 24, 1964, 2, National Archives, RG 12: Records of the Office of Education, Office of the Commissioner, Office Files of the Commissioner of Education, 1939–80, A1, entry 122, box 125.

59. "Preschool Programs for Disadvantaged Children," 4.

60. During his 1964 presidential campaign, Johnson discussed education and poverty at length but did not mention preschool specifically (Vinovskis 2005, 58).

61. "White House Conference on Education: Transcript of Closing Session," remarks of James E. Allen Jr., commissioner of education, State Department of Education, Albany, New York, vice chairman for panels on "Extending Educational Opportunities," 14, National Archives, RG 12: Records of the Office of Education, Office of the Commissioner, Office Files of the Commissioner of Education, 1939–80, A1, entry 122, box 205.

62. J. W. Getzels, "Preschool Education," in *Consultants' Papers, The White House*

Conference on Education, July 20–21, 1965, 2:111, National Archives, RG 12: Records of the Office of Education, Office of the Commissioner, Office Files of the Commissioner of Education, 1939–80, A1, entry 122, box 204.

63. Becker, "Pre-School Education," panel summary of the White House Conference on Education, Washington, DC, July 20–21, 1965, National Archives, RG 12: Records of the Office of Education, Office of the Commissioner, Office Files of the Commissioner of Education, 1939–80, A1, entry 122, box 204. This summary is in a folder labeled "White House Conference on Education: Press Releases."

64. Becker, "Pre-School Education."

65. The memorandum claimed that "what is now known as Project Head Start was originally proposed by Republicans as long ago as 1961" (Carol Khosrov, "The Eradication of Poverty," Task Force on the Functions of Federal, State, and Local Governments, revised draft, May 26, 1966, 4, Minnesota Historical Society, Manuscripts Collection, Albert H. Quie Papers, "1965–1968 Files," box 147, 146.I.19.4F).

66. Milton J. E. Senn, interview with Edward Zigler, June 10, 1972, 26.

67. Milton J. E. Senn, interview with Martha Phillips, November 19, 1973, 29.

68. "Programs and Research in the Facilitation of Development in Young Children," memorandum from Edmund W. Gordon to the President's Task Force on Education, March 24, 1967, 10, National Archives, RG 12: Records of the Office of Education, Office of the Commissioner, Office Files of the Commissioner of Education, 1939–80, A1, entry 122, box 334.

69. During the July 1965 White House Conference on Education, the "one-shot nature" of Head Start emerged as a common critique ("Undated Memorandum: The White House Conference on Education," 4, Minnesota Historical Society, Manuscripts Collection, Albert H. Quie Papers, "House Republican Task Force on Tax Credits for Higher Education Files, 1965," box 56, 146.I.12.11B).

70. "Follow Through," undated program summary, 1, National Archives, RG 12: Records of the Office of Education, Office of the Commissioner, Office Files of the Commissioner of Education, 1939–80, A1, entry 122, box 485. The summary includes estimates of "new obligational authority," the number of children served, and the number of programs for fiscal years 1968, 1969, and 1970. These estimates and the document's reference to the "initial stages" of Follow Through suggest that it was published shortly after the program was launched in 1967. Follow Through was created as a temporary demonstration program, but it lasted for twenty-five years, despite a checkered history and disappointing results (Vinovskis 1999a, chap. 4).

71. "Statement of the Office of Economic Opportunity on the Release of Preliminary Report by Westinghouse Learning Corporation on Head Start Effectiveness," April 14, 1969, O-5 (emphasis in original), Minnesota Historical Society, Manuscripts Collection, Albert H. Quie Papers, "1971–1972 Files," box 150, 146.I.19.7B.

72. The Coleman Report and a research monograph by Albert Jensen also placed Head Start supporters on the defensive. The former argued that schools could do little to reverse the educational disadvantages induced by poverty, and the latter emphasized the impact of genetics and heredity (Zigler and Muenchow 1992, 56–73).

73. "Statement of Secretary Robert H. Finch," April 9, 1969, 2, National Archives, RG 235: General Records of the Department of Health, Education, and Welfare, series 235.3.2: Records of the Office of the Assistant Secretary, Office File of Jule Sugarman, First Director of the Office of Child Development, 1967–69, entry 34, box 4. The state-

ment was one of three enclosures that accompanied a letter of June 2, 1969, from the secretary to Head Start grantees.

74. Office of the White House Secretary, "The White House Press Conference of Robert H. Finch, Secretary of Health, Education, and Welfare; Daniel P. Moynihan, Special Assistant to the President for Urban Affairs; Robert Patricelli, Deputy Assistant Secretary for HEW; Jule Sugarman, Acting Director of the Children's Bureau; and Ron Ziegler, Press Secretary to the President," Roosevelt Room, April 9, 1969, 4, National Archives, RG 235: General Records of the Department of Health, Education, and Welfare, series 235.3.2: Records of the Office of the Assistant Secretary, Office File of Jule Sugarman, First Director of the Office of Child Development, 1967–69, entry 34, box 3.

75. "Head Start: An Overview," undated, 4, National Archives, RG 235: General Records of the Department of Health, Education, and Welfare, series 235.3.2: Records of the Office of the Assistant Secretary, Office File of Jule Sugarman, First Director of the Office of Child Development, 1967–69, entry 34, box 2, folder "H.S./O.C.D., March 1969, #1."

76. "Head Start: An Overview," 5.

77. "Head Start: An Overview," 7.

78. *Head Start Child Development Program: A Manual of Policies and Instructions* (Washington, DC: Community Action Program, Office of Economic Opportunity, 1967), 10, Carl Albert Center, Fred Harris Collection, box 146, folder 4.

79. "Questions and Answers on the Delegation of Head Start to HEW," 3, National Archives, RG 235: General Records of the Department of Health, Education, and Welfare, series 235.3.2: Records of the Office of the Assistant Secretary, Office File of Jule Sugarman, First Director of the Office of Child Development, 1967–69, entry 34, box 4. The statement was one of three enclosures that accompanied a letter of June 2, 1969, from the secretary to Head Start grantees.

80. "Survey Results Revealed: Schools Favored to Run Head Start," *Minneapolis Tribune,* July 24, 1969, Minnesota Historical Society, Manuscripts Collection, Albert H. Quie Papers, "1969–1970 Files," box 149, 146.I.19.6F.

81. Hymes, "Road Ahead for Nursery Schools," 37.

82. Beatrice Rosenberg, *Day Care Facts* (Washington, DC: Women's Bureau, 1970), 1, Carl Albert Center, Fred Harris Collection, box 231, folder 19.

83. "Developmental Day Care," speech by Mrs. Richard M. Lansburgh at White House Conference Forum 17, December 14, 1970, 2, Carl Albert Center, Fred Harris Collection, box 232, folder 5.

84. "Letter from National Women's Political Caucus," July 13, 1971, Minnesota Historical Society, Manuscripts Collection, Albert H. Quie Papers, "1971–1972 Files," box 157, 146.I.19.4F.

85. Statement by Sam Nocella, vice president, Amalgamated Clothing Workers of America, in *A Report of a Conference on Day Care and the Working Mother,* ed. Jeanette Stats (Baltimore, MD: Board of Trustees, Health and Welfare Fund, Baltimore Regional Joint Board, Amalgamated Clothing Workers of America, AFL-CIO, 1967), Minnesota Historical Society, Manuscripts Collection, Albert H. Quie Papers, "1965–1968 Files," box 148, 146.I.19.5B.

86. Senn, interview with Phillips, 4.

87. These two approaches are best thought of as ideal types, as no early childhood program is exclusively custodial or educational.

88. Senn, interview with Zigler, 3.

89. Senn, interview with Zigler, 31.

90. The research of Hunt and Bloom was influential, but the two scholars were not the first to challenge the notion that physical and mental development were predetermined. From the mid-1930s to the early 1950s, the Iowa Child Welfare Research Station was "the leading challenger of the field's twin theses, the maturation theory and the idea of the fixed IQ" (Cravens 1993, 110).

91. Sheldon H. White, "Speculations on the Fate of Early Childhood Education," address before the American Educational Research Association, Washington, DC, April 1975, New York University Archives, John Brademas Congressional Papers, "Child and Family Services: H.R. 2966," box I:04, folder 16.

92. Wortham, *Childhood*, 50.

93. Zigler described himself as a skeptic who believed that the environment affected motivation more profoundly than it affected intelligence. He participated in several heated debates with Hunt that "were advertised somewhat like competitions between rival evangelists" (Zigler and Muenchow 1992, 13–14).

94. Raymond S. Moore and Dennis R. Moore, "The Dangers of Early Schooling," *Harper's* 245 (July 1972): 58–62, at 58, New York University Archives, John Brademas Congressional Papers, "Comprehensive Child Development Act," box I:05, folder 2.

95. Moore and Moore, "Dangers of Early Schooling," 58–59.

96. "The Foundations of Change," address by S. P. Marland Jr., U.S. commissioner of education, Department of Health, Education, and Welfare, before the Lyndon B. Johnson Library Symposium on Education, Austin, Texas, January 24, 1972, 5, National Archives, RG 12: Records of the Office of Education, Office of the Commissioner, Office Files of the Commissioner of Education, 1939–80, A1, entry 122, box 585.

97. The "laboratories of democracy" metaphor can be traced to a dissent by Supreme Court justice Louis Brandeis in *New State Ice Co. v. Liebmann*, 285 U.S. 262 (1932).

98. "A Federal Education Program," memorandum from Hirst Sutton to Messrs. Schultze and Seidman, November 9, 1962, 3, National Archives, RG 51: Records of the Office of Management and Budget, series 61.b: Directors, Deputy Directors, and Assistant Directors Office Files, 1961–68, box 67, folder "Education—A Federal Program For, Nov. 1962."

99. John Brademas, "The National Politics of Education: A View from Capitol Hill," speech before the Harvard Graduate School of Public Administration, June 17, 1968, 6, New York University Archives, John Brademas Congressional Papers, "Speeches: The Politics of Education," box I:10, folder 53.

100. Several historians provide more-comprehensive accounts of the Elementary and Secondary Education Act. See Bailey and Mosher 1968; Graham 1984; Sundquist 1968; Thomas 1975.

101. Harold Howe II, "U.S. Schools: Changing Federal Role Seen—But Not Control," interview with Josephine Ripley, *Christian Science Monitor*, July 13, 1966, Eastern edition, 3, National Archives, RG 12: Records of the Office of Education, Office of the Commissioner, Office Files of the Commissioner of Education, 1939–80, A1, entry 122, box 381.

102. Brademas, "National Politics of Education," 19.

103. Harold Howe II, "U.S. School Aid," *New York Times* annual education review, January 12, 1968, 1, National Archives, RG 12: Records of the Office of Education, Office of the Commissioner, Office Files of the Commissioner of Education, 1939–80, A1, entry 122, box 382.

104. Undated and untitled draft, 17, Minnesota Historical Society, Manuscripts Collection, Albert H. Quie Papers, "House Republican Task Force on Tax Credits for Higher Education Files, 1965," box 56, 146.I.12.11B. The draft appears in a folder with several documents from the first few months of 1965. It may be "A Preschool Program for Republicans," which is referenced by another document in the folder but does not appear in it.

105. Rosenberg, *Day Care Facts*, 3.

106. Getzels, "Preschool Education," 110.

107. "Picking up the Options," address by Harold Howe II, U.S. commissioner of education, Department of Health, Education, and Welfare, before the Annual Meeting of the Department of Elementary School Principals of the National Educational Association, Houston, Texas, April 1, 1968, 6, National Archives, RG 12: Records of the Office of Education, Office of the Commissioner, Office Files of the Commissioner of Education, 1939–80, A1, entry 122, box 382. The speech was read to the principals when Howe could not make the trip to Houston.

CHAPTER 3

1. "Report," memorandum from Robert E. Patricelli, executive secretary of the Advisory Committee on Head Start, to members of the committee, March 4, 1969, 7, National Archives, RG 235: General Records of the Department of Health, Education, and Welfare, series 235.3.2: Records of the Office of the Assistant Secretary, Office File of Jule Sugarman, First Director of the Office of Child Development, 1967–69, entry 34, box 2.

2. "Day Care: It's a Lot More Than Child's Play," *Business Week*, March 21, 1970, 110, Carl Albert Center, Fred Harris Collection, box 193, folder 15.

3. "Statement of Secretary Robert H. Finch," April 9, 1969, 5, National Archives, RG 235: General Records of the Department of Health, Education, and Welfare, series 235.3.2: Records of the Office of the Assistant Secretary, Office File of Jule Sugarman, First Director of the Office of Child Development, 1967–69, entry 34, box 4. The statement was one of three enclosures that accompanied a letter of June 2, 1969, from the secretary to Head Start grantees.

4. Rose K. Wiener, "Some Thoughts on Education for the Poor," April 7, 1967, 8, National Archives, RG 12: Records of the Office of Education, Office of the Commissioner, Office Files of the Commissioner of Education, 1939–80, A1, entry 122, box 335.

5. *Education for the Urban Disadvantaged: From Preschool to Employment* (New York: Committee for Economic Development, 1971), 17, Carl Albert Center, Carl Albert Collection, Department Files, box 93, folder 15. The statement endorsed universal enrollment while placing special emphasis on access for "disadvantaged" children.

6. Milton J. E. Senn, interview with Dr. Julius Richmond, July 12, 1972, 47.

7. Margaret Malone, *Federal Involvement in Day Care* (Washington, DC: Legislative Reference Service of the Library of Congress, 1969), 9–10, Minnesota Historical Society, Manuscripts Collection, Albert H. Quie Papers, "1971–1972 Files," box 157, 146.I.19.14F.

8. Malone, *Federal Involvement in Day Care*, 10–11.

9. "Office of Education: Programs and Activities in Early Childhood Education, Fiscal Year 1969," undated, National Archives, RG 235: General Records of the Department of Health, Education, and Welfare, series 235.3.2: Records of the Office of the Assistant

Secretary, Office File of Jule Sugarman, First Director of the Office of Child Development, 1967–69, entry 34, box 2.

10. "Information Sheet on Federal Assistance for Day Care Programs," prepared by the Office of Child Development, Department of Health, Education, and Welfare, September 1969, Carl Albert Center, Fred Harris Collection, box 193, folder 15.

11. Beatrice Rosenberg, *Day Care Facts* (Washington, DC: Women's Bureau, 1970), 7, Carl Albert Center, Fred Harris Collection, box 231, folder 19.

12. Rosenberg, *Day Care Facts,* 8.

13. Richard D. Jaffe and Evelyn C. Jaffe, *Survey of Available Private and Public Kindergarten Services, Fall, 1968* (Chicago: Richard D. Jaffe and Associates, Institute for Social Action, 1969), 98, National Archives, RG 12: Records of the Office of Education, Office of the Commissioner, Office Files of the Commissioner of Education, 1939–80, A1, entry 122, box 461.

14. Jaffe and Jaffe, *Survey of Available Private and Public Kindergarten Services,* 10, 99.

15. Jaffe and Jaffe, *Survey of Available Private and Public Kindergarten Services,* 103.

16. Malone, *Federal Involvement in Day Care,* 37.

17. Rosenberg, *Day Care Facts,* 12.

18. "Business Takes Care of the Kiddies," *Business Week,* March 21, 1970, 51, Carl Albert Center, Fred Harris Collection, box 193, folder 15.

19. Ann Cook and Herbert Mack, "Business in Education: The Discovery Center Hustle," *Social Policy,* September/October 1970, 6, Carl Albert Center, Fred Harris Collection, box 193, folder 15.

20. Cook and Mack, "Business in Education."

21. "Day Care Programs Authorized by H.R. 12080," memorandum from Lawrence C. Feldman, executive director, National Committee for the Day Care of Children, to staff, Senate Finance Committee, undated, 2, Carl Albert Center, Fred Harris Collection, box 193, folder 15.

22. "For Excellence, Freedom and Diversity," condensation of broadcast, Richard M. Nixon, CBS Radio Network, October 20, 1968, 10, National Archives, RG 12: Records of the Office of Education, Office of the Commissioner, Office Files of the Commissioner of Education, 1939–80, A1, entry 122, box 383.

23. Jule M. Sugarman, "A Summary of Administration Action to Date," draft dated October 31, 1969, 1, National Archives, RG 235: General Records of the Department of Health, Education, and Welfare, series 235.3.2: Records of the Office of the Assistant Secretary, Office File of Jule Sugarman, First Director of the Office of Child Development, 1967–69, entry 34, box 5.

24. Letter from Urie Bronfenbrenner, Cornell University, to the Honorable James Farmer, undersecretary of health, education, and welfare, November 21, 1969, National Archives, RG 235: General Records of the Department of Health, Education, and Welfare, series 235.3.2: Records of the Office of the Assistant Secretary, Office File of Jule Sugarman, First Director of the Office of Child Development, 1967–69, entry 34, box 5.

25. Sugarman, "Summary of Administration Action to Date," 1.

26. Due to tight state budgets, a lack of personnel, and a lack of physical facilities, this provision spurred "relatively little new day care" (Malone, *Federal Involvement in Day Care,* 35–36).

27. *Day Care and Child Development in Your Community* (Washington, DC: Day

Care and Child Development Council of America, 1969), 13 (emphasis in original), Carl Albert Center, Fred Harris Collection, box 193, folder 15.

28. Sugarman, "Summary of Administration Action to Date," 2.

29. Milton J. E. Senn, interview with Stephen Hess, November 19, 1973, 11.

30. "Task Force on Delivery of Services," Developmental Child Care Forum, White House Conference on Children 1970, 5, Carl Albert Center, Fred Harris Collection, box 232, folder 5.

31. Therese W. Lansburgh, "Speech at White House Conference Forum #17: Developmental Day Care," December 14, 1970, 1, Carl Albert Center, Fred Harris Collection, box 232, folder 5.

32. "Results of Balloting by the Delegates to the 1970 White House Conference on Children on Overriding Concerns and Specific Recommendations," undated, National Archives, RG 12: Records of the Office of Education, Office of the Commissioner, Office Files of the Commissioner of Education, 1939–80, A1, entry 122, box 508. The ballot listed sixteen "overriding concerns," with each first-place vote receiving sixteen points, each second-place vote receiving fifteen points, and so forth. "Comprehensive family-oriented child development programs" received the third-highest total of first-place votes.

33. Therese W. Lansburgh, "Report on the White House Conference on Children," memorandum to the Board of Directors, January 5, 1971, 1, Carl Albert Center, Fred Harris Collection. box 232, folder 5.

34. Lansburgh, "Report on the White House Conference," 2.

35. The Select Subcommittee on Education of the House Committee on Education and Labor held hearings on a similar bill with the same title during the Ninetieth Congress.

36. "Dear Colleague" letter from Representative Patsy Mink, January 1969, Carl Albert Center, Jeffery Cohelan Collection, box 77, folder 21.

37. John Brademas, "Testimony before the National Priorities Committee of the Democratic National Committee," April 29, 1970, 7, Carl Albert Center, Carl Albert Collection, Legislative Files, box 115, folder 85.

38. The bills profiled in this paragraph do not provide a comprehensive list of legislation with implications for early childhood policy but highlight the bills whose objectives resonated with those of the Comprehensive Child Development Act of 1971.

39. Jule M. Sugarman, "Legislative Items," memorandum to Tom Joe, special assistant to the undersecretary, June 12, 1969, 1, National Archives, RG 235: General Records of the Department of Health, Education, and Welfare, series 235.3.2: Records of the Office of the Assistant Secretary, Office File of Jule Sugarman, First Director of the Office of Child Development, 1967–69, entry 34, box 4.

40. Sugarman, "Summary of Administration Action to Date," 4.

41. Milton J. E. Senn, interview with Carolyn Harmon, September 14, 1972, 3.

42. Senn, interview with Harmon, 2–3. Harmon did not join the Office of Child Development until July 1970, but she explained that upon joining the agency, she had been told about Sugarman's activities and how they had been perceived.

43. Senn, interview with Harmon, 4.

44. "Federal Block Grant Proposed," ECS Bulletin (Education Commission of the States), May 1969, Carl Albert Center, Jeffery Cohelan Collection, box 77, folder 20.

45. Milton J. E. Senn, interview with Martha Phillips, November 19, 1973, 6.

46. Senn, interview with Phillips, 6–7.

47. Walter F. Mondale, letter to Senator Birch Bayh, May 27, 1971, Minnesota Historical Society, Manuscripts Collection, Walter F. Mondale Papers, "Subcommittee on Children and Youth," box 32, 13.3.0.3B.

48. "Remarks of Senator Walter F. Mondale before the Biennial Meeting of the Society for Research in Child Development," Minneapolis, Minnesota, April 3, 1971, 4, Minnesota Historical Society, Manuscripts Collection, Walter F. Mondale Papers, "Speech Text Files," box 4, 154.K.3.2F.

49. Letter from Walter F. Mondale to Marian Wright Edelman, January 15, 1971, Minnesota Historical Society, Manuscripts Collection, Walter F. Mondale Papers, "Subcommittee on Children and Youth," box 32, 13.3.0.3B.

50. Milton J. E. Senn, interview with Sydney Johnson III, September 15, 1972, 3.

51. Milton J. E. Senn, interview with Marian Wright Edelman, October 4, 1973, 5.

52. Senn, interview with Edelman, 5.

53. Senn, interview with Edelman, 6.

54. Milton J. E. Senn, interview with Judy Assmus, September 14, 1972, 8.

55. Senn, interview with Assmus, 8.

56. Milton J. E. Senn, interview with Dr. Donald Cohen, November 1, 1972, 2.

57. The coalition also included Common Cause, the League of Women Voters, the U.S. Catholic Conference, the National Organization for Women, and organizations representing Latinos and Native Americans (Senn, interview with Johnson, 4).

58. Senn, interview with Assmus, 2–3.

59. Senn, interview with Assmus, 3.

60. Senn, interview with Johnson, 5–6.

61. Senn, interview with Johnson, 5–6.

62. Letter from John Brademas to Wilbur D. Mills, March 31, 1971, Minnesota Historical Society, Manuscripts Collection, Albert H. Quie Papers, "1971–1972 Files," box 157, 146.I.19.14F.

63. "Remarks of Senator Walter F. Mondale before the Biennial Meeting of the Society for Research in Child Development," 6.

64. Letter from Representative Albert H. Quie to Dr. Urie Bronfenbrenner of Cornell University, August 17, 1967, National Archives, RG 235: General Records of the Department of Health, Education, and Welfare, series 235.3.2: Records of the Office of the Assistant Secretary, Office File of Jule Sugarman, First Director of the Office of Child Development, 1967–69, entry 34, box 1.

65. Senn, interview with Edelman, 7.

66. *Comprehensive Child Development Act of 1971*, S. 1512, 92d Cong., 1st sess. (April 5, 1971).

67. "Senate Passes Day Care Bill," Washington memo on federal education programs, NEA Office of Government Relations and Citizenship, September 15, 1971 (emphasis in original), Minnesota Historical Society, Manuscripts Collection, Albert H. Quie Papers, "1971–1972 Files," box 157, 146.I.19.14F.

68. Connaught Coyne Marshner, *Federal Child Development: What's Developing?* (Washington, DC: Heritage Foundation, 1974), 4, New York University Archives, John Brademas Congressional Papers, "Child and Family Services: H.R. 2966," box I:04, folder 34.

69. "Remarks of Senator Walter F. Mondale before the Biennial Meeting of the Society for Research in Child Development," 4.

70. John Brademas, "The Outlook for Child Development Legislation," *National Business Woman*, October 1972, 6–7, at 7, New York University Archives, John Brademas Congressional Papers, "Comprehensive Child Development Act," box I:05, folder 2.

71. Letter from Wilma Scott Heide (president) and Mary Ann Stuart (Child Care Task Force) of the National Organization for Women to secretary of health, education, and welfare Elliot Richardson, November 1, 1971, Carl Albert Center, Fred Harris Collection, box 231, folder 17.

72. Letter from Roy Wilkins, Ralph David Abernathy, Dorothy Height, Vernon Jordan, A. Philip Randolph, Bayard Rustin, Harold Sims, and Andrew Young to President Richard Nixon, November 24, 1971, Carl Albert Center, Cornelius Gallagher Collection, box 21, folder 5.

73. Milton J. E. Senn, interview with Lisbeth Bamberger Schorr and William Smith, April 23, 1974, 12. Schorr made the observation about the political strength of programs for low-income families.

74. Senn, interview with Edelman, 8.

75. Senn, interview with Edelman, 3.

76. Senn, interview with Edelman, 4–5.

77. Senn, interview with Edelman, 9.

78. Letter from Urie Bronfenbrenner, Cornell University, to the Honorable James Farmer, undersecretary of health, education, and welfare, November 21, 1969, National Archives, RG 235: General Records of the Department of Health, Education, and Welfare, series 235.3.2: Records of the Office of the Assistant Secretary, Office File of Jule Sugarman, First Director of the Office of Child Development, 1967–69, entry 34, box 5.

79. Senn, interview with Edelman, 10.

80. Letter from Roy Wilkins et al. to Nixon (emphasis in original).

81. "Remarks of Congressman John Brademas at the Conference on Priorities and Action for Children and Youth," sponsored by the National Committee for Children and Youth, Washington, DC, December 4, 1971, 8, New York University Archives, John Brademas Congressional Papers, "Speeches: Remarks to Select Committee on Education, Conference on Priorities and Action for Children and Youth," box III:11, folder 83.

82. Senn, interview with Phillips, 18.

83. Milton J. E. Senn, interview with Judy Miller, October 12, 1972, 14.

84. Senn, interview with Edelman, 4.

85. Senn, interview with Harmon, 9.

86. "Bipartisan Child Development Bill Introduced," press release, March 24, 1971, Minnesota Historical Society, Manuscript Collections, Albert H. Quie Papers, "1971–1972 Files," box 158, 146.I.20.1B.

87. "Remarks of Congressman John Brademas at the Conference on Priorities and Action for Children and Youth," 4.

88. Jo Ellen Jennette, "Child Care and Child Development: Legislative Developments during the 92nd Congress," Congressional Research Service, December 19, 1972, 3. New York University Archives, John Brademas Congressional Papers, "Child Development: CRS Reports," box I:04, folder 32.

89. Only New York senator James Buckley, representing the Conservative Party, at-

tacked the basic philosophical foundations of the bill. Buckley characterized it as "one of the most radical pieces of legislation ever contemplated by Congress" (McCathren 1981, 111).

90. Jennette, "Child Care and Child Development," 1.

91. "Remarks of Senator Walter F. Mondale before the Biennial Meeting of the Society for Research in Child Development," 2.

92. Jennette, "Child Care and Child Development," 1.

93. Letter from John Brademas to Raymond S. Moore, chief executive officer of Hewitt Research Center, July 18, 1972, 2, New York University Archives, John Brademas Congressional Papers, "Comprehensive Child Development Act," box I:05, folder 2.

94. Raymond S. Moore and Dennis R. Moore, "The Dangers of Early Schooling," *Harper's* 245 (July 1972): 58–62, at 58, New York University Archives, John Brademas Congressional Papers, "Comprehensive Child Development Act," box I:05, folder 2.

95. Jennette, "Child Care and Child Development," 1.

96. "Statement of Senator Fred R. Harris (D-OK) on Child Development Act," February 10, 1971, 1, Carl Albert Center, Fred Harris Collection, box 231, folder 20.

97. "Major Preschool Bill Clears Brademas Subcommittee," press release, Office of Congressman John Brademas, June 21, 1971, New York University Archives, John Brademas Congressional Papers, "H.R. 6748, 92nd Congress, 1st Session," box I:41, folder 50.

98. Jennette, "Child Care and Child Development," 6.

99. "Child Care: Top Priority for Women's Rights Movement," *Voice for Children* (Day Care and Child Development Council of America) 3, no. 8 (September 1970): 1, 8, Carl Albert Center, Fred Harris Collection, box 185, folder 19.

100. "Day Care and Women's Liberation," *Voice for Children* 3, no. 8 (September 1970): 4, Carl Albert Center, Fred Harris Collection, box 185, folder 19.

101. Senn, interview with Phillips, 32.

102. Letter from Agnes T. Marks, coordinator of the Legion of Mothers, to Carl Albert, June 10, 1971, Carl Albert Center, Carl Albert Collection, Legislative Files, box 132, folder 11.

103. Marshner, *Federal Child Development,* 19.

104. Letter from John L. Grady, mayor of Belle Glade, FL, to Cornelius Gallagher, December 8, 1971, Carl Albert Center, Cornelius Gallagher Collection, box 21, folder 5.

105. J. Marie Hosea, "Total Control: A Special Report," *Patriotic Press,* September 1971 (emphasis in original), Carl Albert Center, Fred Harris Collection, box 231, folder 18.

106. Senn, interview with Johnson, 11–12.

107. Marshner, *Federal Child Development,* 14.

108. Marshner, *Federal Child Development,* 27.

109. John Ashbrook, "Should Congress Support a Child Day Care Program? No," *American Legion Magazine,* June 1972, 19, New York University Archives, John Brademas Congressional Papers, "Comprehensive Child Development Act," box I:05, folder 2.

110. See, for example, "Statement of Congressman John Brademas on the National Radio Networks (CBS, NBC, ABC, Mutual, Public) as Spokesman for the Congress in Responding to the Network Address on Education Made by President Nixon One Week Ago," March 30, 1974, New York University Archives, John Brademas Congressional Papers, "Speeches: Education Response to President Nixon," box III:12, folder 23. The date of this particular reference illustrates how advocates cited the presidential message throughout the Nixon presidency.

111. Senn, interview with Assmus, 4.

112. Senn, interview with Johnson, 8.

113. Milton J. E. Senn, interview with Jule Sugarman, November 2, 1972, 23.

114. Senn, interview with Phillips, 6.

115. Senn, interview with Harmon, 9–10.

116. Connie Newman, "Child Care Legislation," undated information memorandum to HEW secretary Elliot Richardson, Minnesota Historical Society, Manuscripts Collection, Albert H. Quie Papers, "1971–1972 Files," box 158, 146.I.20.1B. The memorandum was likely sent in late March or early April.

117. Newman, "Child Care Legislation," 2.

118. Senn, interview with Harmon, 12.

119. Letter from Elliot Richardson to John Brademas, June 8, 1971, New York University Archives, John Brademas Congressional Papers, "Comprehensive Child Development Act," box I:05, folder 2.

120. Senn, interview with Johnson, 8.

121. Senn, interview with Harmon, 12.

122. "Child Care: Who Will Win?" *Washington Memo on Federal Education Programs* (NEA Office of Government Relations and Citizenship), July 19, 1971, 2, Minnesota Historical Society, Manuscripts Collection, Albert H. Quie Papers, "1971–1972 Files," box 158, 146.I.20.1B.

123. "Brief Legislative History of Significant Child Care Proposals," memorandum from Earline Anderson to Walter Campbell, August 10, 1971, 2, Carl Albert Center, Fred Harris Collection, box 231, folder 18.

124. Senn, interview with Harmon, 11.

125. Senn, interview with Schorr and Smith, 16. Smith made this observation about the lobbying campaign.

126. Senn, interview with Edelman, 10.

127. Milton J. E. Senn, interview with Kenneth Keniston, March 7, 1975, 19.

128. "Draft Reply to Letters Criticizing the Child and Family Services Act," undated, Carl Albert Center, Tom Steed Collection, Legislative Series, box 73, folder 4. This document appears in a twelve-page information packet on the child development legislation.

129. Gil Scott, "Day Care—A Choice for Mothers," *Christian Science Monitor,* October 4, 1971, 3, New York University Archives, John Brademas Congressional Papers, "Comprehensive Child Development Act: Comparisons 1971," box I:05, folder 4.

130. Senn, interview with Johnson, 14.

131. Letter from Richardson to Brademas. The quotation appears on the third page of the enclosure accompanying the letter.

132. Walter F. Mondale, "Children's White House Conference Speech (Draft)," December 7, 1970, 64, Minnesota Historical Society, Manuscripts Collection, Walter F. Mondale Papers, "Speech Text Files," box 4, 154.K.3.2F.

133. "Education and Manpower," memorandum from Charles W. Radcliffe, minority counsel for education, to Albert H. Quie, June 23, 1971, Minnesota Historical Society, Manuscripts Collection, Albert H. Quie Papers, "1971–1972 Files," box 157, 146.I.19.14F.

134. Senn, interview with Johnson, 13.

135. Letter from Charles A. Byrley, director of the National Governors' Conference, to Albert H. Quie, June 9, 1971, Minnesota Historical Society, Manuscripts Collection, Albert H. Quie Papers, "1971–1972 Files," box 158, 146.I.20.1B.

136. Senn, interview with Miller, 13.

137. Letter from A. Sidney Johnson III to Urie Bronfenbrenner, September 7, 1971, Minnesota Historical Society, Manuscripts Collection, Walter F. Mondale Papers, "Subcommittee on Children and Youth," box 32, 13.3.0.3B.

138. Senn, interview with Johnson, 9–10.

139. The OEO extension is covered more comprehensively in Cohen 2001, Congressional Quarterly 1972, and Zigler and Muenchow 1992.

140. Senn, interview with Miller, 3.

141. A family could be charged no more than 10 percent on annual incomes between $4,320 and $5,916 and no more than 15 percent on incomes between $5,916 and $6,960. Under this formula, the annual fee for a family of four earning $6,960 would be $316.20 (Congressional Quarterly 1972).

142. Senn, interview with Johnson, 14–15.

143. Letter from Jay M. Arena, president of the American Academy of Pediatrics, to Carl Albert, November 26, 1971, Carl Albert Center, Carl Albert Collection, Legislative Files, box 132, folder 12.

144. Letter from Lucy Wilson Benson, president of the League of Women Voters of the United States, to Carl Albert, November 30, 1971, Carl Albert Center, Carl Albert Collection, Legislative Files, box 132, folder 12.

145. "Press Release from the Office of Senator Walter F. Mondale," November 16, 1971. Minnesota Historical Society, Manuscripts Collection, Walter F. Mondale Papers, "Senate: Press Releases and Newsletters," box 3, 154.K.1.3B.

146. "Press Release from the Office of Senator Walter F. Mondale," December 7, 1971, Minnesota Historical Society, Manuscripts Collection, Walter F. Mondale Papers, "Senate: Press Releases and Newsletters," box 3, 154.K.1.3B.

147. Senn, interview with Assmus, 5.

148. *Veto of the Economic Opportunity Amendments of 1971*, S. Doc. 92-48, 92nd Cong., 1st sess. (1971), 3.

149. *Veto of the Economic Opportunity Amendments of 1971*, 3.

150. *Veto of the Economic Opportunity Amendments of 1971*, 4–5.

151. *Veto of the Economic Opportunity Amendments of 1971*, 5.

152. *Veto of the Economic Opportunity Amendments of 1971*, 5.

153. *Veto of the Economic Opportunity Amendments of 1971*, 5.

154. James J. Kilpatrick, "Incredible Lemon of a Bill, Honey of a Veto," *Evening Star* (Washington, DC), December 16, 1971, A23, Minnesota Historical Society, Manuscripts Collection, Albert H. Quie Papers, "1971–1972 Files," box 157, 146.I.19.14F.

155. John Brademas, "Putting America on the Side of Children," *Early Years Parent*, Winter 1975/76, 8, New York University Archives, John Brademas Congressional Papers, "Child and Family Services: Clippings," box I:04, folder 10.

156. Senn, interview with Assmus, 6.

157. Senn, interview with Johnson, 15–16.

158. Senn, interview with Assmus, 6. See Cohen 2001, chap. 2, for a more expansive discussion of the debate within the Nixon administration over the legislation, the veto, and the press conference that followed the veto.

159. Senn, interview with Harmon, 18–19.

160. Senn, interview with Sugarman, 25–26.

161. Senn, interview with Miller, 10.

162. Senn, interview with Edelman, 12 (emphasis in original).

163. *Veto of the Economic Opportunity Amendments of 1971.*

164. Milton J. E. Senn, interview with Albert Quie, April 25, 1975, 13.

165. Senn, interview with Johnson, 16.

166. Senn, interview with Harmon, 22.

167. Senn, interview with Assmus, 11.

168. Senn, interview with Edelman, 11.

CHAPTER 4

1. Milton J. E. Senn, interview with Dr. Nicholas Hobbs, April 25, 1974, 26.

2. "Implementation of Early Childhood Programs in the States," proposal submitted by Wendell H. Pierce, executive director, Education Commission of the States, to the Office of Child Development and the Office of Education, U.S. Department of Health, Education, and Welfare, time period proposed: September 1, 1971–September 1, 1973, 9, ECS Archives.

3. Early Childhood Project, *State Services in Child Development: Needs Assessment and Planning, Child Abuse, Day Care Issues* (Denver: Education Commission of the States, 1975), ii, ECS Archives.

4. Early Childhood Task Force, *Early Childhood Programs in the States: Report of a December 1972 Conference* (Denver: Education Commission of the States, 1973), 7, ECS Archives.

5. The survey also revealed that public support for kindergarten was provided in the Canal Zone, Puerto Rico, and the Virgin Islands ("Early Childhood Education: Survey of States—1967," 2, ECS Archives; this undated document appears in a folder that also contains a letter of January 18, 1968, and an information packet that was mailed to key figures in each of the states).

6. Early Childhood Task Force, *Early Childhood Programs in the States,* 54.

7. Early Childhood Task Force, *Early Childhood Programs in the States,* 56.

8. The commission was a nonprofit organization formed by interstate compact and designed to establish a partnership between state educators and political leaders ("The Education Commission of the States," *Early Childhood Project Newsletter* 1 [April 1972]: 4, ECS Archives).

9. "Early Childhood Education: Survey of States—1967," 2.

10. The ECS sent the packet to presidents of state education associations, commissioners, majority and minority leaders of state legislatures, chairs of legislative councils, and chairs of finance committees of state legislatures. In preparing the packet, it worked with the American Association of University Women, the Association for Childhood Education International, the National Association for the Education of Young Children, the National Committee for Children and Youth, the National Committee for the Day Care of Children, the National Committee for Support of Public Schools, the National Congress of Parents and Teachers, the National Education Association, and the Department of Elementary-Kindergarten-Nursery Education of the NEA.

11. "Early Childhood Education: Survey of States—1967."

12. Education Commission of the States, *Positions, 1965–77,* pub. no. P2 (Denver: Education Commission of the States, 1977), 4, ECS Archives.

13. Education Commission of the States, *Positions, 1965–77*, 54.

14. Education Commission of the States, *Positions, 1965–77*, 56.

15. "Grant Received for Early Childhood Implementation Project—State Services Planned," *Early Childhood Project Newsletter* 1 (April 1972): 1, ECS Archives.

16. Education Commission of the States, *Positions, 1965–77*, 1.

17. Education Commission of the States, *Positions, 1965–77*, 2.

18. *A Fact Sheet on the ECS Early Childhood Project*, ECS Archives (this undated flyer lists publications from May 1976 and earlier).

19. "Grant Received for Early Childhood Implementation Project," 1.

20. *A Fact Sheet on the ECS Early Childhood Project*.

21. "State Concerns Voiced to Congress," *Early Childhood Project Newsletter* 1 (April 1972): 3, ECS Archives.

22. "Grant Received for Early Childhood Implementation Project," 1.

23. "Task Force Sets Project Priorities," *Early Childhood Project Newsletter* 3 (August 1972): 1, ECS Archives.

24. Early Childhood Task Force, *Early Childhood Programs in the States*, 4.

25. Early Childhood Task Force, *Early Childhood Programs in the States*, 4–5.

26. Early Childhood Task Force, *Early Childhood Programs in the States*, 36.

27. "Grant Enables ECS to Expand Assistance to States," *Early Childhood Project Newsletter* 8 (July 1973): 1, ECS Archives.

28. "Grant Enables ECS to Expand Assistance to States," 1.

29. "Project News: New Staff, New Funds, New Plans," *Early Childhood Project Newsletter* 14 (September 1974): 4, ECS Archives.

30. "Going, Going . . . ," *Early Childhood Project Newsletter* 17 (March 1975): 1, ECS Archives.

31. Early Childhood Project, *The Role of the Family in Child Development: Implications for State Policies and Programs* (Denver: Education Commission of the States, 1975), iii, ECS Archives.

32. Milton J. E. Senn, interview with Judy Miller, October 12, 1972, 20.

33. Milton J. E. Senn, interview with Martha Phillips, November 19, 1973, 33.

34. Milton J. E. Senn, interview with Trude Lash, February 6, 1973, 26.

35. Milton J. E. Senn, interview with Lisbeth Bamberger Schorr and William Smith, April 23, 1974, 13–14. Smith made this observation about the role of the states.

36. Senn, interview with Hobbs, 26.

37. Milton J. E. Senn, interview with Marian Wright Edelman, October 4, 1973, 27.

38. Milton J. E. Senn, interview with Barbara Finberg, undated, 23. Senn conducted ninety-eight interviews between 1967 and 1975. The content of the Finberg interview suggests that it took place sometime in 1974.

39. "Grant Received for Early Childhood Implementation Project," 1.

40. "Grant Received for Early Childhood Implementation Project," 1.

41. Early Childhood Project, *Role of the Family in Child Development*, 1.

42. Early Childhood Project, *State Services in Child Development*, 25.

43. Early Childhood Project, *State Services in Child Development*, 29.

44. Early Childhood Project, *State Services in Child Development*, 22.

45. Early Childhood Project, *State Services in Child Development*, 34.

46. Early Childhood Task Force, *Early Childhood Programs in the States*, 25.

47. Early Childhood Project, *Role of the Family in Child Development*, 42.

48. Early Childhood Project, *Role of the Family in Child Development*, 5 and 8.

49. Early Childhood Task Force, *Early Childhood Programs in the States*, 74.

50. Early Childhood Task Force, *Early Childhood Programs in the States*, 66.

51. Early Childhood Task Force, *Early Childhood Programs in the States*, 70.

52. Early Childhood Project, *State Services in Child Development*, 31.

53. Senn, interview with Edelman, 14.

54. Senn, interview with Schorr and Smith, 14. Smith made this observation about state offices of child development.

55. Education Commission of the States, *Establishing a State Office of Early Childhood Development: Suggested Legislative Alternatives*, Report no. 30, Early Childhood Report no. 3, 2nd printing (Denver: Education Commission of the States, 1973), 21, ECS Archives.

56. Early Childhood Project, *State Offices of Child Development* (Denver: Education Commission of the States, 1975), ix, ECS Archives.

57. Early Childhood Project, "State Offices of Child Development: Do They Work?" preliminary draft for use only at the Early Childhood National Symposium, August 1–2, 1974, 2, ECS Archives.

58. "The States Move in New Directions," *Early Childhood Project Newsletter* 2 (June 1972): 5, ECS Archives.

59. "States Move in New Directions," 6.

60. Early Childhood Project, "State Offices of Child Development: Do They Work?" 2.

61. Early Childhood Task Force, *Early Childhood Programs in the States*, 60. The director of the Idaho office also noted that potential disadvantages to this arrangement included vulnerability to political change and incompatibility between previous political commitments and research.

62. "The States Move Ahead," *Early Childhood Project Newsletter* 3 (August 1972): 2, ECS Archives.

63. "Massachusetts, California Enact Early Childhood Development Legislation," *Early Childhood Project Newsletter* 5 (February 1973): 2, ECS Archives.

64. "States Move Ahead," 3.

65. "Legislation Developed for State Office of Child Development," *Early Childhood Project Newsletter* 4 (January 1973): 2, ECS Archives.

66. "Roundup Reveals 12 States Have Created Child Development Offices," *Early Childhood Project Newsletter* 5 (February 1973): 1, 3, ECS Archives.

67. "State Legislatures Focus on Early Childhood Development in 1973 Sessions," *Early Childhood Project Newsletter* 7 (May 1973): 3, ECS Archives.

68. "State Legislatures Focus on Early Childhood Development," 1.

69. "Hawaii Enacts Child Development Legislation," *Early Childhood Project Newsletter* 8 (July 1973): 2, 4, ECS Archives.

70. "Louisiana Focuses on Children," *Early Childhood Project Newsletter* 8 (July 1973): 3, ECS Archives.

71. "Grant Enables ECS to Expand Assistance to States," 1.

72. "State OCD Directors Organize," *Early Childhood Project Newsletter* 9 (September 1973): 2, ECS Archives.

73. "Directors Urge OCD Appointment," *Early Childhood Project Newsletter* 10 (November 1973): 2, ECS Archives.

74. "About People, Places, Things," *Early Childhood Project Newsletter* 9 (September 1973): 3, ECS Archives.

75. "Nine State Legislatures Act for Child Development," *Early Childhood Project Newsletter* 12 (May 1974): 1, ECS Archives.

76. "Massachusetts Finances Children's Budget and Special Education," *Early Childhood Project Newsletter* 13 (July 1974): 2, ECS Archives.

77. "Changing Times for OCDs," *Early Childhood Project Newsletter* 14 (September 1974): 3, ECS Archives.

78. "Changing Times for OCDs," 2.

79. Early Childhood Project, *Role of the Family in Child Development*, 35.

80. Letter from John B. Himelrick Sr., director, Interagency Council for Child Development Services, Office of the Governor, Charleston, WV, to Congressman John Brademas, September 4, 1975, New York University Archives, John Brademas Congressional Papers, "Child and Family Services: Day Care-Pro," box I:04, folder 12. Himelrick's letter noted that seventeen states had functioning statewide offices of child development, that twelve states had a grant to plan and establish an office, and that eight states had an office of child development functioning in part of the state.

81. Early Childhood Project, *Assessing the Needs of Children in Your State: What Is a Needs Assessment?* (Denver: Education Commission of the States, 1976), ECS Archives.

82. Early Childhood Project, *Role of the Family in Child Development*, 36.

83. Education Commission of the States, *Positions, 1965–77,* 3.

84. Early Childhood Project, *The Children's Needs Assessment Handbook* (Denver: Education Commission of the States, 1976), 4, ECS Archives.

85. Early Childhood Project, *Children's Needs Assessment Handbook,* 75–89.

86. Early Childhood Project, *Early Childhood Programs: A State Survey* (Denver: Education Commission of the States, 1974), 1, ECS Archives.

87. Early Childhood Project, *Early Childhood Programs: A State Survey.*

88. Early Childhood Project, *Early Childhood Programs: A State Survey, 1974–1975* (Denver: Education Commission of the States, 1975), 1.

89. Early Childhood Project, *Early Childhood Programs: A State Survey, 1974–1975,* 1.

90. Early Childhood Project, *Early Childhood Programs: A State Survey, 1974–1975,* 1.

91. "Child Associates Program Develops," *Early Childhood Project Newsletter* 2 (June 1972): 4, ECS Archives.

92. "Day Care Workers Criticize CDA Standards," *Early Childhood Project Newsletter* 11 (January 1974): 4, ECS Archives.

93. Denise Kale Hayas and Doris M. Ross, *The Very Young and Education: 1974 State Activity,* Report no. 68 (Denver: Education Commission of the States Early Childhood Project, 1975), ECS Archives.

94. Early Childhood Project, *State Trends and Priorities in Services for Children and Their Families: A Report of a Telephone Survey* (Denver: Education Commission of the States, 1976), 4, ECS Archives.

95. Early Childhood Project, *State Trends and Priorities,* 8.

96. Early Childhood Project, *State Trends and Priorities,* 2.

97. Early Childhood Project, *State Trends and Priorities,* 2.

98. "Politics and Early Childhood," *Early Childhood Project Newsletter* 10 (November 1973): 3, ECS Archives.

99. Early Childhood Project, *Role of the Family in Child Development,* 1.

100. Senn, interview with Schorr and Smith, 13–14. Smith made this observation about the role of the states.

101. Early Childhood Project, *State Services in Child Development,* 33.

CHAPTER 5

1. Milton J. E. Senn, interview with Carolyn Harmon, September 14, 1972, 22.

2. "Senator Walter F. Mondale Reports to Minnesota," press release from the Office of Senator Walter F. Mondale, May 15, 1972, 1, Minnesota Historical Society, Manuscripts Collection, Walter F. Mondale Papers, "Senate: Press Releases and Newsletters," box 3, 154.K.1.3B.

3. "Senator Walter F. Mondale Reports to Minnesota," 1.

4. "Senator Walter F. Mondale Reports to Minnesota," 2. Mondale issued this press release before the Senate endorsed the controversial Dominick amendment.

5. "Child Development," in an issues book from the 1972 Senate campaign, Minnesota Historical Society, Manuscript Collections, Walter F. Mondale Papers, "1984 Campaign Files," box 1611, 146.L.8.4F. This document describes eleven "criticisms" of Mondale's child development bills and provides "answers" to each of these critiques.

6. "Governor Dunn Wants Bill Amended," *Early Childhood Project Newsletter* 2 (June 1972): 8, ECS Archives.

7. Milton J. E. Senn, interview with Judy Assmus, September 14, 1972, 12–13.

8. Emergency Committee for Children, "What Is Child Development?," undated memorandum, 5, accompanying the booklet "The Comprehensive Headstart, Child Development and Family Services Act of 1972 (S. 3617): Materials, the Case against It," Carl Albert Center, Happy Camp Collection, Legislative Correspondence, box 49, folder 43.

9. Emergency Committee for Children, "What Is Child Development?," 4.

10. Senn, interview with Harmon, 24–25.

11. "Minority Views," undated memorandum, 2, Minnesota Historical Society, Manuscripts Collection, Albert H. Quie Papers, "1971–1972 Files," box 154, 146.I.19.11B.

12. "Minority Views," 4.

13. Milton J. E. Senn, interview with Sydney Johnson III, September 15, 1972, 21. Johnson speculated that Representative Albert Quie (R-MN) was reluctant to negotiate because of the possibility that he would be a committee chair in the next Congress.

14. This summary of congressional activity is based on Margaret Malone, *Child Care Legislation in the 93rd Congress* (Washington, DC: Congressional Research Service, 1975), New York University Archives, John Brademas Congressional Papers, "Child Development: CRS Reports," box I:04, folder 32.

15. "Child Development Bill," memorandum from A. Sidney Johnson III to Walter Mondale, October 26, 1973, 1, Minnesota Historical Society, Manuscripts Collection, Walter F. Mondale Papers, "Subcommittee on Children and Youth," box 32, 13.3.0.3B.

16. Milton J. E. Senn, interview with Trude Lash, February 6, 1973, 27.

17. "Child Development Bill," 1–2.

18. John Brademas, "Child and Family Services Act of 1974," news conference statement, June 26, 1974, 3, New York University Archives, John Brademas Congressional Papers, "Child and Family Services: H.R. 2966," box I:04, folder 13.

19. Milton J. E. Senn, interview with Marian Wright Edelman, October 4, 1973, 18.

20. Brademas, "Child and Family Services Act of 1974," 2.

21. Brademas, "Child and Family Services Act of 1974," 2.

22. "Draft Reply to Letters Criticizing the Child and Family Services Act," undated, Carl Albert Center, Tom Steed Collection, Legislative Series, box 73, folder 4.

23. "Draft Reply to Letters Criticizing the Child and Family Services Act."

24. Milton J. E. Senn, interview with Gilbert Steiner, March 20, 1975, 19–20.

25. Milton J. E. Senn, interview with Martha Phillips, November 19, 1973, 35.

26. "Child Development Bill," 1.

27. John Brademas, "Legislation for Young Children and Their Families," remarks at a meeting of the Fort Worth, Dallas, and Denton Associations for the Education of Young Children, Fort Worth, TX, March 31, 1977, 9, New York University Archives, John Brademas Congressional Papers, "Speeches: Legislation for Young Children and Their Families," box III:15, folder 30.

28. "Working Mothers: Their Child Care Needs," address by Carmen R. Maymi, director of the Women's Bureau, at a meeting of the Chicago Community Coordinated Child Care Committee, Chicago, IL, November 2, 1974, 4, New York University Archives, John Brademas Congressional Papers, "Child Development: Misc. Reports and Clippings," box I:04, folder 34.

29. Sylvia Porter, "Finding Adequate Day Care Increasingly Urgent Need," *South Bend Tribune,* April 8, 1976, 17, New York University Archives, John Brademas Congressional Papers, "Child and Family Services: Clippings," box I:04, folder 10.

30. John Brademas, "Putting America on the Side of Children," *Early Years Parent,* Winter 1975/1976, 11, New York University Archives, John Brademas Congressional Papers, "Child and Family Services: Clippings," box I:04, folder 10.

31. Ann Allman, *Determining the Need* (Washington, DC: Education and Public Welfare Division, Congressional Research Service, 1974), New York University Archives, John Brademas Congressional Papers, "Child and Family Services: H.R. 2966," box I:04, folder 13. The original document is a "draft statement prepared according to the instructions of the Select Education Subcommittee of the House Education and Labor Committee"; it was prepared for "personal use."

32. Milton J. E. Senn, interview with Urie Bronfenbrenner, April 12, 1972, 29.

33. "Remarks of Senator Walter F. Mondale," Minnesota PTA Convention, Duluth, MN, October 15, 1972, 5, Minnesota Historical Society, Manuscripts Collection, Walter F. Mondale Papers, "Subcommittee on Children and Youth," box 32, 13.3.0.3B.

34. "Basic Children's Speech," 11, Minnesota Historical Society, Manuscripts Collection, Walter F. Mondale Papers, "Senate Campaign, 1972," 153.L.16.14F.

35. Onalee McGraw, "Big Brother Child Development Bill Threatens Family, Parental Control," *Battle Line* (American Conservative Union), January 1976, 2, New York University Archives, John Brademas Congressional Papers, "Child and Family Services: Clippings," box I:04, folder 10.

36. Alan Stang, "The Child Care Bill," *American Opinion,* December 1975, 6, New York University Archives, John Brademas Congressional Papers, "Child and Family Services: H.R. 2966," box I:04, folder 15.

37. Letter from Virginia Y. Trotter, assistant secretary of education, to Congressman Carl Perkins, August 17, 1975, New York University Archives, John Brademas Congressional Papers, "Child and Family Services: Day Care-Anti," box I:04, folder 11.

38. Letter from Trotter to Perkins.

39. Letter from Trotter to Perkins.

40. "Summary: Joint House/Senate Hearings on Child and Family Services Bill, H.R. 2966 and S. 626, July 15, 1975," memorandum from staff of the Subcommittee on Select Education to members of the Subcommittee on Select Education, New York University Archives, John Brademas Congressional Papers, "Child and Family Services: Hearings-Memos," box I:04, folder 18.

41. *Child and Family Services Act of 1975: Joint Hearings on S. 626 and H.R. 2966 before the Subcommittee on Children and Youth and the Subcommittee on Employment, Poverty, and Migratory Labor of the Senate Committee on Labor and Public Welfare and the Subcommittee on Select Education of the House Committee on Education and Labor,* 94th Cong., 1st sess. (1975), 2120.

42. *Child and Family Services Act of 1975: Joint Hearings,* 2123.

43. *Child and Family Services Act of 1975: Joint Hearings,* 2121.

44. *Child and Family Services Act of 1975: Joint Hearings,* 2120.

45. "Sensible Opposition," editorial, *Norman (OK) Transcript,* December 17, 1975, 6, Carl Albert Center, Tom Steed Collection, Legislative Files, box 196, folder 3.

46. McGraw, "Big Brother Child Development Bill Threatens Family," 2.

47. "Conservative Coalition Formed to Oppose Pending Child Care Bill," *Day Care and Child Development Reports* 4, no. 20 (October 13, 1975): 8, New York University Archives, John Brademas Congressional Papers, "Child and Family Services: Day Care-Anti," box I:04, folder 11.

48. "The Left's Grand Strategy," editorial, *Indianapolis Star,* June 9, 1974, sec. 2, 2, New York University Archives, John Brademas Congressional Papers, "93rd Congress: Day Care," box I:19, folder 33.

49. "Mr. Carter and the Family," editorial, *Wall Street Journal,* September 15, 1976, 26, New York University Archives, John Brademas Congressional Papers, "Child and Family Services: H.R. 2966," box I:04, folder 15.

50. Stang, "Child Care Bill," 4.

51. Stang, "Child Care Bill," 3.

52. Letter from Josie M. Thomas, Choctaw, OK, to Congressman Carl Albert, October 15, 1975, Carl Albert Center, Carl Albert Collection, Legislative Files, box 196.

53. Letter from Kathy Norcott, Bowlegs, OK, to Congressman Garner Shriver, October 22, 1975, Carl Albert Center, Carl Albert Collection, Legislative Files, box 196.

54. Letter from Roy L. Miller, Oklahoma City, OK, to Congressman Carl Albert, October 30, 1975, Carl Albert Center, Carl Albert Collection, Legislative Files, box 196.

55. Letter from Nancy Freeland, Oklahoma City, OK, to Congressman Carl Albert, October 29, 1975, Carl Albert Center, Carl Albert Collection, Legislative Files, box 196.

56. The correspondence that Speaker Albert received on the Child and Family Services Act fills eleven folders.

57. John Brademas, "HR 2966, Child and Family Services Act," memorandum to members of the Indiana Congressional Delegation, November 4, 1975, 1, New York University Archives, John Brademas Congressional Papers, "Child and Family Services: Rebuttal," box I:04, folder 23.

58. "A Ranting Mail Campaign," *Washington Post,* February 19, 1976, New York University Archives, John Brademas Congressional Papers, "Child and Family Services: Clippings," box I:04, folder 10.

59. Robert P. Sigman, "Misleading Charges against Child Care Act," *Kansas City Star,*

November 30, 1975, New York University Archives, John Brademas Congressional Papers, "Child and Family Services: Clippings," box I:04, folder 10.

60. Martha Angle, "Even Nonexistent Parts of Child Bill Draw Fire," *Washington Star,* February 3, 1976, A-7, New York University Archives, John Brademas Congressional Papers, "Child and Family Services: Clippings," box I:04, folder 10.

61. Letter from Charles A. Moser, Emergency Committee for Children, to Congressman John Brademas, February 4, 1976, New York University Archives, John Brademas Congressional Papers, "Child and Family Services: Rebuttal," box I:04, folder 23.

62. Brademas, "HR 2966, Child and Family Services Act," 2–3.

63. Brademas, "Putting America on the Side of Children," 11.

64. John W. Baker and Rosemary Brevard, "The Charges Being Made about Child Services Act," *Baptist Messenger,* December 11, 1975, 5, Carl Albert Center, Tom Steed Collection, Legislative Files, box 75, folder 3.

65. Brademas, "Putting America on the Side of Children," 11.

66. Statement by Congressman John Brademas on the Child and Family Services Bill, November 1, 1975, 2, New York University Archives, John Brademas Congressional Papers, "Child and Family Services: Rebuttal," box I:04, folder 23.

67. Letter from Walter F. Mondale to Cheryl Crooker, October 28, 1976, Minnesota Historical Society, Manuscripts Collection, Walter F. Mondale Papers, "Subject Files on Children and Youth," box 1789, 29.A.0.8F.

68. "Our Point of View: Child-Family Services," editorial, *Norman (OK) Transcript,* December 1, 1975, 6, Carl Albert Center, Tom Steed Collection, Legislative Files, box 75, folder 3.

69. Baker and Brevard, "Charges Being Made about Child Services Act."

70. "Child Care Opposition Mounts—and Sinks," editorial, *Minneapolis Tribune,* January 23, 1976, 6A, Minnesota Historical Society, Manuscripts Collection, Walter F. Mondale Papers, "Senate: Press Releases and Newsletters," box 3, 154.K.1.3B.

71. "Interreligious Statement on Child and Family Services Bill, 1975," Minnesota Historical Society, Manuscripts Collection, Walter F. Mondale Papers, "Senate: Press Releases and Newsletters," box 3, 154.K.1.3B.

72. Letter from Congressman Michael T. Blouin to Congressman John Brademas, April 6, 1976, New York University Archives, John Brademas Congressional Papers, "Child and Family Services: Clippings," box I:04, folder 10.

73. Edith K. Roosevelt, "Flyer Claims Bill Imperils U.S. Families," *Manchester (NH) Union Leader,* December 27, 1975, New York University Archives, John Brademas Congressional Papers, "Child and Family Services: Clippings," box I:04, folder 10.

74. Remarks of Senator Walter F. Mondale at the Midwestern Conference on Early Childhood Education, Omaha, NE, October 5, 1975, 11, Minnesota Historical Society, Manuscripts Collection, Walter F. Mondale Papers, "Speech Text Files," box 7, 154.K.3.5B.

75. Howard Flieger, "False Alarm," *U.S. News and World Report,* March 1, 1976, 80, New York University Archives, John Brademas Congressional Papers, "Child and Family Services: Clippings," box I:04, folder 10.

76. Current Population Survey, "Table A-1: School Enrollment of the Population 3 Years Old and Over, by Level and Control of School, Race, and Hispanic Origin: October 1955 to 2010," http://www.census.gov/hhes/school/data/cps/historical/index.html (accessed March 13, 2012). The increasing role of the private sector in early childhood

was not limited to nursery schools, and the figures cited in this paragraph are suggestive of broader changes.

77. "Child and Family Services Act: Analysis of Testimony on H.R. 2966 and S. 626," Congressional Research Service, New York University Archives, John Brademas Congressional Papers, "Child and Family Services: Hearings-Testimony," box I:04, folder 20.

78. "Child and Family Services Act: Analysis of Testimony."

79. "Child and Family Services Act: Analysis of Testimony."

80. "Child and Family Services Act: Analysis of Testimony."

81. "Child and Family Services Act: Analysis of Testimony."

82. "Child and Family Services Act: Analysis of Testimony."

83. Of the seventeen functional state offices of child development, only three were part of departments of education; the others were in governors' offices or in departments of social or community services (Sally V. Allen, "Growing National Debate: The Schools Can/Can't Be Trusted with Child Development," *Compact*, February 1975, 22, New York University Archives, John Brademas Congressional Papers, "Child and Family Services: H.R. 2966," box I:04, folder 13). This variation foreshadowed the looming battle over the appropriate role of the public schools.

84. Letter from John B. Himelrick Sr., director, Interagency Council for Child Development Services, Office of the Governor, Charleston, WV, to Congressman John Brademas, September 4, 1975, New York University Archives, John Brademas Congressional Papers, "Child and Family Services: Day Care-Pro," box I:04, folder 12.

85. "Dilemma for Working Mothers: Not Enough Day-Care Centers," *U.S. News and World Report*, April 12, 1976, 50, New York University Archives, John Brademas Congressional Papers, "Child and Family Services: Clippings," box I:04, folder 10.

86. Emergency Committee for Children, "What Is Child Development?," 6.

87. "Summary: Joint House/Senate Hearings." Weinberger "did not know offhand of any programs to be eliminated" when questioned about this programmatic duplication.

88. "American Families: Trends, Pressures, and Recommendations," preliminary report to Governor Jimmy Carter by Joseph A. Califano Jr., undated, 5, New York University Archives, John Brademas Congressional Papers, "Child and Family Services: H.R. 2966," box I:04, folder 15.

89. The contest between Shanker and Selden for control of the American Federation of Teachers is described in more detail in Kahlenberg 2007.

90. Shanker referred to comments by Edwin W. Martin, acting deputy commissioner of the U.S. Bureau of Education for the Handicapped, who had compared the fragmentation of early childhood policy to a "Buddhist approach to gardening."

91. Albert Shanker, "Early Childhood Education Is a Job for the Public Schools," *New York Times*, September 8, 1974.

92. "Highlights of Meeting with Ed Zigler on October 28, 1975," memorandum from "Mike" to "Jack," New York University Archives, John Brademas Congressional Papers, "Child and Family Services: H.R. 2966," box I:04, folder 15. The recipient of this memorandum was likely Jack G. Duncan, counsel to the House Subcommittee on Select Education.

93. U.S. OECD Forum of Education Organization Leaders, "A Call for Federal Funding of Early Childhood Development Programs," press release, January 28, 1976, New York University Archives, John Brademas Congressional Papers, "Child and Family Services: Rebuttal," box I:04, folder 23.

94. U.S. OECD Forum of Education Organization Leaders, "Statement in Support of Federal Funding of Early Childhood Development Programs," undated, New York University Archives, John Brademas Congressional Papers, "Child and Family Services: Rebuttal," box I:04, folder 23. This statement was presumably issued at the forum's news conference on January 29, 1976.

95. "Bell Wants Education in Child Care Bill," *Education Daily,* April 30, 1975, 5–6. New York University Archives, John Brademas Congressional Papers, "Child and Family Services," box I:18, folder 15.

96. Senn, interview with Steiner, 12.

97. William V. Shannon, "Government and Families," *New York Times,* September 14, 1975, New York University Archives, John Brademas Congressional Papers, "Child and Family Services: Clippings," box I:04, folder 10.

98. Charles A. Moser for the Emergency Committee for Children, "Letters to the Editor," December 1, 1975, New York University Archives, John Brademas Congressional Papers, "Child and Family Services: Rebuttal," box I:04, folder 23.

99. The rift over the appropriate role of the public schools began to emerge before the publication of Shanker's essay. Two members of the ECS task force debated each other at an August 1974 symposium on child development. The event was characterized as "the first public airing of these contrasting views by prominent persons in the field" ("Martin and Sugarman Debate Public Schools as Delivery System," *Early Childhood Project Newsletter* 14 [September 1974]: 1, ECS Archives).

100. Shannon, "Government and Families."

101. Allen, "Growing National Debate," 23.

102. Allen, "Growing National Debate," 23.

103. Letter from Jack T. Waters, major and city commander, Salvation Army, Tulsa, OK, to Congressman Carl Albert, April 2, 1975, Carl Albert Center, Carl Albert Collection, Legislative Files, box 196.

104. Quoted in Brademas, "Legislation for Young Children and Their Families," 12.

105. Brademas, "Legislation for Young Children and Their Families," 12.

106. Steiner (1981, 42–43) speculates that Cohen withdrew due to the controversy over Patricia Fleming's appointment as executive director and the fact that he "could look ahead to trouble because of his belief in public intervention to prevent large families."

107. However, the administration did create the Office for Families in the Department of Health and Human Services, in October 1979 (Beck 1982, 328).

108. Cranston's cosponsors included Harrison Williams Jr. (D-NJ), Donald Reigle Jr. (D-MI), Jacob Javits (R-NY), and George McGovern (D-SD).

109. Representative Edward Roybal (D-CA) introduced a companion bill in the House of Representatives (Beck 1982, 328).

110. *Child Care Act of 1979: Hearings before the Subcommittee on Child and Human Development of the Senate Committee on Labor and Human Resources,* 96th Cong., 1st sess. (1979), 4.

111. *Child Care Act of 1979: Hearings before the Subcommittee on Child and Human Development,* 3.

112. Draft letter from Governor Jerry Apodaca to President Jimmy Carter, February 10, 1977. National Archives, RG 12: Records of the Office of Education, Office of the Commissioner, Office Files of the Commissioner of Education, 1939–80, A1, entry 122, box 941.

113. *Child Care Act of 1979: Hearings before the Subcommittee on Child and Human Development*, 398.

114. *Child Care Act of 1979: Hearings before the Subcommittee on Child and Human Development*, 4.

115. *Child Care Act of 1979: Hearings before the Subcommittee on Child and Human Development*, 223.

116. *Child Care Act of 1979: Hearings before the Subcommittee on Child and Human Development*, 238.

117. *Child Care Act of 1979: Hearings before the Subcommittee on Child and Human Development*, 238. Vice President Mondale later remarked that Cranston's queries had been "inartfully answered" and that the testimony might have been less controversial had the lack of administration support been attributed to budgetary constraints (interview with former vice president Walter F. Mondale, December 3, 2010, Minneapolis, MN).

118. "Draft Head Start Assessment Report—Final Draft," memorandum from James F. Mellody, principal regional official, Department of Health, Education, and Welfare, May 15, 1978, 1, National Archives, RG 12: Records of the Office of Education, Office of the Commissioner, Office Files of the Commissioner of Education, 1939–80, A1, entry 122, box 1133.

119. "Draft Head Start Assessment Report," 1.

120. "Draft Head Start Assessment Report," 5.

121. "Draft Head Start Assessment Report," 10.

122. "Draft Head Start Assessment Report," 11.

123. "Draft Head Start Assessment Report," 10–11.

124. "Draft Head Start Assessment Report," 11.

125. *Child Care Act of 1979: Hearings before the Subcommittee on Child and Human Development*, 39.

126. House Committee on Ways and Means, *1990 Green Book: Background Material and Data on Programs within the Jurisdiction of the Committee on Ways and Means*, 101st Cong., 2d sess. (Committee Print, 1990), 840.

127. *Veto of the Economic Opportunity Amendments of 1971*, 92nd Cong., 1st sess. (1971), S. Doc. 92-48, 3–4.

128. *Veto of the Economic Opportunity Amendments of 1971*, 3.

129. *Statistics of Income, 1973: Individual Income Tax Returns*, Internal Revenue Service Publication 79 (11-76) (Washington, DC: Department of the Treasury, 1976), tables 1B, 2A, and 2.9.

130. House Committee on Ways and Means, *1990 Green Book*, 840. The Revenue Act of 1978 modified the rules governing payments to relatives but did not fundamentally alter the treatment of dependent care expenses in the tax code.

131. House Committee on Ways and Means, *1990 Green Book*, 842.

132. House Committee on Ways and Means, *1990 Green Book*, 842.

133. *Child Care Act of 1979: Hearings before the Subcommittee on Child and Human Development*, 274.

134. *Child Care Act of 1979: Hearings before the Subcommittee on Child and Human Development*, 290.

135. *Child Care Act of 1979: Hearings before the Subcommittee on Child and Human Development*, 286–87.

CHAPTER 6

1. Examining initiatives that were not adopted also provides a useful contrast with the recent state-level changes that are profiled in chapter 8. Those successful campaigns generally accommodated existing stakeholders, illustrating how the long-term impact of decisions made in the 1970s constrained policymakers' options.

2. *Early Childhood Education and Development Act: Hearing on H.R. 3 before the House Committee on Education and Labor,* 101st Cong., 2d sess. (1990), 47.

3. Several studies examine these changes in more detail. See Manna 2006; McDermott 2011; McGuinn 2006.

4. The Child Care Development and Block Grant Act of 1990 did not focus on educational services. Instead, it sought to make child care resources available to low-income families beyond those receiving welfare. It limited the national government's role to "providing subsidies to low-income families and helping states upgrade the quality of existing [child care] services" (E. Rose 2010, 79). For more on this landmark legislation, see Cohen 2001; Lombardi 2003; E. Rose 2010.

5. At a hearing on another piece of legislation in 1988, Kennedy said, "I do not expect that as comprehensive a program as Smart Start will be enacted in this session of Congress" (*Prekindergarten Early Dropout Intervention Act of 1988: Hearing on S. 2034 before the Senate Committee on Labor and Human Resources,* 100th Cong., 2d sess. [1988], 2).

6. *Smart Start: The Community Collaborative for Early Childhood Development Act of 1988; Hearing on S. 2270 before the Senate Committee on Labor and Human Resources,* 100th Cong., 2d sess. (1988), 75.

7. *Smart Start,* 329.

8. *Smart Start,* 63.

9. *Smart Start,* 259.

10. *Smart Start,* 240.

11. *Smart Start,* 253.

12. *Smart Start,* 226.

13. *Smart Start,* 335 (emphasis in original).

14. One exception was Lawrence J. Schweinhart of the High/Scope Educational Research Foundation, who described underfunded, low-quality programs as "a reckless gamble with our nation's most precious commodity—the lives and futures of our children" (*Smart Start,* 318).

15. "For Children: A Fair Chance," *New York Times,* September 6, 1987, reprinted in *Smart Start,* 173.

16. *Smart Start,* 76.

17. *Smart Start,* 161.

18. *Smart Start,* 272.

19. *Smart Start,* 230.

20. *Smart Start,* 219.

21. *Smart Start,* 42.

22. *Smart Start,* 42–43.

23. *Smart Start,* 237.

24. *Smart Start,* 303.

25. *Smart Start,* 152.
26. *Smart Start,* 304.
27. *Smart Start,* 105.
28. *Smart Start,* 264.
29. *Smart Start,* 31.
30. *Smart Start,* 2.
31. *Smart Start,* 304. The witness, Lawrence J. Schweinhart of the High/Scope Educational Research Foundation, argued that Head Start should also strive to develop stronger ties with the states.
32. *Smart Start,* 31.
33. *Smart Start,* 305.
34. *Smart Start,* 157.
35. *Smart Start,* 269.
36. *Smart Start,* 295.
37. *Smart Start,* 307.
38. *Smart Start,* 154.
39. *Smart Start,* 187.
40. *Smart Start,* 280.
41. *Smart Start,* 57.
42. *Smart Start,* 107.
43. *Smart Start,* 122.
44. *Smart Start,* 238–39.
45. *Prekindergarten Early Dropout Intervention Act,* 6.
46. *Prekindergarten Early Dropout Intervention Act,* 35.
47. *Prekindergarten Early Dropout Intervention Act,* 56–57.
48. *Prekindergarten Early Dropout Intervention Act,* 14.
49. *Prekindergarten Early Dropout Intervention Act,* 48.
50. *Prekindergarten Early Dropout Intervention Act,* 125.
51. *Prekindergarten Early Dropout Intervention Act,* 42.
52. *Prekindergarten Early Dropout Intervention Act,* 33.
53. *Prekindergarten Early Dropout Intervention Act,* 43.
54. *Prekindergarten Early Dropout Intervention Act,* 50–51.
55. *Prekindergarten Early Dropout Intervention Act,* 130.
56. *Prekindergarten Early Dropout Intervention Act,* 49.
57. *Prekindergarten Early Dropout Intervention Act,* 131.
58. *Early Childhood Education and Development Act,* 148.
59. See Morgan 2006 for a more detailed discussion of the tax policy changes of the 1980s and their political implications.
60. *Early Childhood Education and Development Act,* 42.
61. *Early Childhood Education and Development Act,* 163.
62. One minor policy change occurred in 1989, when the Early Start program was established. Early Start "invests in early literacy programs for very low-income families, particularly during the years leading up to a child's third birthday" (Maeroff 2006, 29). Early Start illustrates the constraining effect of the existing policy repertoire, because both its name and its primary constituency are clearly extensions of Head Start.
63. *Early Childhood Education and Development Act,* 131.

64. Policy and Priorities Committee, *The Evolving Reform Agenda: The Three-Year Plan of the Education Commission of the States with Priorities for 1987–88* (Denver: Education Commission of the States, 1987), 7 (emphasis in original), ECS Archives.

65. Those who support additional public investment in early childhood programs frequently cite the Perry Preschool Program and other initiatives, but the quality of these acclaimed programs exceeds that of most other preschool programs in the United States (Vinovskis 1999a, 75). Furthermore, these multifaceted initiatives "had many moving parts, and no one can say for sure which (if any) of them mattered more than others" (Finn 2009, 49).

66. These programs are described in *Why Policymakers Should Be Concerned about Brain Research*, ECS Policy Brief: Early Childhood Education (Denver: Education Commission of the States, 1998), 2, ECS Archives.

67. "Federal/State Relations," memorandum from Frank Newman, president of the Education Commission of the States, to Governor Garrey Carruthers, Governor Bill Clinton, and Governor Ted Sanders, September 25, 1989, 2, ECS Archives.

68. "Education Leaders Praise Agenda Set at Education Summit," *White House Wire on Education*, November 8, 1989, 4, ECS Archives.

69. "'A Jeffersonian Compact': The Statement by the President and Governors." *New York Times*, October 1, 1989.

70. Despite widespread public support for the goal of promoting school readiness, its numerous and shifting meanings meant that "attempts to implement [the goal] faced major conceptual and practical problems" (Dombkowski 2001, 541). For an excellent account of the politics surrounding school readiness and the effort by the National Education Goals Panel and the National Governors Association to achieve it, see Vinovskis 1999b.

71. "Early Childhood Education Getting More Attention," *State Education Leader* 15, no. 1 (Winter 1997), 13, ECS Archives.

72. "Early Childhood Education Programs," February 15, 1997, ECS Archives.

73. Janelle Miller, "Education Practices Conflict with Brain Research," *State Education Leader* 15, no. 1 (Winter 1997): 3–4, at 4, ECS Archives.

CHAPTER 7

1. Education Commission of the States, *Starting Early, Starting Now: A Policymaker's Guide to Early Care and Education and School Success* (Denver: Education Commission of the States, 2001), 5, ECS Archives. These estimates came from the Bureau of Labor Statistics. According to another estimate, 64 percent of women with preschool children participated in the labor market in 1999 (Lombardi 2003, 2).

2. Education Commission of the States, *Starting Early, Starting Now*, 10.

3. Sharon Lynn Kagan, *Giving America's Young Children a Better Start: A Change Brief* (Denver: Education Commission of the States, 2001), 1, ECS Archives.

4. Policy and Priorities Committee, *The Evolving Reform Agenda: The Three-Year Plan of the Education Commission of the States with Priorities for 1987–88* (Denver: Education Commission of the States, 1987), 8–9, ECS Archives.

5. Education Commission of the States, *Starting Early, Starting Now*, 4.

6. *Why Policymakers Should Be Concerned about Brain Research* (Denver: Education Commission of the States, 1998), 1–2, ECS Archives.

7. Frank Newman, "Is First Grade Too Late?" *State Education Leader* 15, no. 1 (Winter 1997): 1–2, at 2, ECS Archives.

8. Education Commission of the States, *Early Learning: Improving Results for Young Children* (Denver, CO: Education Commission of the States, 2000), 3, ECS Archives.

9. "Early Childhood Education Getting More Attention," *State Education Leader* 15, no. 1 (Winter 1997): 13, ECS Archives.

10. This focus on early childhood programs extended to those serving children between birth and age three. The ECS, the National Governors Association, and several foundations launched initiatives on the topic in the late 1990s.

11. Roy Romer, "The Importance of Early Childhood," *State Education Leader* 15, no. 1 (Winter 1997): 9–10, at 9, ECS Archives.

12. *Multiple Program Coordination in Early Childhood Education: Hearings before the Senate Subcommittee on Oversight of Government Management, Restructuring, and the District of Columbia,* 106th Cong., 1st sess. (1999), 3.

13. The Early Head Start National Resource Center, "What Is Early Head Start?" http://www.ehsnrc.org/AboutUs/ehs.htm (accessed February 14, 2011).

14. Senate Committee on Labor and Human Resources, *Are Our Children Ready to Learn? Hearing of the Senate Committee on Labor and Human Resources,* 105th Cong., 2d sess. (1998), 44.

15. *Are Our Children Ready to Learn?,* 27.

16. *Are Our Children Ready to Learn?,* 28.

17. *Multiple Program Coordination,* 21.

18. *Multiple Program Coordination,* 46.

19. *Multiple Program Coordination,* 3.

20. *Multiple Program Coordination,* 23.

21. *Multiple Program Coordination,* 16.

22. *Multiple Program Coordination,* 38.

23. *Multiple Program Coordination,* 32.

24. *Multiple Program Coordination,* 11.

25. *Multiple Program Coordination,* 12.

26. *Multiple Program Coordination,* 18.

27. *Multiple Program Coordination,* 37.

28. *Multiple Program Coordination,* 36.

29. *Early Education: From Science to Practice; Hearing of the Senate Committee on Health, Education, Labor, and Pensions,* 107th Cong., 1st sess. (2002), 21.

30. *Early Education: From Science to Practice,* 68.

31. Manna (2006) and McGuinn (2006) examine the politics, provisions, and implications of NCLB in greater detail.

32. Kristie Kauerz and Jessica McMaken, *Implications for the Early Learning Field,* ECS No Child Left Behind Policy Brief (Denver: Education Commission of the States, 2004), ECS Archives.

33. *Early Education and Care: What Is the Federal Government's Role? Hearing before the Senate Subcommittee on Education and Early Childhood Development of the Committee on Health, Education, Labor, and Pensions,* 109th Cong., 1st sess. (2005), 15.

34. *Early Education: From Science to Practice,* 5.

35. *Forum on Early Learning: Investing in Our Children, Investing in Our Future; Hearing of the Senate Committee on Health, Education, Labor, and Pensions,* 107th Cong., 2d sess. (2002), 12.

36. *Early Education: From Science to Practice,* 4.

37. *Forum on Early Learning,* 4.

38. *Forum on Early Learning,* 6.

39. *Early Education: From Science to Practice,* 37.

40. *Early Education and Care,* 32.

41. *Early Education: From Science to Practice,* 35.

42. *Early Education: From Science to Practice,* 40.

43. *Early Education: From Science to Practice,* 12.

44. *Early Childhood Education: Improvement through Integration; Hearing before the House Subcommittee on Education Reform of the Committee on Education and the Workforce,* 109th Cong., 1st sess. (2005), 21.

45. *Early Childhood Education: Improvement through Integration,* 33.

46. *Early Childhood Education: Improvement through Integration,* 8.

47. *The School Readiness Act of 2003: Hearing on H.R. 2210 before the House Subcommittee on Education Reform of the Committee on Education and the Workforce,* 108th Cong., 1st sess. (2003), 26.

48. *School Readiness Act of 2003,* 60.

49. *School Readiness Act of 2003,* 93.

50. *School Readiness Act of 2003,* 8.

51. *School Readiness Act of 2003,* 37.

52. *School Readiness Act of 2003,* 36.

53. *School Readiness Act of 2003,* 43.

54. *School Readiness Act of 2003,* 45.

55. *School Readiness Act of 2003,* 45.

56. *School Readiness Act of 2003,* 94.

57. *School Readiness Act of 2003,* 5.

58. *School Readiness Act of 2003,* 13.

59. *School Readiness Act of 2003,* 35.

60. *School Readiness Act of 2003,* 94.

61. *School Readiness Act of 2003,* 64.

62. *School Readiness Act of 2003,* 85.

63. *School Readiness Act of 2003,* 89.

64. *Early Childhood Education: Improvement through Integration,* 2.

65. During the debate over reauthorization, Democrats and Republicans were also divided on language that would have allowed faith-based providers of Head Start services to take religion into account when hiring employees for the program. This language, which the Bush administration endorsed, was not in the final bill.

66. For more information on the content and politics of Head Start reauthorization, see "Long-Sought Head Start Bill Clears," in *CQ Almanac 2007,* 63rd ed., ed. Jan Austin, (Washington, DC: Congressional Quarterly, 2008), 8-6–8-7, available at http://library .cqpress.com/cqalmanac/cqal07-1066-44917-2048087.

67. *Providing Resources Early for Kids Act,* HR 3289, 110th Cong., 1st sess., *Congressional Record* 153 (August 1, 2007): H9282.

68. The Library of Congress: THOMAS, "Bill Summary and Status, 110th Congress: H.R. 3289," http://www.thomas.gov/cgi-bin/bdquery/z?d110:HR03289:@@@L&summ2 =m& (accessed March 14, 2011).

69. Sam Dillon, "Obama Pledge Stirs Hope in Early Education," *New York Times*, December 17, 2008.

70. Dillon, "Obama Pledge Stirs Hope."

71. Valerie Strauss, "Early Childhood Again in Spotlight," *Washington Post*, October 9, 2011.

72. Title I distributes funds to local education agencies and public schools that have high numbers or high percentages of poor children. The funds can be used for preschool or to supplement or expand other early childhood programs. See Steffanie Clothier, *Economic Recovery Funding Opportunities for Early Care and Education* (Denver: National Conference of State Legislatures, 2009), 2.

73. Clothier, *Economic Recovery Funding Opportunities*, 3.

74. Clothier, *Economic Recovery Funding Opportunities*, 6.

75. *Race to the Top Program Executive Summary* (Washington, DC: Department of Education, 2009), 2.

76. Twelve of the sixteen finalists in the first phase of Race to the Top completed the early education section of the application. See Chrisanne L. Gayl, *Pre-K and the Race to the Top: A Review of Early Education Proposals in States' Phase 1 Grant Applications* (Washington, DC: Pre-K Now, 2010), 2.

77. Gayl, *Pre-K and the Race to the Top*, 2–3.

78. Gayl, *Pre-K and the Race to the Top*, 6.

79. Gayl, *Pre-K and the Race to the Top*, 8.

80. *Race to the Top–Early Learning Challenge* (Washington, DC: Department of Education and Department of Human Resources, 2011), 2.

81. *Race to the Top–Early Learning Challenge*, 3.

82. *Race to the Top–Early Learning Challenge*, 2.

83. Strauss, "Early Childhood Again in Spotlight."

84. Letter from Mary Jane Wallner, Wes Keller, John Goedde, and Roy Takumi to Arne Duncan and Kathleen Sebelius, July 6, 2011, http://www.ncsl.org/issues-research/human-services/letter-to-hhs-re-race-to-the-top-early-learni32.aspx (accessed March 7, 2012).

85. Department of Health and Human Services, "We Can't Wait: Nine States Awarded Race to the Top–Early Learning Challenge Grants," news release, December 16, 2011.

CHAPTER 8

1. "We Are Listening to You: 1999 ECS Constituent Needs Survey Results," August 1999, 1, ECS Archives.

2. Education Commission of the States, *Early Learning: Improving Results for Young Children* (Denver: Education Commission of the States, 2000), 7, ECS Archives.

3. Education Commission of the States, *Early Learning*, 8.

4. Education Commission of the States, *Early Learning*, 9.

5. Education Commission of the States, *Starting Early, Starting Now: A Policymaker's Guide to Early Care and Education and School Success* (Denver: Education Commission of the States, 2001), 6, ECS Archives.

6. Gloria Zradicka, "2003 State-of-the-State Addresses: Early Learning," State Notes: Early Learning, March 17, 2003, ECS Archives.

7. For more on the role of the Pew Charitable Trusts, see Bushouse 2009 and E. Rose 2010, chap. 5.

8. A similar rhetorical transformation occurred in the context of kindergarten, where several developments in the late twentieth century "progressively recast the purpose of kindergarten education from a vehicle for young children's development to the foundation for the individual child's future academic achievement" (Russell 2011, 256).

9. Supporters of increased public investment carefully considered how to frame the issue. For example, focus groups in four states suggested greater public comfort with "universally available, voluntary prekindergarten" than "universal pre-K," because the latter sounded like a mandatory program. They also suggested a preference for "government-assisted" rather than "government-run" programs, possibly due to the existing mélange of service providers (Education Commission of the States, *Starting Early, Starting Now*, 23).

10. Kristie Kauerz and Jessica McMaken, *Implications for the Early Learning Field*, ECS No Child Left Behind Policy Brief (Denver: Education Commission of the States, 2004), 2, ECS Archives.

11. Samuel J. Meisels and Abigail M. Jewkes, "'School Readiness' Not Easy to Determine," *State Education Leader* 19, no. 2 (Summer 2001): 15, ECS Archives.

12. "Assessment," *The Progress of Education Reform, 1999–2001: Early Care and Education* 2, no. 6 (June–July 2001): 4, ECS Archives.

13. Jessica McMaken, "Eligibility Requirements for Students," ECS State Notes: State Funded Prekindergarten Programs, March 2002, ECS Archives.

14. "'P-16': The Next Great Education Reform," *State Education Leader* 20, no. 1 (Winter 2002): 1–2, at 2, ECS Archives.

15. Louise Stoney, "Financing Early Care and Education: Key Issues," *State Education Leader* 19, no. 2 (Summer 2001): 3–4, at 3, ECS Archives.

16. Mimi Howard, *Emerging Issues 2006*, ECS Policy Brief: Early Learning (Denver: Education Commission of the States, 2006), 3, ECS Archives.

17. Education Commission of the States, *Starting Early, Starting Now*, 2.

18. Sharon Lynn Kagan, *Giving America's Young Children a Better Start: A Change Brief* (Denver: Education Commission of the States, 2001), 5, ECS Archives.

19. Education Commission of the States, *Starting Early, Starting Now*, 8.

20. Education Commission of the States, *Starting Early, Starting Now*, 3.

21. "Early Childhood Education Resource Materials," Education Commission of the States Education Legislative Workshop, October 3, 2005, 2, ECS Archives.

22. "Early Learning Shows Benefits," *The Progress of Education Reform, 1999–2001: Early Care and Education* 2, no. 6 (June–July 2001): 1, ECS Archives.

23. Education Commission of the States, *Early Learning*, 4.

24. Jane Wiechel, "Eliminating the 'Nonsystem' of Governance," *State Education Leader* 19, no. 2 (Summer 2001): 8–9, at 9, ECS Archives.

25. Kagan, *Giving America's Young Children a Better Start*, 5.

26. The relevant service providers included child care facilities (18 percent), Head Start centers (7 percent), family-based care (1 percent), and other organizations (3 percent) ("Early Childhood Education Resource Materials," 2).

27. "From Potty Gate to Popularity," *State Education Leader* 15, no. 1 (Winter 1997): 14, ECS Archives.

28. See Bushouse 2009 for a more comprehensive description of developments in Georgia and Oklahoma.

29. Howard, *Emerging Issues 2006*, 1.

30. Education Commission of the States, *Starting Early, Starting Now*, 17.

31. Education Commission of the States, *Starting Early, Starting Now*, 12.

32. For more on the social scientific rationale behind this approach and the perils of failing to examine multiple outcomes, see Geddes 1990 and King, Keohane, and Verba 1994.

33. In addition to the quantitative approach employed here, one can increase confidence in the conclusions drawn from primarily historical accounts by paying more-careful attention to causal mechanisms, relying on counterfactual analysis, or examining multiple policy areas (Hacker 2002).

34. Rigby 2007 describes the data on which these figures are based.

35. Two policy alignments will not be examined here. One might hypothesize that a strong Head Start community will lead states to fund only Head Start supplements. Very few states undertake such a funding approach, however, making a systematic analysis impossible. In addition, the analysis in this chapter does not examine the relationship between Head Start strength and a mixed funding approach, because its impact is unclear. Head Start supporters might appreciate the supplemental funding but worry that the simultaneous existence of a freestanding program represents a long-term threat. In addition, Head Start supplements often come with "strings attached." Some supplements fund extended days or enrollment expansions, but in other cases, the state assumes some administrative responsibility for Head Start (Barnett et al. 2006, 31). As a result, Head Start supporters might resist the establishment of a mixed funding approach.

36. Data on Head Start enrollment come from Administration for Children and Families, "Head Start Program Fact Sheet: Fiscal Year 2002," http://www.acf.hhs.gov/programs/ohs/about/fy2002.html (accessed March 12, 2009). Data on overall preschool enrollment come from U.S. Census Bureau, "Table P053: School Enrollment by Level of School for the Population 3 Years and Over," in *Census 2000 Supplementary Survey* (Washington, DC: U.S. Census Bureau, 2001).

37. U.S. Census Bureau, "SC-EST2005-2: Population Estimates by State: Age and Sex for States and for Puerto Rico, April 1, 2000 to July 1, 2006," (accessed September 20, 2012 http://www.census.gov/popest/data/state/asrh/2006/SC-EST2006-02.html).

38. References to anticipated "positive" or "negative" relationships merit further explanation. The first dependent variable indicates whether a state does not fund preschool education. Any characteristic expected to have a "positive" impact on preschool spending will be expected to have a negative relationship with this specific outcome. The second dependent variable indicates whether a state exclusively funds a freestanding program. The expected relationships are therefore expected to hold as they are described here. For ease of interpretation, tables 2 and 3 include the expected direction of the relationship under examination.

39. The analysis in this section uses state per capita income as its proxy for the economic resources. The specific measure is per capita income (Bureau of Economic Analysis, http://www.bea.gov/regional/docs/income [accessed September 20, 2012]) divided

by the implicit price deflator ("Gross Domestic Product: Implicit Price Deflator," http://www.research.stlouisfed.org/fred2/series/GDPDEF/ [accessed January 19, 2013]) and then logged.

40. The measure is a percentage of the state population aged twenty-five and over, from U.S. Census Bureau. "QT-P20: Educational Attainment by Sex, 2000," in *Census 2000 Summary File 3 (SF-3) Sample Data* (Washington, DC: U.S. Census Bureau, 2001).

41. U.S. Census Bureau, "SC-EST2006-6RACE: Annual State Population Estimates with Sex, 6 Race Groups (5 Race Alone Groups and One Group with Two or More Race Groups) and Hispanic Origin, April 1, 2000 to July 1, 2006," http://www.census.gov/popest/states/asrh/stasrh.html (accessed March 11, 2010).

42. The party control measure is an updated, annual version of the data presented in Klarner 2003.

43. The "first differences" displayed in tables 2 and 3 are predicted probabilities rather than the coefficients of the original analysis. They were derived by setting all continuous variables to their means and all dichotomous variables to their modes and manipulating the quantity of interest. For such variables as the size of the Head Start community, the values in the tables display the change in the predicted probability when the quantity of interest shifts from one standard deviation below its mean to one standard deviation above its mean. For dichotomous variables like unified Democratic government, the values in the tables display the change in predicted probability when the quantity of interest shifts from zero to one. The values were derived using the statistical simulation technique and computer software described in King, Tomz, and Wittenberg 2000. The "confidence intervals" presented in the tables are 2.5 percent, 97.5 percent of the posterior distributions.

44. Technically, the results presented in table 2 indicate that wealthy states, liberal states, and states with a unified Democratic government are all significantly less likely not to allocate public funds to preschool. The formulations used in the text have been employed for ease of interpretation.

45. The effects of the remaining three variables included in the model—percentage of the state population under age five (positive), state education level (positive), and population homogeneity (positive)—do not conform to our predictions. Of these three variables, only the relationship between the state education level and the decision not to fund preschool education achieves conventional levels of statistical significance.

46. The effects of the remaining four variables included in the model—percentage of the state population under age five (negative), state wealth (negative), state education level (negative), and population homogeneity (negative)—do not conform to our predictions. Of these four variables, only the relationship between state education level and the exclusive funding of a freestanding state program achieves conventional levels of statistical significance. The negative relationships between education and preschool funding in tables 2 and 3 might reflect regional patterns. Southern states' populations generally have less formal education, but states like Georgia and Oklahoma have been policy leaders. This southern leadership dates to the 1980s, when several regional associations called for increased investment in public schools, including early childhood programs, as part of a long-term economic growth strategy (Bushouse 2009, 19).

47. The key relationship identified in this section is robust to changes in model specification. In models using alternative measures of partisanship, population homogene-

ity, and education levels, the relationship between Head Start strength and preschool funding remains in the expected direction and achieves conventional levels of statistical significance. These results suggest that neither the absence of a relationship between ethnic and racial diversity and preschool funding nor the unexpected relationship between education levels and preschool funding decisions is an artifact of the proxies used to measure these state attributes. In another test of the robustness of the results reported here, the analysis was also performed using a random effects model. The substantive effects of the analysis hold, as the interest group variable achieves conventional levels of statistical significance in both models.

48. It might also be useful to extend the present analysis to other dimensions of preschool policy, such as curricular standards, personnel credentials, and classroom regulations. The contemporary debate over preschool education is multidimensional, and the size of the Head Start community may not be relevant in every context.

49. Steffanie Clothier and Julie Poppe, "Preschool Rocks: Policymakers around the Country Are Investing in Preschool," *State Legislatures,* January 2007, 28–30.

50. Elizabeth McNichol, Phil Oliff, and Nicholas Johnson, *States Continue to Feel Recession's Impact* (Washington, DC: Center on Budget and Policy Priorities, 2012), 1.

51. McNichol, Oliff, and Johnson, *States Continue to Feel Recession's Impact.*

52. McNichol, Oliff, and Johnson, *States Continue to Feel Recession's Impact,* 2.

53. Nicholas Johnson, Phil Oliff, and Erica Williams, *An Update on State Budgets: At Least 46 States Have Imposed Cuts That Hurt Vulnerable Residents and Cause Job Loss* (Washington, DC: Center on Budget and Policy Priorities, 2011), 3.

54. Johnson, Oliff, and Williams, *An Update on State Budgets,* 10–11.

55. *Child Care and Early Education 2009 Legislative Action* (Denver: National Conference of State Legislatures, 2010), 1.

56. *Child Care and Early Education 2009 Legislative Action,* 2.

57. *Child Care and Early Education 2010 Legislative Action* (Denver: National Conference of State Legislatures, 2012), 1.

58. *Child Care and Early Education 2010 Legislative Action,* 4.

59. *Transforming Public Education: Pathway to a Pre-K–12 Future* (Washington, DC: Pew Center on the States, 2011), 14.

60. Amanda Szekely, *State Early Childhood Advisory Councils: An Overview of Implementation across the States* (Washington, DC: National Governors Association, 2011), 2.

61. Szekely, *State Early Childhood Advisory Councils,* 6.

62. "Teacher Training," *The Progress of Educational Reform, 1999–2001: Early Care and Education* 2, no. 6 (June–July 2001): 6–7, at 7, ECS Archives. Many scholarly studies, however, find no connection between teacher credentials and academic outcomes (Early et al. 2006; Early et al. 2007; LoCasale-Crouch et al. 2007).

63. *The Best of Head Start: Learning from Model Programs; Hearing before the House Subcommittee on Education Reform of the Committee on Education and the Workforce,* 109th Cong., 1st sess. (2005), 32.

64. National Head Start Association, *Position Paper: Our View of the U.S. Senate Reauthorization Bill, S. 1940* (Alexandria, VA: National Head Start Association, 2004), 8. In the late 1990s and early 2000s, many states provided scholarships and financial incentives to help address the fiscal barriers that accompany new training requirements (Ackerman 2004).

65. National Head Start Association, *Position Paper,* 8.

66. "Teacher Training," 6.

67. Some observers view programmatic diversity as a benefit of the status quo because it promotes parental choice and is potentially responsive to families' divergent priorities (Finn 2009; Fuller 2007).

68. Quoted in "Georgia: Ahead of the Game in Early Childhood Education," *State Education Leader* 20, no. 1 (Winter 2002): 10, ECS Archives.

CONCLUSION

1. Melinda Henneberger, "'Princess Nancy' Pelosi Calls Cain 'Clueless,' Vows to Do More for Child Care," *Washington Post,* November 17, 2011.

2. *Transforming Public Education: Pathway to a Pre-K–12 Future* (Washington, DC: Pew Center on the States, 2011), 12.

3. Duane Benson, "Lessons Learned While Pushing for Preschool," *Star Tribune,* December 11, 2011, A15.

4. *Transforming Public Education,* 5.

5. In recent years, scholarship in comparative politics has devoted more attention to the politics of education, often through the lens of political economy (Ansell 2010; Iversen and Stephens 2008).

6. One exception is Skocpol 1992, which examines the evolution of maternalist public policies at both the national and the state level in the late nineteenth and early twentieth centuries.

7. Scholars of state politics bear equal responsibility for this lack of scholarly engagement. The theoretical advances and key concepts of the policy development approach have generally not been incorporated into state politics research (Howard 1999).

8. Interview with former vice president Walter F. Mondale, December 3, 2010, Minneapolis, MN.

Bibliography

Ackerman, Debra J. 2004. "States' Efforts in Improving the Qualifications of Early Care and Education Teachers." *Educational Policy* 18:311–37.

Ansell, Ben W. 2010. *From the Ballot to the Blackboard: The Redistributive Political Economy of Education.* Cambridge: Cambridge University Press.

Bailey, Stephen K. 1975. *Education Interest Groups in the Nation's Capital.* Washington, DC: American Council on Education.

Bailey, Stephen K., and Edith K. Mosher. 1968. *ESEA: The Office of Education Administers a Law.* Syracuse, NY: Syracuse University Press.

Bainbridge, Jay, Marcia K. Meyers, Sakiko Tanaka, and Jane Waldfogel. 2005. "Who Gets an Early Education? Family Income and the Enrollment of Three- to Five-Year-Olds from 1968 to 2000." *Social Science Quarterly* 86:724–45.

Barnett, W. Steven, Dale J. Epstein, Megan E. Carolan, Jen Fitzgerald, Debra J. Ackerman, and Allison H. Friedman. 2010. *The State of Preschool 2010: State Preschool Yearbook.* New Brunswick, NJ: National Institute on Early Education Research.

Barnett, W. Steven, Dale J. Epstein, Allison H. Friedman, Rachel A. Sansanelli, and Jason T. Hustedt. 2009. *The State of Preschool 2009: State Preschool Yearbook.* New Brunswick, NJ: National Institute on Early Education Research.

Barnett, W. Steven, and Jason T. Hustedt. 2003. "Preschool: The Most Important Grade." *Educational Leadership* 60:54–57.

Barnett, W. Steven, Jason T. Hustedt, Laura E. Hawkinson, and Kenneth B. Robin. 2006. *The State of Preschool: 2006 State Preschool Yearbook.* New Brunswick, NJ: National Institute on Early Education Research.

Baumgartner, Frank R., Jeffrey M. Berry, Marie Hojnacki, David C. Kimball, and Beth L. Leech. 2009. *Lobbying and Policy Change: Who Wins, Who Loses, and Why.* Chicago: University of Chicago Press.

Baumgartner, Frank R., and Bryan D. Jones. 1991. "Agenda Dynamics and Policy Subsystems." *Journal of Politics* 53:1044–74.

Baumgartner, Frank R., and Bryan D. Jones. 1993. *Agendas and Instability in American Politics.* Chicago: University of Chicago Press.

Beatty, Barbara. 1995. *Preschool Education in America: The Culture of Young Children from the Colonial Era to the Present.* New Haven: Yale University Press.

Beatty, Barbara. 2001. "The Politics of Preschool Advocacy: Lessons from Three Pioneering Organizations." In *Who Speaks for America's Children? The Role of Child*

Advocates in Public Policy, ed. Carol J. DeVita and Rachel Mosher-Williams. Washington, DC: Urban Institute Press.

Beck, Rochelle. 1982. "Beyond the Stalemate in Child Care Public Policy." In *Day Care: Scientific and Social Policy Issues,* ed. Edward F. Zigler and Edmund W. Gordon. Boston: Auburn House.

Berkowitz, Edward D. 2006. *Something Happened: A Political and Cultural Overview of the Seventies.* New York: Columbia University Press.

Berry, William D., Evan J. Ringquist, Richard C. Fording, and Russell L. Hanson. 1998. "Measuring Citizen and Government Ideology in the American States, 1960–1993." *American Journal of Political Science* 42:327–48.

Bloom, Benjamin. 1964. *Stability and Change in Human Characteristics.* New York: Wiley.

Bonoli, Giuliano, and Frank Reber. 2010. "The Political Economy of Childcare in OECD Countries: Explaining Cross-National Variation in Spending and Coverage Rates." *European Journal of Political Research* 49:97–118.

Bradbury, Dorothy E. 1936. "The Case for Nursery Schools." *Childhood Education* 12:406–8, 429.

Brademas, John. 1986. *Washington, D.C. to Washington Square.* New York: Weidenfeld and Nicolson.

Brademas, John. 1987. *The Politics of Education: Conflict and Consensus on Capitol Hill.* With Lynne P. Browne. Norman: University of Oklahoma Press.

Bushouse, Brenda K. 2009. *Universal Preschool: Policy Change, Stability, and the Pew Charitable Trusts.* Albany: State University of New York Press.

Cahan, Emily D. 1989. *Past Caring: A History of U.S. Preschool Care and Education for the Poor, 1820–1965.* New York: National Center for Children in Poverty.

Cammisa, Anne Marie. 1995. *Governments as Interest Groups: Intergovernmental Lobbying and the Federal System.* Westport, CT: Praeger.

Campbell, Andrea Louise. 2002. "Self-Interest, Social Security, and the Distinctive Participation Patterns of Senior Citizens." *American Political Science Review* 96:565–74.

Campbell, Andrea Louise. 2003. "Participatory Reactions to Policy Threats: Senior Citizens and the Defense of Social Security and Medicare." *Political Behavior* 25:29–49.

Cibulka, James G. 2001. "The Changing Role of Interest Groups in Education: Nationalization and the New Politics of Education Productivity." *Educational Policy* 15:12–40.

Clifford, Richard M., Oscar Barbarin, Florence Chang, Diane Early, Donna Bryant, Carollee Howes, Margaret Burchinal, and Robert Pianta. 2005. "What Is Pre-Kindergarten? Characteristics of Public Pre-Kindergarten Programs." *Applied Developmental Science* 9:126–43.

Cobb, Clifford W. 1992. *Responsive Schools, Renewed Communities.* San Francisco: ICS Press.

Cohen, Sally S. 2001. *Championing Child Care.* New York: Columbia University Press.

Collier, Ruth Berins, and David Collier. 1991. *Shaping the Political Arena: Critical Junctures, the Labor Movement, and Regime Dynamics in Latin America.* Princeton: Princeton University Press.

Congressional Quarterly. 1972. *Congressional Quarterly Almanac, 1971.* Washington, DC: Congressional Quarterly.

Cravens, Hamilton. 1993. *Before Head Start: The Iowa Station and America's Children.* Chapel Hill: University of North Carolina Press.

Cuban, Larry. 1992. "Why Some Reforms Last: The Case of Kindergarten." *American Journal of Education* 100:166–94.

Daly, Mary. 2010. "Families versus State and Market." In *The Oxford Handbook of the Welfare State,* ed. Frances G. Castles, Stephan Liebfried, Jane Lewis, Herbert Obinger, and Christopher Pierson. New York: Oxford University Press.

Dombkowski, Kristen. 2001. "Will the Real Kindergarten Please Stand Up? Defining and Redefining the Twentieth-Century US Kindergarten." *History of Education* 30:527–45.

Dye, Thomas R. 1966. *Politics, Economics, and the Public: Policy Outcomes in the American States.* Chicago: Rand McNally.

Early, Diane M., Donna M. Bryant, Robert C. Pianta, Richard M. Clifford, Margaret R. Burchinal, Sharon Ritchie, Carolle Howes, and Oscar Barbarin. 2006. "Are Teachers' Education, Major, and Credentials Related to Classroom Quality and Children's Academic Gains in Pre-Kindergarten?" *Early Childhood Research Quarterly* 21:174–95.

Early, Diane M., Kelly L. Maxwell, Margaret Burchinal, Soumya Alva, Randall H. Bender, Donna Bryant, Karen Cai, Richard M. Clifford, Caroline Ebanks, James A. Griffin, Gary T. Henry, Carollee Howes, Jeniffer Iriondo-Perez, Hyun-Joo Jeon, Andrew J. Mashburn, Ellen Peisner-Feinberg, Robert C. Pianta, Nathan Vandergrift, and Nicholas Zill. 2007. "Teachers' Education, Classroom Quality, and Young Children's Academic Skills: Results from Seven Studies of Preschool Programs." *Child Development* 78:558–80.

Educational Policies Commission. 1966. *Universal Opportunity for Early Childhood Education.* Washington, DC: Educational Policies Commission of the National Education Association and American Association of School Administrators.

Eliot, Thomas H. 1959. "Toward an Understanding of Public School Politics." *American Political Science Review* 53:1032–51.

Elmore, Richard R., and Milbrey Wallin McLaughlin. 1983. "The Federal Role in Education: Learning from Experience." *Education and Urban Society* 15:309–30.

Erikson, Robert S., Gerald C. Wright, and John P. McIver. 1993. *Statehouse Democracy: Public Opinion and Public Policy in the American States.* Cambridge: Cambridge University Press.

Esping-Andersen, Gosta. 1990. *The Three Worlds of Welfare Capitalism.* Princeton: Princeton University Press.

Fellowes, Matthew C., and Gretchen Rowe. 2004. "Politics and the New American Welfare States." *American Journal of Political Science* 48:362–73.

Finn, Chester E., Jr. 2009. *Reroute the Preschool Juggernaut.* Stanford, CA: Hoover Institution Press.

Fishhaut, Erna H., and Donald Pastor. 1977. "Should the Public Schools Be Entrusted with Preschool Education: A Critique of the AFT Proposals." *School Review* 86:38–49.

Fishhaut, Erna H., and Donald Pastor. 1978. "A Response to a Response to a Response: Comments on the Berk and Berson Reply." *School Review* 87:120–24.

Frum, David. 2000. *How We Got Here: The 70's; The Decade That Brought You Modern Life (For Better or Worse).* New York: Basic Books.

Fuller, Bruce. 2007. *Standardized Childhood: The Political and Cultural Struggle over Early Education.* Stanford, CA: Stanford University Press.

Fusarelli, Lance D. 2002. "The Political Economy of Gubernatorial Elections: Implications for Education Policy." *Educational Policy* 16:139–60.

Geddes, Barbara. 1990. "How the Cases You Choose Affect the Answers You Get: Selection Bias in Comparative Politics." *Political Analysis* 2:131–50.

Gesell, Arnold. 1924. "The Significance of the Nursery School." *Childhood Education* 1:11–20.

Gilles, Stephen. 1996. "On Educating Children: A Paternalist Manifesto." *University of Chicago Law Review* 63:937–1034.

Gormley, William T., Jr., and Deborah Phillips. 2005. "The Effects of Universal Pre-K in Oklahoma: Research Highlights and Policy Implications." *Policy Studies Journal* 33:65–82.

Gormley, William T., Jr., Deborah Phillips, and Ted Gayer. 2008. "Preschool Programs Can Boost School Readiness." *Science* 320:1723–24.

Gornick, Janet C., and Marcia K. Meyers. 2003. *Families That Work: Policies for Reconciling Parenthood and Employment.* New York: Russell Sage Foundation.

Gottschalk, Marie. 2000. *The Shadow Welfare State: Labor, Business, and the Politics of Health Care in the United States.* Ithaca, NY: Cornell University Press.

Graham, Hugh Davis. 1984. *The Uncertain Triumph: Federal Education Policy in the Kennedy and Johnson Years.* Chapel Hill: University of North Carolina Press.

Gray, Virginia. 2008. The Socioeconomic and Political Context of States. In *Politics in the American States: A Comparative Analysis,* ed. Virginia Gray and Russell L. Hanson. 9th ed. Washington, DC: CQ Press.

Grotberg, Edith H. 1981. "The Federal Role in Family Policies." In *Approaches to Child and Family Policy,* ed. Harold C. Wallach. Boulder, CO: Westview.

Grubb, W. Norton. 1987. *Young Children Face the States: Issues and Options for Early Childhood Education.* New Brunswick, NJ: Center for Policy Research in Education.

Hacker, Jacob S. 2002. *The Divided Welfare State: The Battle over Public and Private Social Benefits in the United States.* Cambridge: Cambridge University Press.

Hacker, Jacob S. 2005. "Bringing the Welfare State Back In: The Promise (and Perils) of the New Social Welfare History." *Journal of Policy History* 17:125–54.

Hacker, Jacob S., and Paul Pierson. 2002. "Business Power and Social Policy: Employers and the Formation of the American Welfare State." *Politics and Society* 30:277–325.

Haider, Donald H. 1974. *When Governments Come to Washington: Governors, Mayors, and Intergovernmental Lobbying.* New York: Free Press.

Hales, Dawson. 1954. *Federal Control of Public Education: A Critical Appraisal.* New York: Bureau of Publications, Teachers College, Columbia University.

Hatch, Orrin G. 1982. "Families, Children, and Child Care." In *Day Care: Scientific and Social Policy Issues,* ed. Edward F. Zigler and Edmund W. Gordon. Boston: Auburn House.

Heclo, Hugh. 1974. *Modern Social Policy in Britain and Sweden: From Relief to Income Maintenance.* New Haven: Yale University Press.

Henry, Gary T., Craig S. Gordon, and Dana K. Rickman. 2006. "Early Education Policy Alternatives: Comparing Quality and Outcomes of Head Start and State Prekindergarten." *Educational Evaluation and Policy Analysis* 28:77–99.

Hero, Rodney E., and Caroline J. Tolbert. 1996. "A Racial/Ethnic Interpretation of Politics and Policy in the States of the U.S." *American Journal of Political Science* 40:851–71.

Hinitz, Blythe F. 1998. "Credentialing Early Childhood Paraprofessionals in the United States: The Child Development Associate and Other Frameworks." *International Journal of Early Years Education* 6:87–103.

Holyoke, Thomas T. 2003. "Choosing Battlegrounds: Interest Group Lobbying across Multiple Venues." *Political Research Quarterly* 56:325–36.

Howard, Christopher. 1997. *The Hidden Welfare State: Tax Expenditures and Social Policy in the United States.* Princeton: Princeton University Press.

Howard, Christopher. 1999. "The American Welfare State, or States?" *Political Research Quarterly* 52:421–42.

Howard, Christopher. 2007. *The Welfare State Nobody Knows: Debunking Myths about U.S. Social Policy.* Princeton: Princeton University Press.

Huber, Evelyne, Charles Ragin, and John D. Stephens. 1993. "Social Democracy, Constitutional Structure, and the Welfare State." *American Journal of Sociology* 99:711–49.

Hunt, Joseph McVicker. 1961. *Intelligence and Experience.* New York: Ronald.

Hymes, James L., Jr. 1979. *Early Childhood Education: Living History Interviews.* Carmel, CA: Hacienda.

Iversen, Torben, and John D. Stephens. 2008. "Partisan Politics, the Welfare State, and Three Worlds of Human Capital Formation." *Comparative Political Studies* 41:600–637.

Jones-Correa, Michael. 2000–2001. "The Origins and Diffusion of Racial Restrictive Covenants." *Political Science Quarterly* 115:541–68.

Kaestle, Carl F., and Maris A. Vinovskis. 1978. "From Apron Strings to ABCs: Parents, Children, and Schooling in Nineteenth-Century Massachusetts." *American Journal of Sociology* 84:S39-S80.

Kagan, Sharon L., and Michelle J. Neuman. 2003. "Integrating Early Care and Education." *Educational Leadership* 60:58–63.

Kahlenberg, Richard D. 2007. *Tough Liberal: Albert Shanker and the Battles over Schools, Unions, Race, and Democracy.* New York: Columbia University Press.

Kamerman, Sheila, and Shirley Gatenio. 2003. "Overview of the Current Policy Context." In *Early Childhood Education and Care in the USA*, ed. Debby Cryer and Richard M. Clifford. Baltimore: Paul H. Brookes.

Katznelson, Ira. 2003. "The Possibilities of Analytical Political History." In *The Democratic Experiment: New Directions in American Political History,* ed. Meg Jacobs, William J. Novak, and Julian E. Zelizer. Princeton: Princeton University Press.

Kelly, Erin L. 2003. "The Strange History of Employer-Sponsored Child Care: Interested Actors, Uncertainty, and the Transformation of Law in Organizational Fields." *American Journal of Sociology* 109:606–49.

Kennedy, Edward M. 1982. "Child Care—a Commitment to Be Honored." In *Day Care: Scientific and Social Policy Issues,* ed. Edward F. Zigler and Edmund W. Gordon. Boston: Auburn House.

King, Anthony. 1973. "Ideas, Institutions, and the Policies of Governments: A Comparative Analysis." Part 3. *British Journal of Political Science* 3:409–23.

King, Gary, Robert O. Keohane, and Sidney Verba. 1994. *Designing Social Inquiry: Scientific Inference in Qualitative Research.* Princeton: Princeton University Press.

King, Gary, Michael Tomz, and Jason Wittenberg. 2000. "Making the Most of Statistical Analyses: Improving Interpretation and Presentation." *American Journal of Political Science* 44:347–61.

Kingdon, John W. 1995. *Agendas, Alternatives, and Public Policies.* 2nd ed. New York: HarperCollins College.

Kirp, David L. 2004. "You're Doing Fine, Oklahoma! The Universal Pre-K Movement Takes Off in Unlikely Places." *American Prospect Online,* November 1.

Kirp, David L. 2007. *The Sandbox Investment: The Preschool Movement and Kids-First Politics.* Cambridge, MA: Harvard University Press.

Klarner, Carl E. 2003. "The Measurement of the Partisan Balance of State Government." *State Politics and Policy Quarterly* 3:309–19.

Lazerson, Marvin. 1972. "The Historical Antecedents of Early Childhood Education." In *Early Childhood Education,* ed. Ira J. Gordon. Chicago: University of Chicago Press.

LoCasale-Crouch, Jennifer, Tim Konold, Robert Pianta, Carollee Howes, Margaret Burchinal, Richard Clifford, Diane Early, and Oscar Barbarin. 2007. "Observed Classroom Quality Profiles in State-Funded Pre-Kindergarten Programs and Associations with Teacher, Program, and Classroom Characteristics." *Early Childhood Research Quarterly* 22:3–17.

Lombardi, Joan. 2003. *Time to Care: Redesigning Child Care to Promote Education, Support Families, and Build Communities.* Philadelphia: Temple University Press.

Lowry, Robert C. 2009. "Reauthorization of the Federal Higher Education Act and Accountability for Student Learning: The Dog That Didn't Bark." *Publius* 39:506–26.

Maeroff, Gene I. 2006. *Building Blocks: Making Children Successful in the Early Years of School.* New York: Palgrave Macmillan.

Manna, Paul. 2006. *School's In: Federalism and the National Education Agenda.* Washington, DC: Georgetown University Press.

May, Dean, and Maris A. Vinovskis. 1977. "A Ray of Millennial Light: Early Education and Social Reform in the Infant School Movement in Massachusetts, 1826–1840." In *Family and Kin in Urban Communities, 1700–1930,* ed. Tamara K. Hareven. New York: New Viewpoints.

Mayes, Rick. 2004. *Universal Coverage: The Elusive Quest for National Health Insurance.* Ann Arbor: University of Michigan Press.

Mayhew, David R. 1974. *Congress: The Electoral Connection.* New Haven: Yale University Press.

Mazzoni, Tim L. 1993. "The Changing Politics of State Education Policy Making: A 20-Year Minnesota Perspective." *Educational Evaluation and Policy Analysis* 15:357–79.

Mazzoni, Tim L. 1995. "State Policymaking and School Reform: Influences and Influentials." In *The Study of Educational Politics,* ed. Jay D. Scribner and Donald H. Layton. Washington, DC: Falmer.

McCathren, Randall R. 1981. "The Demise of Federal Categorical Child Care Legislation: Lessons for the '80s from the Failures of the '70s." In *Approaches to Child and Family Policy,* ed. Harold C. Wallach. Boulder, CO: Westview.

McDermott, Kathryn A. 2011. *High-Stakes Reform: The Politics of Educational Accountability.* Washington, DC: Georgetown University Press.

McDonnell, Lorraine M. 2005. "No Child Left Behind and the Federal Role in Education: Evolution or Revolution?" *Peabody Journal of Education* 80:19–38.

McGill-Franzen, Anne. 1993. *Shaping the Preschool Agenda: Early Literacy, Public Policy, and Professional Beliefs.* Albany: State University of New York Press.

McGuinn, Patrick J. 2006. *No Child Left Behind and the Transformation of Federal Education Policy, 1965–2005.* Lawrence: University Press of Kansas.

Melnick, R. Shep. 1994. *Between the Lines: Interpreting Welfare Rights*. Washington, DC: Brookings Institution.

Mettler, Suzanne, and Jeffrey M. Stonecash. 2008. "Government Program Usage and Political Voice." *Social Science Quarterly* 89:273–93.

Michel, Sonya. 1999. *Children's Interests/Mothers' Rights*. New Haven: Yale University Press.

Mondale, Walter F. 1975. "The Need for Child and Family Services." *Day Care and Early Education* 3:14–15.

Mondale, Walter F. 2010. *The Good Fight: A Life in Liberal Politics*. New York: Scribner.

Mooney, Christopher Z. 2001. "*State Politics and Policy Quarterly* and the Study of State Politics: The Editor's Introduction." *State Politics and Policy Quarterly* 1:1–4.

Morgan, Kimberly J. 2001. "A Child of the Sixties: The Great Society, the New Right, and the Politics of Federal Child Care." *Journal of Policy History* 13:215–50.

Morgan, Kimberly J. 2006. *Working Mothers and the Welfare State: Religion and the Politics of Work-Family Policies in Western Europe and the United States*. Stanford, CA: Stanford University Press.

Nelson, John R., Jr. 1982. The Politics of Federal Day Care Regulation. In *Day Care: Scientific and Social Policy Issues*, ed. Edward F. Zigler and Edmund W. Gordon. Boston: Auburn House.

Nice, David C. 1994. *Policy Innovation in State Government*. Ames: Iowa State University Press.

Olmsted, Patricia. 1992. "Where Did Our Diversity Come From? A Profile of Early Childhood Care and Education in the U.S." *High Scope Resource* 11:4–9.

Organization for Economic Cooperation and Development. 2001. *Starting Strong: Early Childhood Education and Care*. Paris: OECD.

Orloff, Ann Shola. 1988. "The Political Origins of America's Belated Welfare State." In *The Politics of Social Policy in the United States*, ed. Margaret Weir, Ann Shola Orloff, and Theda Skocpol. Princeton: Princeton University Press.

Patashnik, Eric M. 1997. "Unfolding Promises: Trust Funds and the Politics of Precommitment." *Political Science Quarterly* 112:431–52.

Patashnik, Eric M. 2003. "After the Public Interest Prevails: The Political Sustainability of Policy Reform." *Governance* 16:203–34.

Patashnik, Eric M. 2008. *Reforms at Risk: What Happens after Major Policy Changes Are Enacted*. Princeton: Princeton University Press.

Peterson, Paul E. 1995. *The Price of Federalism*. Washington, DC: Brookings Institution.

Pierson, Paul. 1993. When Effect Becomes Cause: Policy Feedback and Political Change. *World Politics* 45:595–628.

Pierson, Paul. 1995. "Fragmented Welfare States: Federal Institutions and the Development of Social Policy." *Governance* 8:449–78.

Pierson, Paul. 1996. "The Path to European Integration: A Historical Institutionalist Analysis." *Comparative Political Studies* 29:123–63.

Pierson, Paul. 2000. "Increasing Returns, Path Dependence, and the Study of Politics." *American Political Science Review* 94:251–68.

Pierson, Paul. 2004. *Politics in Time: History, Institutions, and Social Analysis*. Princeton: Princeton University Press.

Pierson, Paul. 2005. "The Study of Policy Development." *Journal of Policy History* 17:34–51.

Quadagno, Jill. 2005. *One Nation Uninsured: Why the U.S. Has No National Health Insurance*. New York: Oxford University Press.

Reese, Ellen. 1996. "Maternalism and Political Mobilization: How California's Postwar Child Care Campaign Was Won." *Gender and Society* 10:566–89.

Rigby, Elizabeth. 2007. "Same Policy Area, Different Politics: How Characteristics of Policy Tools Alter the Determinants of Early Childhood Education Policy." *Policy Studies Journal* 35:653–70.

Robertson, David Brian. 1989. "The Bias of American Federalism: Federal Institutions and the Development of Social Policy." *Journal of Policy History* 1:261–91.

Roh, Jongho, and Donald P. Haider-Markel. 2003. "All Politics Is Not Local: National Forces in State Abortion Initiatives." *Social Science Quarterly* 84:15–31.

Rose, Elizabeth. 1999. *A Mother's Job: The History of Day Care, 1890–1960*. New York: Oxford University Press.

Rose, Elizabeth. 2010. *The Promise of Preschool: From Head Start to Universal Prekindergarten*. New York: Oxford University Press.

Rose, Richard. 1989. "How Exceptional Is the American Political Economy?" *Political Science Quarterly* 104:91–115.

Rose, Richard. 1990. "Inheritance before Choice in Public Policy." *Journal of Theoretical Politics* 2:263–91.

Ross, Elizabeth Dale. 1976. *The Kindergarten Crusade: The Establishment of Preschool Education in the United States*. Athens: Ohio University Press.

Rothman, Sheila M. 1973. "Other People's Children: The Day Care Experience in America." *Public Interest* 30:11–27.

Russell, Jennifer Lin. 2011. "From Child's Garden to Academic Press: The Role of Shifting Institutional Logics in Redefining Kindergarten Education." *American Educational Research Journal* 48:236–67.

Schneider, Anne, and Helen Ingram. 1993. "Social Construction of Target Populations: Implications for Politics and Policy." *American Political Science Review* 87:334–47.

Schneider, Anne, and Mara Sidney. 2009. "What Is Next for Policy Design and Social Construction Theory?" *Policy Studies Journal* 37:103–19.

Schulman, Bruce J. 2001. *The Seventies: The Great Shift in American Culture, Society, and Politics*. New York: Free Press.

Scribner, Jay D., Pedro Reyes, and Lance D. Fusarelli. 1995. "Educational Politics and Policy: And the Game Goes On." In *The Study of Educational Politics*, ed. Jay D. Scribner and Donald H. Layton. Washington, DC: Falmer.

Sealander, Judith. 2003. *The Failed Century of the Child: Governing America's Young in the Twentieth Century*. Cambridge: Cambridge University Press.

Sealander, Judith. 2004. "The History of Childhood Policy: A Philippic's Wish List." *Journal of Policy History* 16:175–87.

Skocpol, Theda. 1991. "Targeting within Universalism: Politically Viable Policies to Combat Poverty in the United States." In *The Urban Underclass*, ed. Christopher Jencks and Paul E. Peterson. Washington, DC: Brookings Institution.

Skocpol, Theda. 1992. *Protecting Soldiers and Mothers: The Political Origins of Social Policy in the United States*. Cambridge, MA: Harvard University Press.

Slobdin, Carol. 1975. "When the U.S. Paid for Day Care." *Day Care and Early Education* 3:22–25, 49.

Soss, Joe. 1999. "Lessons of Welfare: Policy Design, Political Learning, and Political Action." *American Political Science Review* 101:111–27.

Soss, Joe, Sanford F. Schram, Thomas P. Vartanian, and Erin O'Brien. 2001. "Setting the Terms of Relief: Explaining State Policy Choices in the Devolution Revolution." *American Journal of Political Science* 45:378–95.

Spill, Rorie L., Michael J. Licari, and Leonard Ray. 2001. "Taking on Tobacco: Policy Entrepreneurship and the Tobacco Litigation." *Political Research Quarterly* 54:605–22.

Sroufe, Gerald E. 1995. "Politics of Education at the Federal Level." In *The Study of Educational Politics,* ed. Jay D. Scribner and Donald H. Layton. Washington, DC: Falmer.

Steiner, Gilbert Y. 1981. *The Futility of Family Policy.* Washington, DC: Brookings Institution.

Steinfels, Margaret O'Brien. 1973. *Who's Minding the Children? The History and Politics of Day Care in America.* New York: Simon and Schuster.

Steinmo, Sven, and Jon Watts. 1995. "It's the Institutions Stupid! Why Comprehensive National Health Insurance Always Fails in America." *Journal of Health Politics, Policy, and Law* 20:329–72.

Stimson, James A. 1991. *Public Opinion in America: Moods, Cycles, and Swings.* Boulder, CO: Westview.

Stimson, James A., Michael B. MacKuen, and Robert Erikson. 1995. "Dynamic Representation." *American Political Science Review* 89:543–65.

Stipek, Deborah. 2006. "No Child Left Behind Comes to Preschool." *Elementary School Journal* 105:455–65.

Stout, Robert T., Marilyn Tallerico, and Kent Paredes Scribner. 1995. "Values: The 'What' of the Politics of Education." In *The Study of Educational Politics,* ed. Jay D. Scribner and Donald H. Layton. Washington, DC: Falmer.

Sundquist, James L. 1968. *Politics and Policy: The Eisenhower, Kennedy, and Johnson Years.* Washington, DC: Brookings Institution.

Takanishi, Ruby. 1977. "Federal Involvement in Early Education (1933–1973): The Need for Historical Perspectives." In *Current Topics in Early Childhood Education,* ed. Lilian G. Katz, vol. 1. Norwood, NJ: Ablex.

Thelen, Kathleen. 1999. "Historical Institutionalism in Comparative Politics." *American Review of Political Science* 2:369–404.

Thomas, Norman C. 1975. *Education in National Politics.* New York: David McKay.

Thomas, Norman C. 1983. "The Development of Federal Activism in Education: A Contemporary Perspective." *Education and Urban Society* 15: 271–90.

Tsebelis, George. 1995. "Decision Making in Political Systems: Veto Players in Presidentialism, Parliamentarism, Multicameralism, and Multipartyism." *British Journal of Political Science* 25:289–325.

Tweedie, Jack. 1994. "Resources rather than Needs: A State-Centered Model of Welfare Policymaking." *American Journal of Political Science* 38:651–72.

Tyack, David, and Larry Cuban. 1995. *Tinkering toward Utopia: A Century of Public School Reform.* Cambridge, MA: Harvard University Press.

Verba, Sidney, and Gary R. Orren. 1985. *Equality in America: The View from the Top.* Cambridge, MA: Harvard University Press.

Vinovskis, Maris A. 1999a. *History and Educational Policymaking.* New Haven: Yale University Press.

Vinovskis, Maris A. 1999b. *The Road to Charlottesville: The 1989 Education Summit.* Washington, DC: National Education Goals Panel.

Vinovskis, Maris A. 2005. *The Birth of Head Start: Preschool Education Policies in the Kennedy and Johnson Administrations.* Chicago: University of Chicago Press.

Viteritti, Joseph P. 2004. "From Excellence to Equity: Observations on Politics, History, and Policy." *Peabody Journal of Education* 79:64–86.

Walker, Jack L., Jr. 1969. "The Diffusion of Innovations among the American States." *American Political Science Review* 63:880–99.

Walker, Jack L., Jr. 1991. *Mobilizing Interest Groups in America: Patrons, Professions, and Social Movements.* Ann Arbor: University of Michigan Press.

White, Ann Dryden. 2005. "The Structure of Early Care and Education in the United States: Historical Evolution and International Comparisons." *Tax Policy and the Economy* 19:1–37.

White, Linda A. 2002. "Ideas and the Welfare State: Explaining Child Care Policy Development in Canada and the United States." *Comparative Political Studies* 35:713–43.

White, Linda A. 2004. "Trends in Child Care/Early Childhood Education/Early Childhood Development Policy in Canada and the United States." *American Review of Canadian Studies* 34:665–87.

Wilensky, Harold. 1975. *The Welfare State and Equality.* Berkeley: University of California Press.

Wong, Kenneth K. 1995. "The Politics of Education: From Political Science to Multi-Disciplinary Inquiry." In *The Study of Educational Politics,* ed. Jay D. Scribner and Donald H. Layton. Washington, DC: Falmer.

Wong, Kenneth K. 2008. "The Politics of Education." In *Politics in the American States: A Comparative Analysis,* ed. Virginia Gray and Russell L. Hanson. 9th ed. Washington, DC: CQ Press.

Zelizer, Julian E. 2004. "History and Political Science: Together Again?" *Journal of Policy History* 16:126–36.

Zigler, Edward, and Susan Muenchow. 1992. *Head Start: The Inside Story of America's Most Successful Educational Experiment.* New York: Basic Books.

Zigler, Edward, and Sally J. Styfco. 2010. *The Hidden History of Head Start.* New York: Oxford University Press.

Zimmerman, Joseph F. 1991. *Federal Preemption: The Silent Revolution.* Ames: Iowa State University Press.

Index

LoCasale-Crouch, Jennifer, 197n62
Lombardi, Joan, 44, 85, 137, 156n1
Los Angeles, 41, 186
Louisiana, 6, 97–98
Lowry, Robert C., 207

MacKuen, Michael B., 18n4
Maeroff, Gene I., 149n62, 157, 178, 183, 187
Maine, 98, 102
Manna, Paul, 26–27, 136n3, 163n31, 207
Marland, S. P., Jr., 54
Maryland, 98, 103
Massachusetts, 34n2, 42n48, 88, 93, 97, 98–99, 102, 153, 195
maternal roles, 34–35, 38, 41, 44. *See also* female labor force participation
May, Dean, 34n2
Mayes, Rick, 7, 24, 28, 194
Mayhew, David R., 29
Mazzoni, Tim L., 150, 151
McCathren, Randall R., 19, 71–72, 79, 111, 117, 120, 121, 125–26, 127, 130
McCaughey, Betsy, 157
McDermott, Kathryn A., 136n3, 150
McDonnell, Lorraine M., 26, 56
McGill-Franzen, Anne, 50, 110, 120, 126, 152, 153
McGovern, George, 109, 125n108
McGuinn, Patrick J., 28, 136n3, 163n31, 207
McIver, John P., 18n4, 191
McLaughlin, Milbrey Wallin, 149
McNair, Robert, 87
Medicaid, 205
Medicare, 28, 84
Melnick, R. Shep, 26
Mettler, Suzanne, 205
Meyers, Marcia K., 51
Michel, Sonya, 3n10, 4, 12, 16n1, 20, 23, 27, 33n1, 34, 36, 43, 44, 75, 106, 114, 132, 134, 136, 138
Michigan, 144, 153, 177
Midcentury White House Conference on Children and Youth (1950), 43
Middle class: children, 68–69; families, 69, 126, 132, 134, 159; tax credit and, 4, 11, 132, 134; women, 136

Miller, Zell, 184
Mink, Patsy T., 64
Minneapolis, 49
Minnesota, 97, 98, 101, 142, 151, 196
Minnesota Early Learning Foundation, 200
Mississippi, 70–71, 96, 97, 182, 189
Missouri, 98, 102, 151
Mondale, Walter, 19–20, 208–9; Child and Family Services Act of 1975 and, 110–11, 113, 117–18, 121; Comprehensive Child Development Act of 1971 and, 66–68, 72, 79, 81; and other congressional initiatives, 64, 107–9; as vice president, 123–24, 128
Montavon, William F., 38
Mooney, Christopher Z., 188
Moore, Arch, 88
Moral Majority, 137
Morgan, Kimberly J., 11, 19n5, 20, 27, 132, 134, 148n59
Mormon Church, 83
Mosher, Edith K., 55, 56
mothers. *See* maternal roles
mothers' pensions, 44
Moynihan, Daniel Patrick, 75–76
Muenchow, Susan, 10, 44n57, 45, 46, 47, 48n72, 49, 53, 68, 71, 77, 80–81, 82, 124, 128, 136, 205

Napolitano, Janet, 177
Nathan, Richard, 75–76
National Alliance of Pupil Services Organizations, 141
National Association for Child Development, 133
National Association for the Education of Young Children, 67, 88n10, 104, 142, 152, 159, 167
National Association for Nursery Education, 41, 42
National Association of State Boards of Education (NASBE), 141, 152
National Association of State Directors of Child Development, 98, 99
National Black Child Development Institute, 141, 152